The Law and Society Anthology

Justice in 21st Century America and Beyond

First Edition

Edited by Paul Lohse
Arizona State University

cognella
SAN DIEGO

Bassim Hamadeh, CEO and Publisher
Peaches diPierro, Acquisitions Editor
Skyler Van Valkenburgh, Project Editor
Rachel Kahn, Production Editor
Emely Villavicencio, Senior Graphic Designer
Laura Duncan, Licensing Coordinator
Natalie Piccotti, Director of Marketing
Kassie Graves, Senior Vice President, Editorial
Alia Bales, Director, Project Editorial and Production

Printed in the United States of America.

cognella® ACADEMIC PUBLISHING
320 South Cedros Ave., Ste. 400, Solana Beach, CA 92075

Contents

Introduction

First, as you might suspect, I teach Law and Society. The course has become my most enrolled in and possibly most popular class. Second, let me tell you that I'm a political scientist. Finally, I never personally took the course as an undergraduate or graduate student, where I studied the American courts as a policymaking institution.

When I first taught the class, I found it to be an odd creature, not unlike some of the animals that inhabit Australia. The body parts seemed to be there, but the proportions were off and incoherent, as if the animal were some mythical creature made from different animals. Law and Society is different. It is interdisciplinary, drawing from many academic fields including political science, economics, psychology, anthropology, sociology, law, philosophy, political theory, criminology, and others. You may, as I was, be a little disoriented at first.

My next observation about the study of Law and Society is that it can be very dark. At times it feels like you're walking through the hall of horrors at a wax museum. Most of us acknowledge that we live in a less than perfect world. This course, nonetheless, seems to drive home that point particularly well, whether it's through learning that Clarence Earl Gideon was unable to have an attorney represent him for a criminal offense more than 150 years after the US Constitution declared that defendants have a right to "the Assistance of Council" or many states' efforts to secure lethal injection drugs after the European Union banned the export of drugs such as sodium thiopental.

For this anthology, I've chosen readings that reinforce important concepts and provide insight into debates in Law and Society. So, you might read that Justice Oliver believed that the interpretation of law should consider factors other than the law itself. Reading the first lecture of *The Common Law* will give you a firsthand account of why he came to this conclusion. Likewise, a course in Law and Society will most likely introduce you to the Two

Hemispheres of Law. Reading some of Carlin's account in *Lawyers on Their Own* will show you how it often feels to not get a job in corporate law.

I've also chosen readings that I think you can take with you to law school, graduate school, or wherever your personal journey takes you. These authors changed how we think about law and society in very important ways. If, for example, you decide to pursue a career in criminal justice, it will help you to have read Barbara Babcock's personal account of being a defense attorney and why she likes her job despite a popular assumption that she is letting criminals off the hook.

That said, many of these readings may not be particularly easy. Some of the works are older and have different writing styles. My advice to you is to be patient. Read the pieces more than once. Highlight or mark what you see as important. Think about what you read and ask whether you personally agree. See if you can also make connections between what you read and the positions taken by other thinkers.

I've organized this anthology into seven chapters that hopefully either parallel or fit into a Law and Society class. The first chapter asks what law is and includes stories about disputes that E. Adamson Hoebel and Karl N. Llewellyn give in their classic study of the Cheyenne. Chapter 2 addresses law and theory by including the first lecture from Justice Oliver Wendell Holmes's *The Common Law.* The next chapter considers the often challenging life of an attorney with readings from Jerome E. Carlin's *Lawyers on Their Own*, while chapter 4 includes readings from Barbara Babcock, who examines why defense attorneys do their jobs. In chapter 5, a piece by law professor Erwin Chemerinsky offers an overlooked perspective on the debate over whether there is too much litigation in America. Chapter 6 also includes an unexpected point of view by anthropologist Stanley Diamond in the debate on whether law follows society or vice versa. The final chapter includes a reading by Professor Frank Baumgartner and colleagues on racial profiling and policing.

Let me end by wishing you happy travels through these readings. I hope that you gain new insights and perspectives and become someone who stands for justice even when it conflicts with your own self-interest.

Chapter 1

What is Law?

IMAGINE THAT I'M AN INTERVIEWER ON the street. I greet you and ask your permission to ask a question, which you graciously give. I hold a microphone out to you and ask a seemingly simple question: What is law? You breathe a sigh of relief knowing that this is a question that you can respond to. With the camera rolling, you pause for a second and then give your answer.

There are many answers that you might give. You might tell me that law is official rules, passed by the government and enforced by the police and courts. This is law's authoritative dimension, described by law scholar Donald Black (1972). Or you might tell me that the law is rules about right and wrong (see Selznick 1992). This is the moral dimension. Or you might describe its integrative function. Law builds trust and cooperation, as anthropologist Bronislaw Malinowski ([1926] 2013) discovered in his study of South Pacific Islanders.

Go ahead and answer this question for yourself: What is law? Regardless of how you answer, you are most likely able to identify some important quality of law. Good job. Unfortunately, I suspect that you only described part of the law, much like the blind men who each describe an elephant by touching a part of it. Law, then, is complex and cannot be fully understood from a single perspective.

There are many approaches to try to fully understand law. One way is to study statutes, rules, and regulations. This is sometimes called *black-letter law.* In law school you might take a course in contracts, and this is one example of black-letter law. In the class, your instructor will most likely also describe changes in the interpretation of contract law. This is *jurisprudence.* A class in constitutional law is a good example of this type of study.

Many scholars believe that we cannot disentangle law from society. To understand law, we must understand society, and vice versa. *Law and society* are bound together, joined at the hip. This is our approach to studying law in this book and perhaps in a course that you are taking.

Those who study law and society think about law broadly. For them, law is much more than written rules. Expectations about personal behavior and consequences exist outside of formal law. To illustrate this broad perspective, think about the personal judgments that you make regarding behavior each day. For a more specific example, imagine that it's your child's birthday and the company that you work for will not give you the day off. Is it appropriate to call in and use one of your sick days to attend the party?

These informal expectations or *norms* are not the same. They're based on commonly held values, yet people respond differently when these rules are broken. A *folkway* is a social norm that's part of tradition. If one disregards a folkway, people might take minor offense. This is not true with *mores*, which are based on moral convictions. Breaking a more is generally very offensive. These norms include *taboos*, which are norms that create disgust when broken (Sumner [1906] 2019).

Law, like informal norms, is based on commonly held values. The law that you're most likely familiar with is written law. Unwritten law also exists. Anthropologist E. Adamson Hoebel argues that informal norms become law when a society responds to an offense with force or the threat of force (1979, 28). Sometimes, informal norms become formal law. Legal anthropologist Paul Bohanan uses the word *reinstitutionalization* to describe this (quoted in Kidder 1983, 30–31). In this chapter's readings, Hoebel and law professor Karl N. Llewellyn give an example of this when they discuss Cheyenne chiefs who formally declared that people could not take horses from their owners and that those who did would be punished.

When we think about law, we most likely think about the system of law that we practice today. So, we think about what lawyers, judges, detectives, police, and others employed by the justice system do. This understanding of law most likely comes to us through television, movies, and other media, unless we have studied law or participate in the legal system.

Yet people practiced law long before modern law. And studying other legal systems can help us to understand law.

In 1935, Hoebel and Llewellyn did exactly this. They ventured West to what is today the Northern Cheyenne Indian Reservation in southeastern Montana, where the duo made use of their combined expertise in anthropology and law to study the unwritten laws or law-ways of the Cheyenne people. In their book, *The Cheyenne Way* (1941), they retell many instances where members of the tribe struggled with the meaning of law and what justice required.

As you read through some of these stories, see if you can identify the role that values and informal norms like folkways, mores, and taboos play. See if you can identify instances where these informal norms become law-ways through *reinstitutionalization*. Pay attention also to how the Cheyenne people resolved disputes when the meaning of law was unclear. Do you see parallels with legal disputes today, particularly those that make their way to the US Supreme Court?

Reading 1.1

Selection from "Five Histories"

Karl N. Llewellyn
E. Adamson Hoebel

Case 1. When Two Twists Led the Cheyennes Against the Crows.[1]

Red Robe's two sons were killed by the Crows quite a while back; their father in his grief stood before his lodge in mourning and called out, "All of my horses are for those who take them." He threw the whole herd away, not keeping even one for himself to ride upon.

The Dog Soldiers went out to herd his horses together, because they simply were not going to see the old man afoot. "No one is going to take these horses," they said. Then they sent an old man to see Red Robe.

"Your sons died like men," this messenger reminded him. "They died the glorious death, not in bed sick. Why don't you take back some ponies?"

"No," Red Robe replied, "Maiyun [the Supernatural] wanted my sons to die in battle and it wants that I should be afoot awhile." Whatever they said, they could not budge him.

Finally, four soldier troops [the Elk, Bowstring, Dog, and Fox] decided to go talk to him. He had been a good man in the tribe and here he was destitute. When the camp moved, he was the last to come along. He had nothing to camp with, but just stayed in the open. This had gone on three or four months when the soldiers got together. They all came to Red Robe, but one or two did the talking for them all. "We are begging you to do what we ask you—we are not alone—see them all—every company among us is here. We still have your horses. Come in among the people."

Still he was unmoved by all their pleading. At last Two Twists,[2] a chief of the Bowstring Soldiers, came forward. "Say yes," he implored the old man. "Say yes, and we will promise you to go to war against the Crows wherever they may be. Say yes, and I'll get revenge for you whatever the risks. If they be in breastworks, I'll drive them out."

"I accept," the bereaved old man finally answered. "I did not want to take those horses back after giving them away. It's like taking back a thing given to a friend."

---

1 Informant: Stump Horn. [...]

2 An earlier Two Twists than the one who had the squabble with Last Bull.

"No, it is not like that to us," the soldiers all assured him.

So Red Robe came into camp. In the days which followed after, Two Twists prepared his pipe, taking it to all the soldier societies. Everyone smoked, whole troops pledging themselves to vengeance on the Crows. When all was ready the societies moved to the raid in a body. Women and children went too, for the whole tribe was on the march. Two Twists was the leader of them all.[3]

When they had come close to the enemy, Two Twists rode about the camp accompanied by his crier, who called for the people to listen. Two Twists spoke in this vein. "Look at me now. Soon I am about to follow the two sons of Red Robe. My friends, behold me; I shall never return from this raid."

The women all came out of their lodges to gaze at him. They sang him many heartening songs of which one was this—"Only the rocks lie here and never move. The human being vapors away." That night Two Twists sang the war songs of the Bowstring Soldiers.

The people were anxious to face the enemy, but the chiefs held them in. In the meantime the Crow scouts had spotted the Cheyennes and warned their camp. That night they built a breastwork of all their tipis arranged in a semi-circle.

The next morning Two Twists was out in the camp again. "I sing for the last time," he cried. "People, behold me! This is my last time to walk on earth."

From all around folks brought him feathers, to help him in the thing he was to do. They tied them to his war bonnet, to his horse's mane, and to its tail.

At last the fighters went toward the Crow camp. Two Twists led them, armed only with a sabre. When they were before the enemy, he ordered his followers to hold back; he had his promise to fulfill. And so they all watched as he rode out alone toward the waiting enemy.

Straight at the tipis and into the breastwork he charged, slashing off the head of a Crow warrior as he broke through. He wheeled about, charging into the thick of them again, working havoc where his sword fell. The Crows shot, but missed and missed. Then our people saw Two Twists disappear among them in hand-to-hand struggle.

---

3 This moving of the entire tribe against an enemy was a rare occurrence. According to George Bird Grinnell in *The Fighting Cheyennes* (New York, C. Scribner's Sons, 1915), 69, there were but six such movements in the nineteenth century. It is likely that the story given here was the action against the Crows which took place in 1820 as a punitive expedition for the annihilation of thirty-two Cheyenne warriors in the previous year. Grinnell (*ibid.*, 22–27) gives an account of this affair. It was the greatest of many encounters with the Crows and the second remembered move of the Medicine Arrows against a hostile tribe. No mention was made of the Arrows by the informant, but the taking of the Medicine Hat indicates that this was one of the important tribal movement occasions.

Then the Cheyennes charged into the Crows killing them on all sides. Red Robe's wife charged with an ax. Wherever she found a Crow dead or wounded she split his skull to smear the blood of the enemy upon her face and arms [pantomimed by the informant with proper gusto]. Red Robe joined in by cutting the arm from a dead Crow. He carried it into the scalp dance to scare the women with. E-E-E-E—he would hit them in the back with it; they would run screaming.

Two Twists was not killed, and from his deeds he derived the greatest honor. People said he had done his work; they would never let him do so again; he need not fulfill his vow to die. Back in camp, Two Twists sent for Red Robe and his two wives and children. He himself stripped them of their mourning rags and dressed them well. Many things were given to the women, and now Red Robe took back his horses. They, too, participated in the victory joy of the camp.

Red Robe went back to his lodge and in his turn sent for a crier to get Two Twists. Red Robe was accepting felicitations from everybody. To each person who came to greet him he gave a horse. He painted the faces of all adult comers with black charcoal—the symbol of joy in the death of the enemy. Of all his horses he kept only a few for himself, and this time he was not stopped by the soldiers.

At the end, he adopted Two Twists for his son. Two Twists was not a tribal chief then, only the leader of a soldier society; later he was made a big chief, but on that one occasion he had charge of the whole tribe. He had wanted to wear the Medicine Hat in the battle, and he had told the keeper he wished to wear it, but the keeper gave no answer. It was the keeper's wife who refused him. "You are going to war never to return. I do not think it right for us to give you the Hat. You will get it bloody; you would bring us great trouble; blood on the Hat would mean blood for all the tribe."

Case 2. Pawnee Punished by the Bowstring Soldiers and Rehabilitated by High Backed Wolf.[4]

Pawnee was a Southern Cheyenne when he was a very young man, but in his later years he lived up here with us. He was all the time looking out after the people's morals and counseling the boys on good behavior. I have heard him tell his story many times when I was a youth, because he was always telling it to us as a lesson. He had been an awful rascal down there in Oklahoma when he was young, stealing meat from people's racks, taking their horses for joy-rides without asking them for them, and then when he got to where he was going he would just turn the horse loose and let it wander back to its owner—if it did. He

4 Informant: Black Wolf. [...]

was disrespectful to people and sassed them back. Everyone thought he was a mean boy, and whatever happened in the camp he got blamed for it. This story I am going to tell happened just after that trouble Wolf Lies Down had over the borrowed horse when the soldiers made the rule that no one in the camp could take another person's horse without permission. This is what Pawnee used to tell us:

Down there [in Oklahoma] were two spotted horses well liked in their family. One day I took them and headed west. Three days passed and I found myself still safe. Now I was out of trouble's way, so I began to feel pretty good. On the fourth day, as I looked back I saw some people coming up. "It is nothing," I thought, "just some people traveling." When they overtook me, I saw they were Bowstring Soldiers out after me.

"You have stolen those horses," they cried as they pulled me from my horse. "Now we have trailed you down." They threw me on the ground and beat me until I could not stand; they broke up my weapons and ruined my saddle; they cut my blankets, moccasins, and kit to shreds. When they had finished they took all my food and went off with the horses, leaving me alone on the prairie, sore and destitute, too weak and hurt to move.

The next day I started back, traveling as best I could all day long. I knew there was a small camp of buffalo hunters out and for them I was looking. I travelled all day. The next day I thought I would die. I had no food, only water. Late in the afternoon I camped on a creek. My feet were bleeding and I could not walk farther. I crawled slowly on my hands and knees to the brow of a high hill to find a place to die. I waited in mourning. Far to the south of me I could see the rolling country; to the west my view was blocked. My pipe and tobacco were gone. Without smoke I sat there thinking of a great many things as I watched the blood drip from my swollen feet.

As I gazed steadfastly into the south, a hunter came up the hill from behind me. When he saw me he stopped and watched me for a long time. After three days and two nights in my condition I must have been nearly deaf, for I did not hear him until he spoke from his horse right behind me. I was naked. I fell over in a fright when I heard his voice start out in the silence.

This man dismounted and hugged me. He wept, he felt so bad at seeing my plight. It was High Backed Wolf,[5] a young man, but a chief. He put his blanket about me and took me home. The camp was on the creek below, hidden just around a bend where I had not seen it. His wife gave me food and nourished me.

Then High Backed Wolf sent for the chiefs who were in the camp. Four or five came, one of whom was a soldier chief.

---

5 Later a famous chief killed in a skirmish with American troops at the Platte Bridge, July 25, 1865. Grinnell, *The Fighting Cheyennes*, 218.

High Backed Wolf spoke to the soldier chief first. "This is the first time since I have become a big [tribal] chief that I have happened upon such a poor man; now I am going to outfit him. Until he is fixed up, I shall ask no questions. Then we shall learn how he came to be naked. I am not going to ask you to give anything unless you wish to do so. I know this man," he said. "He is a great smoker. But I shall give him no smoke until he has first eaten." (In my own mind I said, "I'd rather smoke first.")

First they gave me a little soup; then some meat.

High Backed Wolf then filled the pipe. As he held it to the five directions he prayed, "This is my first good act as a chief. Help this man to tell the truth." Then he held the pipe for me to smoke; then he gave it to the next man and to the others. Now he faced me again. "Now you tell the truth. Have you been caught by enemies and stripped? Or was it something else? You saw me smoke this pipe; you have touched it with your own lips. That is to help you tell the truth. If you tell us straightly, Maiyun will help you."

I told them the whole story. I told them whose horses they were, and I told them it was the Bowstrings who had punished me.

High Backed Wolf knew I was a rascal, so he lectured to me. "You are old enough now to know what is right," he preached. "You have been to war. Now leave off this foolishness. If it had been that I had not ridden out into the hills today you would have died. No one would have known the end of you. You know how we Cheyennes try to live. You know how we hunt, how we go to war. When we take horses, we take them from enemies, not from Cheyennes. You had better join a military society. You can learn good behavior from the soldiers. Yet I ask only one thing of you. Be decent from now on! Stop stealing! Stop making fun of people! Use no more bad language in the camp! Lead a good life!

"Now I am going to help you out. That is what I am here for, because I am a chief of the people. Here are your clothes. Outside are three horses. You may take your choice!" He gave me a six-shooter. "Here is a mountain-lion skin. I used to wear this in the parades. Now I give it to you." He offered me all these things and I took them.

The others gave me beaver skins to braid in my hair, beads, and extra moccasins, and two more horses.

Then High Backed Wolf ended it. "Now I am not going to tell you to leave this camp. You may stay here as long as you wish. I shall not tell you which direction to go, west or south."

I had a sweetheart in the south, but when these people did this for me, I felt ashamed. I had all those things with which to look beautiful, but I did not dare to go back, for I knew she would have heard what the Bowstrings had done to me. I thought it wisest to go north until the thing was dead.

When the Arrows were next renewed, the Foxes put up their lodge to get more men. I went in [joined]. Still, I never got it out of my heart that it had been those Bowstrings. Whenever my Fox troop was on duty I was out looking for those men or their families to do something wrong. I always looked for a Bowstring to slip, so I could beat him well. I stayed with the Northern Cheyennes a long, long time, until the Horse Creek Treaty.[6] Though I came to be a chief of the Fox Soldiers among the Northern people, I never amounted to much with the Southern bands. Those people always remembered me as a no-good.

You boys remember that. You may run away, but your people always remember. You just obey the rules of the camp, and you'll do all right.

Case 3. The Tribal Ostracism and Reinstatement of Sticks Everything Under His Belt.[7]

Once, at a time when all the Cheyenne tribe was gathered together, Sticks Everything Under His Belt went out hunting buffalo alone. "I am hunting for myself," he told the people. He was implying that the rules against individual hunting did not apply to him because he was declaring himself out of the tribe—a man on his own.

All the soldier chiefs and all the tribal chiefs met in a big lodge to decide what to do in this case, since such a thing had never happened before. This was the ruling they made: no one could help Sticks Everything Under His Belt in any way, no one could give him smoke, no one could talk to him. They were cutting him off from the tribe. The chiefs declared that if anyone helped him in any way that person would have to give a Sun Dance.

When the camp moved, Sticks Everything Under His Belt moved with it, but the people would not recognize him. He was left alone and it went to his heart, so he took one of his horses (he had many) and rode out to the hilltops to mourn.

His sister's husband was a chief in the camp. This brother-in-law felt sorry for him out there mourning, with no more friends. At last he took pity on his poor brother-in-law; at last he spoke to his wife, "I feel sorry for your poor brother out there and now I am going to do something for him. Cook up all those tongues we have! Prepare a good feast!"

Then he invited the chiefs to his lodge and sent for his brother-in-law to come in. This was after several years had passed, not months.

---

6 Horse Creek Treaty—a famous occasion when in the summer of 1851 Siouxs, Assiniboines, Gros Ventres, Crows, Shoshones, Arikaras, Arapahoes, and Cheyennes to the number of eight to twelve thousand met under the aegis of two American agents to agree to peace among themselves and toward the whites. The treaties, though not ratified by Congress, were observed for several years by the Indians. Pierre-Jean De Smet, *Western Missions and Missionaries* (New York, J. B. Kirker, 1863), 101 ff.

7 Informant: Black Wolf. [...]

When the chiefs had assembled, the brother-in-law spoke. "Several years ago you passed a ruling that no one could help this man. Whoever should do so you said would have to give a Sun Dance. Now is the time to take pity on him. *I* am going to give a Sun Dance to bring him back in. I beg you to let him come back to the tribe, for he has suffered long enough. This Sun Dance will be a great one. I declare that every chief and all the soldiers must join in. Now I put it up to you. Shall we let my brother-in-law smoke before we eat, or after?"

The chiefs all answered in accord, "Ha-ho, ha-ho [thank you, thank you]. We are very glad you are going to bring back this man. However, let him remember that he will be bound by whatever rules the soldiers lay down for the tribe. He may not say he is outside of them. He has been out of the tribe for a long time. If he remembers these things, he may come back."

Then they asked Sticks Everything Under His Belt whether he wanted to smoke before or after they had eaten. Without hesitation he replied, "Before," because he had craved tobacco so badly that he had split his pipe stem to suck the brown gum inside of it.

The lodge was not big enough to hold all the chiefs who had come to decide this thing, so they threw open the door, and those who could not get in sat in a circle outside. Then they filled a big pipe and when it was lighted they gave it to Sticks Everything Under His Belt. It was so long since he had had tobacco that he gulped in the smoke and fell over in a faint. As he lay there the smoke came out of his anus, he was so empty. The chiefs waited silently for him to come to again and then the pipe was passed around the circle.

When all had smoked, Sticks Everything Under His Belt talked. "From now on I am going to run with the tribe. Everything the people say, I shall stay right by it. My brother-in-law has done a great thing. He is going to punish himself in the Sun Dance to bring me back. He won't do it alone, for I am going in, too."

After a while the people were getting ready for the Sun Dance. One of the soldiers began to get worried because he had an ugly growth on his body which he did not want to reveal to the people. He was a good-looking young man named Black Horse. Black Horse went to the head chiefs asking them to let him sacrifice himself alone on the hilltops as long as the Sun Dance was in progress.

"We have nothing to say to that," they told him. "Go to the pledger. This is his Sun Dance."

Black Horse went to the brother-in-law of Sticks Everything Under His Belt, who was a brother-in-law to him as well.[8] "Brother-in-law," he begged, "I want to be excused from going into the lodge. Can't you let me go into the hills to sacrifice myself as long as you are in there, to make my own bed?"

"No," he was rebuffed, "you know my rule is that all must be there."

---

8 This means he was a classificatory brother to the pledger's wife.

"Well, brother-in-law, won't it be all right if I set up a pole on the hill and hang myself to it through my breasts? I shall hang there for the duration of the dance."

This brother-in-law of his answered him in these words, "Why didn't you take that up when all the chiefs were in the lodge? I have agreed with them that everyone must be in the lodge. I don't want to change the rule. I won't give you permission to go outside."

Then Black Horse replied, "You will not make the rules my way. Now *I* am going to put in a rule for everybody. Everyone in there has to swing from the pole as I do."

"No," countered the brother-in-law. "That was not mentioned in the meeting. If you want to swing from the pole, that is all right, but no one else has to unless he wishes to."

When they had the Sun Dance everyone had a good time. Black Horse was the only one on the pole, and there were so many in the lodge that there was not room enough for all to dance. Some just had to sit around inside the lodge. Though they did not dance, they starved themselves for four days. This dance took place near Sheridan, Wyoming, seven years before Custer.[9] I was only a year old at that time, but what I have said here I was told by Elk River and others. We call this place "Where The Chiefs Starved Themselves."

Case 4. Cries Yia Eya Banished for the Murder of Chief Eagle.[10]

Cries Yia Eya had been gone from the camp for three years because he had killed Chief Eagle in a whiskey brawl. The chiefs had ordered him away for his murder, so we did not see anything of him for that time. Then one day he came back, leading a horse packed with bundles of old-time tobacco. He stopped outside the camp and sent a messenger in with the horse and tobacco who was to say to the chiefs for him, "I am begging to come home."

The chiefs all got together for a meeting, and the soldier societies were told to convene, for there was an important matter to be considered. The tobacco was divided up and chiefs' messengers were sent out to invite the soldier chiefs to come to the lodge of the tribal council, for the big chiefs wanted to talk to them. "Here is the tobacco that that man sent in," they told the soldier chiefs. "Now we want you soldiers to decide if you think we should accept his request. If you decide that we should let him return, then it is up to you to convince his family that it is all right." (The relatives of Chief Eagle had told everybody that they would kill Cries Yia Eya on sight if they ever found him. "If we set eyes on him, he'll never make another track," they had vowed.) The soldier chiefs took the tobacco and went out to gather

9 The Northern Cheyennes date most events from the 1860's to the nineties as so many years before or after the annihilation of the Custer command at the Indian village on the Little Big Horn, June 25, 1876.

10 Informant: Calf Woman. [...]

their troops. Each society met in its own separate lodge to talk among themselves, but the society servants kept passing back and forth between their different lodges to report on the trend of the discussion in the different companies.

At last one man said, "I think it is all right. I believe the stink has blown from him.[11] Let him return!" This view was passed around, and this is the view that won out among the soldiers. Then the father of Chief Eagle was sent for and asked whether he would accept the decision. "Soldiers," he replied, "I shall listen to you. Let him return! But if that man comes back, I want never to hear his voice raised against another person. If he does, we come together. As far as that stuff of his is concerned, I want nothing that belonged to him. Take this share you have set aside for me and give it to someone else."

Cries Yia Eya had always been a mean man, disliked by everyone, but he had been a fierce fighter against the enemies. After he came back to the camp, however, he was always good to the people.

Case 5. When Walking Rabbit Raised a Problem.[12]

A war party was organizing. Walking Rabbit approached the leader with a question. "Is it true that you have declared we must all go afoot? If so, I would like to be able to lead a horse to pack my moccasins and possibles." The leader gave him an answer. "There is a reason for my ruling. I want no horses, that it may be easier for us to conceal our movements. However, you may bring one horse." Then Walking Rabbit asked for instructions concerning the location of the first and second nights' camps, for he would start late and overtake the party.

Walking Rabbit's sweetheart had been married only recently to another. "My husband is not the man I thought he was," she told her former suitor. So Walking Rabbit took her to join the war party. [The Cheyennes have a phrase for the single man who marries a one-time married woman—"putting on the old moccasin."] In this way, it turned out that the "moccasin" he was packing was a big woman.

When they saw this woman there, the warriors got excited. The party turned into the hills and stopped. The leader opened his pipe. The leader's pipe was always filled before they left the camp, but it was not smoked until the enemy was seen or their tracks reported. Now the leader spoke. "When we take a woman with us it is usually known in the camp. Here is a man who has sneaked off with another's wife. Now what is going to happen?" That is what they were talking about.

---

11 On this supernatual physical effect of murder, see below [...]

12 Informant: Black Wolf. [...]

The leader declared, "The only thing this man can do is return and make a settlement with the husband. Then he may follow us up."

One warrior was for aiding Walking Rabbit. "Why can't we let him stay?" was his proposal. "If we take any horses, we can give them to her husband." That was rejected.

The decision was that he had to go back. "If you had told us you wanted her so badly, we might have waited for you to settle for her. Then we could have taken her the right way. If you really want to go to war with us, you will be able to overtake us. We are afoot."

Then three or four warriors spoke up, each promising Walking Rabbit a horse to send to the husband. Everyone gave one or two arrows to be sent as well.

In the meantime Walking Rabbit's father had fixed it up with the aggrieved husband. Since he and his wife were incompatible, he was willing to release her. When Walking Rabbit came in and told his father the story of the soldiers' action, the father said, "Just let that stand. The thing is fixed. When those fighters come back they may want to give to the girl's parents. You go back after your party." But Walking Rabbit preferred to stay at home.

When Walking Rabbit did not go out, his closest relatives raised a big tipi. When they heard of the approach of the returning war. party, everything was in readiness.

The warriors came charging in, shooting; they had taken many horses. The first coup-counters were in the van.[12] Walking Rabbit's father had a right to harangue; he was a crier. "Don't go to your homes! Don't go to your own lodges! Come here to the lodge of Walking Rabbit, your friend!"

When they were all in this lodge the old man entered and told them his story. "I had this thing all settled before my son returned. You have sent arrows and promised horses. Now I have kept this girl here pending your return. I shall send her back to her parents with presents. I have waited to see what you are going to do."

The leader replied for his followers. "Yes, we will help you. We promised to help your son. When you send her back, we'll send presents with her." The men who had promised horses went out to get them. Others gave captured horses.

Sending her back with these presents was giving wedding gifts. Her relatives got them all. They gathered up their goods to send back. The war party was called together once more; to them this stuff was given. It was a great thing for the people to talk about. It was the first and last time a woman was sent home on enemy horses the day they came in.

Such is the Cheyenne material as it comes from the informants. If one goes back over the accounts, not as stories merely, but as indicators of Cheyenne law-ways, one finds that even these five are rich no less with perplexity than with illumination.

[...]

Reading 1.2

Selection from "The Military Societies"

Karl N. Llewellyn
E. Adamson Hoebel

[...]

In the first history there is Wolf Lies Down, owner of horses.[1]

« « « While Wolf Lies Down was away, a friend took one of his horses to ride to war. This man had brought his bow and arrow and left them in the lodge of the horse's owner. When Wolf Lies Down returned, he knew by this token security who had his horse, so he said nothing.

A year passed without the horse's return, and then Wolf Lies Down invited the Elk Soldier chiefs to his lodge, because he was in their society. "There is this thing," he told them. "My friend borrowed my horse, leaving his bow and arrow; there they are yet. Now I want to know what to do. I want you to tell me the right thing. Will you go over and ask him his intentions?"

The borrower was in another camp well distant, yet the chiefs agreed. "We'll send a man to bring him in, get his word, or receive his presents," they promised.

The camp moved while the messenger was gone, but he knew of course where it would be on his return. The soldier returned with the borrower, who was leading two horses, "one spotted, one ear-tipped." He called for the four Elk chiefs on his arrival. The chiefs laid before him the story told by Wolf Lies Down.

"That is true," the man assented. "My friend is right. I left my bow and arrow here. I intended to return his horse, but I was gone longer than I expected. I have had good luck with that horse, though. I have treated it better than my own. However, when I got back to camp I found my folks there. Our camps were far apart and I just could not get away. I was waiting for his camp and mine to come together. Now, I always intended to do the right thing. I have brought two good horses with me. My friend can have his choice. In addition I give his own horse back, and further, I am leaving my bow and arrow."

Then up spoke Wolf Lies Down, "I am glad to hear my friend say these things. Now I feel better. I shall take one of those horses, but I am giving him that one he borrowed to keep. From now on we shall be bosom friends."

---

1 Informant: Black Wolf, to whom this story was told by Elk River.

The chiefs declared, "Now we have settled this thing. Our man is a bosom friend of this man. Let it be that way among all of us. Our society and his shall be comrades. Whenever one of us has a present to give, we shall give it to a member of his soldier society.

"Now we shall make a new rule. There shall be no more borrowing of horses without asking. If any man takes another's goods without asking, we will go over and get them back for him. More than that, if the taker tries to keep them, we will give him a whipping." » » »

[...]

CHAPTER 1 QUESTIONS

In my introduction to *The Cheyenne Way*, I describe the different types of norms. Below, I recount moments in the book when the authors address expectations about behavior. Tell me whether you think that a folkway, more, or taboo best describes each expectation that I describe. Give a reason for your answer.

1. In preparation for war with the Crows, Two Twists prepares his pipe, which he presents to the soldiers in the war societies.
2. Two Twists wishes to wear the Medicine Hat into battle. The hat keeper's wife refuses his request, telling him that getting the hat bloody will bring bad luck to the tribe.
3. Pawnee steals two horses while traveling through Oklahoma. He is pursued by two Bowstring Soldiers.
4. High Backed Wolf tells Pawnee that he should join a military society to improve his moral character.
5. Sticks Everything Under His Belt decides to hunt buffalo alone, to the dismay of the tribal members.
6. Black Horse goes to the head chiefs to ask their permission to sacrifice himself rather than go into the lodge and reveal an ugly growth on his body during the sun dance.
7. Cries Yia Eya murders Chief Eagle in a whisky brawl. The chiefs banish him from the tribe.
8. The leader of the war party packs his pipe before leaving for battle. The pipe is not to be smoked until the enemy was seen or their tracks spotted.
9. White Rabbit sneaks off with a woman who is unhappily married. The party leader demands that he return to the husband to make a settlement.

Chapter 2

Justice Oliver Wendell Holmes and the Living Law

MANY AMERICANS TODAY EXPRESS DISPLEASURE THAT judges make law when they establish new legal precedents. Judges, we are often told, should only interpret law.

Sometimes these judges are labeled activist judges. In today's politics, the term is used to describe judges who decide cases based on their personal ideologies rather than the law.[1] It's a negative label.

However, Justice Oliver Wendell Holmes would most likely not agree with this popular sentiment. Holmes would see judges making law as inevitable and perhaps even necessary.

In *The Common Law*, Holmes argues that law changes with society. While long-standing legal principles persist, the reasons for them and their content changes. Holmes writes, "The life of the law has not been logic: it has been experience" (lect. 1, par. 1).

Holmes's perspective is called *legal realism*. It contrasts with *legal formalism*, which argues that judges decide cases based on a logical analysis of law, where existing legal precedents are mechanically applied to new cases. With legal formalism, law is discovered rather than made. With legal realism, the law is guided by changes in society.

How, then, might these perspectives see a case like *Griswold v. Connecticut* (1965)? In this case, the US Supreme Court decided that Americans had a constitutional right to privacy. The US Constitution, nonetheless, does not give this explicit right.

If Holmes were to vote on the case, he might not take the liberal position. It fair to say, however, that he would be sympathetic to the justices' broader reading of the Constitution and their efforts to consider the changing society of the 1960s.

1 Nonetheless, those who study politics define judicial activism as judges using the power of judicial review to overturn laws created by legislative bodies.

Today, we associate the less strict reading of the law with modern liberalism. It might seem ironic, then, that Justice Oliver Wendell Holmes studied, practiced, and presided over law more than a century and a half ago.

Justice Oliver Wendell Holmes was born in Boston, Massachusetts, in 1841. He later attended Harvard University and enlisted in his senior year in the Massachusetts militia at the beginning of the US Civil War, which he fought in as a second lieutenant.

Holmes returned from war in 1864 and enrolled in Harvard Law School. Two years later, he graduated and passed the Massachusetts Bar Exam. Holmes went into private legal practice, where he practiced admiralty and commercial law. It was during this time that he served as the editor of the *American Law Review* and continued his scholarly study of the law.

In his studies, Holmes searched for a way to categorize and explain law. At first, he attempted to use "arrangements of the law" to organize and understand it. He was unsuccessful, finding no philosophic basis for categorizing it despite many efforts (introduction, par. 28).

In 1872, Holmes observed that the American courts did not often abandon the legal structures and rules that they had created. They did, nonetheless, embrace new reasons for their rules. Consequently, Holmes came to believe that law was a collection of rationales that happened to exist at a point in time. For Holmes, public policy and history were the rationales that causes existing legal precedent to change.

This observation sparked Holmes's belief that the law was ephemeral, as rationales changed (intro., par. 31). For Holmes, these rationales represented the law's "form," while the unchanging legal rules represented its "structure" or "machinery." Strong tension exists, according to Holmes, between form and structure (lecture 1, par. 1).

These thoughts culminated in a series of lectures that were published as *The Common Law* in 1881.

In the first lecture, Holmes explores the legal development of liability. Liability is legal responsibility. This may be for an action taken or not taken. Liability is a legal concept that we still have with us today. The machinery of liability law, then, still exists even after well over a millennium in English law alone.

But what about its form? Toward the beginning of the first lecture, Holmes provides a medley of scenarios showing how the meaning of liability was no longer consistent. It had taken on new meanings with its historical progression.

Holmes then describes the growth of liability law in situations where an animal, person, or thing had caused injury. He first explores instances where something living had caused harm and then gives his attention to inanimate objects, like ships, for example.

Ancient law initially took vengeance against the animal or person that caused the injury. To illustrate this principle, Holmes cites a verse in Exodus, which decrees that an ox causing injury be put to death and its owner forgiven (English Standard Version 21:28).[2]

Holmes then discovered similar legal traditions in Greek and Roman society. In Greece, the owner of a slave or animal had to take personal responsibility only when he failed to surrender the slave or animal to the injured party for retribution. We discover the exact same principle of *noxae deditio*, or noxious surrender, in Roman law under the Twelve Tables.

The form of liability nonetheless changed with the Aquiline Law, which took away the privilege of surrender and made the master of a slave or animal responsible. Later, the Romans made shipowners and innkeepers personally responsible for damages caused by employees as well.

Holmes tells us that English law similarly gave greater liability to an employer or owner. For example, in the case of an employer, if the king fined the servant of a lord, and the servant ran away, the lord had to pay the fine. With animals, liability over time became based on "the right of property" or ownership. This "ownership" existed for certain animals but not others. A cow, for example, was owned while a dog was not.

Holmes finds that liability law involving inanimate objects changed less than it did with people and animals. With maritime law, Holmes discovered that the principle of *noxae deditio* had remained in effect, as a ship rather than its owner or even a captain or pilot was made liable for collisions and other misfortunes.

The interaction between form and substance sent maritime liability on a unique trajectory, one that Holmes thought that people of his time might see as odd given the changes to other types of liability. Holmes writes, "If a livery-stable lets a horse and wagon to a customer, who runs a man down by careless driving, no one would think of claiming the right to seize the horse and wagon" (lect. 1, par. 48).

As you read through the Reading 2.1, consider who or what is held accountable for an offense. Also consider reparations or payment. How did these change with time? Do you think that the old or more recent legal interpretations of liability are fairer? What are your reasons?

---

2 Later verses in this chapter of Exodus do tell us that owners of livestock had some personal liability in certain cases, such as when the owner knew the animal had acted violently in the past. While that verse illustrates *noxae deditio*, Jewish liability law was ostensibly more complex.

Reading 2.1

Lecture I—Early Forms of Liability

Oliver Wendell Holmes Jr.

The object of this book is to present a general view of the Common Law. To accomplish the task, other tools are needed besides logic. It is something to show that the consistency of a system requires a particular result, but it is not all. The life of the law has not been logic: it has been experience. The felt necessities of the time, the prevalent moral and political theories, intuitions of public policy, avowed or unconscious, even the prejudices which judges share with their fellow-men, have had a good deal more to do than the syllogism in determining the rules by which men should be governed. The law embodies the story of a nation's development through many centuries, and it cannot be dealt with as if it contained only the axioms and corollaries of a book of mathematics. In order to know what it is, we must know what it has been, and what it tends to become. We must alternately consult history and existing theories of legislation. But the most difficult labor will be to understand the combination of the two into new products at every stage. The substance of the law at any given time pretty nearly corresponds, so far as it goes, with what is then understood to be convenient; but its form and machinery, and the degree to which it is able to work out desired results, depend very much upon its past.

In Massachusetts today, while, on the one hand, there are a great many rules which are quite sufficiently accounted for by their manifest good sense, on the other, there are some which can only be understood by reference to the infancy of procedure among the German tribes, or to the social condition of Rome under the Decemvirs.

I shall use the history of our law so far as it is necessary to explain a conception or to interpret a rule, but no further. In doing so there are two errors equally to be avoided both by writer and reader. One is that of supposing, because an idea seems very familiar and natural to us, that it has always been so. Many things which we take for granted have had to be laboriously fought out or thought out in past times. The other mistake is the opposite one of asking too much of history. We start with man full grown. It may be assumed that the earliest barbarian whose practices are to be considered, had a good many of the same feelings and passions as ourselves.

The first subject to be discussed is the general theory of liability civil and criminal. The Common Law has changed a good deal since the beginning of our series of reports, and the search after a theory which may now be said to prevail is very much a study of tendencies. I believe that it will be instructive to go back to the early forms of liability, and to start from them.

Oliver Wendell Holmes Jr., "Early Forms of Liability," The Common Law, 1881.

It is commonly known that the early forms of legal procedure were grounded in vengeance. Modern writers have thought that the Roman law started from the blood feud, and all the authorities agree that the German law begun in that way. The feud led to the composition, at first optional, then compulsory, by which the feud was bought off. The gradual encroachment of the composition may be traced in the Anglo-Saxon laws, /1/ and the feud was pretty well broken up, though not extinguished, by the time of William the Conqueror. The killings and house-burnings of an earlier day became the appeals of mayhem and arson. The appeals de pace et plagis and of mayhem became, or rather were in substance, the action of trespass which is still familiar to lawyers. /2/ But as the compensation recovered in the appeal was the alternative of vengeance, we might expect to find its scope limited to the scope of vengeance. Vengeance imports a feeling of blame, and an opinion, however distorted by passion, that a wrong has been done. It can hardly go very far beyond the case of a harm intentionally inflicted: even a dog distinguishes between being stumbled over and being kicked.

Whether for this cause or another, the early English appeals for personal violence seem to have been confined to intentional wrongs. Glanvill /3/ mentions melees, blows, and wounds,—all forms of intentional violence. In the fuller description of such appeals given by Bracton /4/ it is made quite clear that they were based on intentional assaults. The appeal de pace et plagis laid an intentional assault, described the nature of the arms used, and the length and depth of the wound. The appellor also had to show that he immediately raised the hue and cry. So when Bracton speaks of the lesser offences, which were not sued by way of appeal, he instances only intentional wrongs, such as blows with the fist, flogging, wounding, insults, and so forth. /1/ The cause of action in the cases of trespass reported in the earlier Year Books and in the Abbreviatio Plaeitorum is always an intentional wrong. It was only at a later day, and after argument, that trespass was extended so as to embrace harms which were foreseen, but which were not the intended consequence of the defendant's act. /2/ Thence again it extended to unforeseen injuries. /3/

It will be seen that this order of development is not quite consistent with an opinion which has been held, that it was a characteristic of early law not to penetrate beyond the external visible fact, the damnum corpore corpori datum. It has been thought that an inquiry into the internal condition of the defendant, his culpability or innocence, implies a refinement of juridical conception equally foreign to Rome before the Lex Aquilia, and to England when trespass took its shape. I do not know any very satisfactory evidence that a man was generally held liable either in Rome /4/ or England for the accidental consequences even of his own act. But whatever may have been the early law, the foregoing account shows the starting-point of the system with which we have to deal. Our system of private liability for the consequences of a man's own acts, that is, for his trespasses, started from the notion of actual intent and actual personal culpability.

The original principles of liability for harm inflicted by another person or thing have been less carefully considered hitherto than those which governed trespass, and I shall therefore devote the rest of this Lecture to discussing them. I shall try to show that this liability also had its root in the passion of revenge, and to point out the changes by which it reached its present form. But I shall not confine myself strictly to what is needful for that purpose, because it is not only most interesting to trace the transformation throughout its whole extent, but the story will also afford an instructive example of the mode in which the law has grown, without a break, from barbarism to civilization. Furthermore, it will throw much light upon some important and peculiar doctrines which cannot be returned to later.

A very common phenomenon, and one very familiar to the student of history, is this. The customs, beliefs, or needs of a primitive time establish a rule or a formula. In the course of centuries the custom, belief, or necessity disappears, but the rule remains. The reason which gave rise to the rule has been forgotten, and ingenious minds set themselves to inquire how it is to be accounted for. Some ground of policy is thought of, which seems to explain it and to reconcile it with the present state of things; and then the rule adapts itself to the new reasons which have been found for it, and enters on a new career. The old form receives a new content, and in time even the form modifies itself to fit the meaning which it has received. The subject under consideration illustrates this course of events very clearly.

I will begin by taking a medley of examples embodying as many distinct rules, each with its plausible and seemingly sufficient ground of policy to explain it.

A man has an animal of known ferocious habits, which escapes and does his neighbor damage. He can prove that the animal escaped through no negligence of his, but still he is held liable. Why? It is, says the analytical jurist, because, although he was not negligent at the moment of escape, he was guilty of remote heedlessness, or negligence, or fault, in having such a creature at all. And one by whose fault damage is done ought to pay for it.

A baker's man, while driving his master's cart to deliver hot rolls of a morning, runs another man down. The master has to pay for it. And when he has asked why he should have to pay for the wrongful act of an independent and responsible being, he has been answered from the time of Ulpian to that of Austin, that it is because he was to blame for employing an improper person. If he answers, that he used the greatest possible care in choosing his driver, he is told that that is no excuse; and then perhaps the reason is shifted, and it is said that there ought to be a remedy against some one who can pay the damages, or that such wrongful acts as by ordinary human laws are likely to happen in the course of the service are imputable to the service.

Next, take a case where a limit has been set to liability which had previously been unlimited. In 1851, Congress passed a law, which is still in force, and by which the owners of ships in all the more common cases of maritime loss can surrender the vessel and her freight then pending to the losers; and it is provided that, thereupon, further proceedings against the owners shall cease. The legislators to whom we owe this act argued that, if a merchant embark a portion of his property upon a hazardous venture, it is reasonable that his stake should be confined to what he puts at risk,—a principle similar to that on which corporations have been so largely created in America during the last fifty years.

It has been a rule of criminal pleading in England down into the present century, that an indictment for homicide must set forth the value of the instrument causing the death, in order that the king or his grantee might claim forfeiture of the deodand, "as an accursed thing," in the language of Blackstone.

I might go on multiplying examples; but these are enough to show the remoteness of the points to be brought together.—As a first step towards a generalization, it will be necessary to consider what is to be found in ancient and independent systems of law.

There is a well-known passage in Exodus, /1/ which we shall have to remember later: "If an ox gore a man or a woman, that they die: then the ox shall be surely stoned, and his flesh shall not be eaten; but the owner of the ox shall be quit." When we turn from the Jews to the Greeks, we find the principle of the passage just quoted erected into a system. Plutarch, in his Solon, tells us that a dog that had bitten a man was to be delivered up bound to a log four cubits long. Plato made elaborate provisions in his Laws for many such cases. If a slave killed a man, he was to be given up to the relatives of the deceased. /2/ If he wounded a man, he was to be given up to the injured party to use him as he pleased. /3/ So if he did damage to which the injured party did not contribute as a joint cause. In either case, if the owner failed to surrender the slave, he was bound to make good the loss. /1/ If a beast killed a man, it was to be slain and cast beyond the borders. If an inanimate thing caused death, it was to be cast beyond the borders in like manner, and expiation was to be made. /2/ Nor was all this an ideal creation of merely imagined law, for it was said in one of the speeches of Aeschines, that "we banish beyond our borders stocks and stones and steel, voiceless and mindless things, if they chance to kill a man; and if a man commits suicide, bury the hand that struck the blow afar from its body." This is mentioned quite as an every-day matter, evidently without thinking it at all extraordinary, only to point an antithesis to the honors heaped upon Demosthenes. /3/ As late as the second century after Christ the traveller Pausanias observed with some surprise that they still sat in judgment on inanimate things in the Prytaneum. /4/ Plutarch attributes the institution to Draco. /5/

In the Roman law we find the similar principles of the noxoe deditio gradually leading to further results. The Twelve Tables (451 B.C.) provided that, if an animal had done damage, either the animal was to be surrendered or the damage paid for. /6/ We learn from Gains that the same rule was applied to the torts of children or slaves, /7/ and there is some trace of it with regard to inanimate things.

The Roman lawyers, not looking beyond their own system or their own time, drew on their wits for an explanation which would show that the law as they found it was reasonable. Gaius said that it was unjust that the fault of children or slaves should be a source of loss to their parents or owners beyond their own bodies, and Ulpian reasoned that a fortiori this was true of things devoid of life, and therefore incapable of fault. /1/ This way of approaching the question seems to deal with the right of surrender as if it were a limitation of a liability incurred by a parent or owner, which would naturally and in the first instance be unlimited. But if that is what was meant, it puts the cart before the horse. The right of surrender was not introduced as a limitation of liability, but, in Rome and Greece alike, payment was introduced as the alternative of a failure to surrender.

The action was not based, as it would be nowadays, on the fault of the parent or owner. If it had been, it would always have been brought against the person who had control of the slave or animal at the time it did the harm complained of, and who, if any one, was to blame for not preventing the injury. So far from this being the course, the person to be sued was the owner at the time of suing. The action followed the guilty thing into whosesoever hands it came. /2/ And in curious contrast with the principle as inverted to meet still more modern views of public policy, if the animal was of a wild nature, that is, in the very case of the most ferocious animals, the owner ceased to be liable the moment it escaped, because at that moment he ceased to be owner. /3/ There seems to have been no other or more extensive liability by the old law, even where a slave was guilty with his master's knowledge, unless perhaps he was a mere tool in his master's hands. /1/ Gains and Ulpian showed an inclination to cut the noxoe deditio down to a privilege of the owner in case of misdeeds committed without his knowledge; but Ulpian is obliged to admit, that by the ancient law, according to Celsus, the action was noxal where a slave was guilty even with the privity of his master. /2/

All this shows very clearly that the liability of the owner was merely a way of getting at the slave or animal which was the immediate cause of offence. In other words, vengeance on the immediate offender was the object of the Greek and early Roman process, not indemnity from the master or owner. The liability of the owner was simply a liability of the offending thing. In the primitive customs of Greece it was enforced by a judicial process expressly directed against the object, animate or inanimate. The Roman Twelve Tables made the owner, instead of the thing itself, the defendant, but did not in any way change the ground of liability, or affect its limit. The change was simply a device to allow the owner to protect his interest. /3/

But it may be asked how inanimate objects came to be pursued in this way, if the object of the procedure was to gratify the passion of revenge. Learned men have been ready to find a reason in the personification of inanimate nature common to savages and children, and there is much to confirm this view. Without such a personification, anger towards lifeless things would have been transitory, at most. It is noticeable that the commonest example in the most primitive customs and laws is that of a tree which falls upon a man, or from which he falls and is killed. We can conceive with comparative ease how a tree might have been put on the same footing with animals. It certainly was treated like them, and was delivered to the relatives, or chopped to pieces for the gratification of a real or simulated passion. /1/

In the Athenian process there is also, no doubt, to be traced a different thought. Expiation is one of the ends most insisted on by Plato, and appears to have been the purpose of the procedure mentioned by Aeschines. Some passages in the Roman historians which will be mentioned again seem to point in the same direction. /2/

Another peculiarity to be noticed is, that the liability seems to have been regarded as attached to the body doing the damage, in an almost physical sense. An untrained intelligence only imperfectly performs the analysis by which jurists carry responsibility back to the beginning of a chain of causation. The hatred for anything giving us pain, which wreaks itself on the manifest cause, and which leads even civilized man to kick a door when it pinches his finger, is embodied in the noxoe deditio and other kindred doctrines of early Roman law. There is a defective passage in Gaius, which seems to say that liability may sometimes be escaped by giving up even the dead body of the offender. /1/ So Livy relates that, Brutulus Papins having caused a breach of truce with the Romans, the Samnites determined to surrender him, and that, upon his avoiding disgrace and punishment by suicide, they sent his lifeless body. It is noticeable that the surrender seems to be regarded as the natural expiation for the breach of treaty, /2/ and that it is equally a matter of course to send the body when the wrong-doer has perished. /3/

The most curious examples of this sort occur in the region of what we should now call contract. Livy again furnishes an example, if, indeed, the last is not one. The Roman Consul Postumius concluded the disgraceful peace of the Caudine Forks (per sponsionem, as Livy says, denying the common story that it was per feedus), and he was sent to Rome to obtain the sanction of the people. When there however, he proposed that the persons who had made the contract, including himself, should be given up in satisfaction of it. For, he said, the Roman people not having sanctioned the agreement, who is so ignorant of the jus fetialium as not to know that they are released from obligation by surrendering us? The formula of surrender seems to bring the case within the noxoe deditio. /1/ Cicero narrates a similar surrender of Mancinus by the pater-patratus to the Numantines, who, however, like the Samnites in the former case, refused to receive him. /2/

It might be asked what analogy could have been found between a breach of contract and those wrongs which excite the desire for vengeance. But it must be remembered that the distinction between tort and breaches of contract, and especially between the remedies for the two, is not found ready made. It is conceivable that a procedure adapted to redress for violence was extended to other cases as they arose. Slaves were surrendered for theft as well as for assault; /1/ and it is said that a debtor who did not pay his debts, or a seller who failed to deliver an article for which he had been paid, was dealt with on the same footing as a thief. /2/ This line of thought, together with the quasi material conception of legal obligations as binding the offending body, which has been noticed, would perhaps explain the well-known law of the Twelve Tables as to insolvent debtors. According to that law, if a man was indebted to several creditors and insolvent, after certain formalities they might cut up his body and divide it among them. If there was a single creditor, he might put his debtor to death or sell him as a slave. /3/

If no other right were given but to reduce a debtor to slavery, the law might be taken to look only to compensation, and to be modelled on the natural working of self-redress. /4/ The principle of our own law, that taking a man's body on execution satisfies the debt, although he is not detained an hour, seems to be explained in that way. But the right to put to death looks like vengeance, and the division of the body shows that the debt was conceived very literally to inhere in or bind the body with a vinculum juris.

Whatever may be the true explanation of surrender in connection with contracts, for the present purpose we need not go further than the common case of noxoe deditio for wrongs. Neither is the seeming adhesion of liability to the very body which did the harm of the first importance. The Roman law dealt mainly with living creatures,—with animals and slaves. If a man was run over, it did not surrender the wagon which crushed him, but the ox which drew the wagon. /1/ At this stage the notion is easy to understand. The desire for vengeance may be felt as strongly against a slave as against a freeman, and it is not without example nowadays that a like passion should be felt against an animal. The surrender of the slave or beast empowered the injured party to do his will upon them. Payment by the owner was merely a privilege in case he wanted to buy the vengeance off.

It will readily be imagined that such a system as has been described could not last when civilization had advanced to any considerable height. What had been the privilege of buying off vengeance by agreement, of paying the damage instead of surrendering the body of the offender, no doubt became a general custom. The Aquilian law, passed about a couple of centuries later than the date of the Twelve Tables, enlarged the sphere of compensation for bodily injuries. Interpretation enlarged the Aquilian law. Masters became personally liable for certain wrongs committed by their slaves with their knowledge, where previously they were only bound to surrender the slave. /2/ If a pack-mule threw off his burden upon a passer-by because he had been improperly overloaded, or a dog which might have been restrained escaped from his master and bit any one, the old noxal action, as it was called, gave way to an action under the new law to enforce a general personal liability. /3/ Still later, ship-owners and innkeepers were made liable as if they were wrong-doers for wrongs committed by those in their employ on board ship or in the tavern, although of course committed without their knowledge. The true reason for this exceptional responsibility was the exceptional confidence which was necessarily reposed in carriers and innkeepers. /1/ But some of the jurists, who regarded the surrender of children and slaves as a privilege intended to limit liability, explained this new liability on the ground that the innkeeper or ship-owner was to a certain degree guilty of negligence in having employed the services of bad men? This was the first instance of a master being made unconditionally liable for the wrongs of his servant. The reason given for it was of general application, and the principle expanded to the scope of the reason.

The law as to ship-owners and innkeepers introduced another and more startling innovation. It made them responsible when those whom they employed were free, as well as when they were slaves. /3/ For the first time one man was made answerable for the wrongs of another who was also answerable himself, and who had a standing before the law. This was a great change from the bare permission to ransom one's slave as a privilege. But here we have the history of the whole modern doctrine of master and servant, and principal and agent. All servants are now as free and as liable to a suit as their masters. Yet the principle introduced on special grounds in a special case, when servants were slaves, is now the general law of this country and England, and under it men daily have to pay large sums for other people's acts, in which they had no part and for which they are in no sense to blame. And to this day the reason offered by the Roman jurists for an exceptional rule is made to justify this universal and unlimited responsibility. /1/

So much for one of the parents of our common law. Now let us turn for a moment to the Teutonic side. The Salic Law embodies usages which in all probability are of too early a date to have been influenced either by Rome or the Old Testament. The thirty-sixth chapter of the ancient text provides that, if a man is killed by a domestic animal, the owner of the animal shall pay half the composition (which he would have had to pay to buy off the blood feud had he killed the man himself), and for the other half give up the beast to the complainant. /2/ So, by chapter thirty-five, if a slave killed a freeman, he was to be surrendered for one half of the composition to the relatives of the slain man, and the master was to pay the other half. But according to the gloss, if the slave or his master had been maltreated by the slain man or his relatives, the master had only to surrender the slave. /3/ It is interesting to notice that those Northern sources which Wilda takes to represent a more primitive stage of German law confine liability for animals to surrender alone. /4/ There is also a trace of the master's having been able to free himself in some cases, at a later date, by showing that the slave was no longer in his possession. /1/ There are later provisions making a master liable for the wrongs committed by his slave by his command. /2/ In the laws adapted by the Thuringians from the earlier sources, it is provided in terms that the master is to pay for all damage done by his slaves. /4/

In short, so far as I am able to trace the order of development in the customs of the German tribes, it seems to have been entirely similar to that which we have already followed in the growth of Roman law. The earlier liability for slaves and animals was mainly confined to surrender; the later became personal, as at Rome.

The reader may begin to ask for the proof that all this has any bearing on our law of today. So far as concerns the influence of the Roman law upon our own, especially the Roman law of master and servant, the evidence of it is to be found in every book which has been written for the last five hundred years. It has been stated already that we still repeat the reasoning of the Roman lawyers, empty as it is, to the present day. It will be seen directly whether the German folk-laws can also be followed into England.

In the Kentish laws of Hlothhaere and Eadrie (A.D. 680) it is said, "If any one's slave slay a freeman, whoever it be, let the owner pay with a hundred shillings, give up the slayer," &c. /1/ There are several other similar provisions. In the nearly contemporaneous laws of Ine, the surrender and payment are simple alternatives. "If a Wessex slave slay an Englishman, then shall he who owns him deliver him up to the lord and the kindred, or give sixty shillings for his life." /2/ Alfred's laws (A.D. 871–901) have a like provision as to cattle. "If a neat wound a man, let the neat be delivered up or compounded for." /3/ And Alfred, although two hundred years later than the first English lawgivers who have been quoted, seems to have gone back to more primitive notions than we find before his time. For the same principle is extended to the case of a tree by which a man is killed. "If, at their common work, one man slay another unwilfully, let the tree be given to the kindred, and let them have it off the land within thirty nights. Or let him take possession of it who owns the wood." /4/

It is not inapposite to compare what Mr. Tylor has mentioned concerning the rude Kukis of Southern Asia. "If a tiger killed a Kuki, his family were in disgrace till they had retaliated by killing and eating this tiger, or another; but further, if a man was killed by a fall from a tree, his relatives would take their revenge by cutting the tree down, and scattering it in chips." /5/

To return to the English, the later laws, from about a hundred years after Alfred down to the collection known as the laws of Henry I, compiled long after the Conquest, increase the lord's liability for his household, and make him surety for his men's good conduct. If they incur a fine to the king and run away, the lord has to pay it unless he can clear himself of complicity. But I cannot say that I find until a later period the unlimited liability of master for servant which was worked out on the Continent, both by the German tribes and at Rome. Whether the principle when established was an indigenous growth, or whether the last step was taken under the influence of the Roman law, of which Bracton made great use, I cannot say. It is enough that the soil was ready for it, and that it took root at an early day. /1/ This is all that need be said here with regard to the liability of a master for the misdeeds of his servants.

It is next to be shown what became of the principle as applied to animals. Nowadays a man is bound at his peril to keep his cattle from trespassing, and he is liable for damage done by his dog or by any fierce animal, if he has notice of a tendency in the brute to do the harm complained of. The question is whether any connection can be established between these very sensible and intelligible rules of modern law and the surrender directed by King Alfred.

Let us turn to one of the old books of the Scotch law, where the old principle still appears in full force and is stated with its reasons as then understood, /2/

"Gif ane wylde or head-strang horse, carries ane man against his will over an craig, or heuch, or to the water, and the man happin to drowne, the horse sall perteine to the king as escheit.

"Bot it is otherwise of ane tame and dantoned horse; gif any man fulishlie rides, and be sharp spurres compelles his horse to take the water, and the man drownes, the horse sould not be escheit, for that comes be the mans fault or trespasse, and not of the horse, and the man has receaved his punishment, in sa farre as he is perished and dead; and the horse quha did na fault, sould not be escheit.

"The like reason is of all other beastes, quhilk slayes anie man, [it is added in a later work, "of the quhilk slaughter they haue gilt,"] for all these beasts sould be escheit." /1/

"The Forme and Maner of Baron Courts" continues as follows:—

"It is to witt, that this question is asked in the law, Gif ane lord hes ane milne, and any man fall in the damne, and be borne down with the water quhill he comes to the quheill, and there be slaine to death with the quheill; quhither aught the milne to be eseheir or not? The law sayes thereto nay, and be this reason, For it is ane dead thing, and ane dead thing may do na fellony, nor be made escheit throw their gilt. Swa the milne in this case is not culpable, and in the law it is lawfull to the lord of the land to haue ane mylne on his awin water quhere best likes him." /2/

The reader will see in this passage, as has been remarked already of the Roman law, that a distinction is taken between things which are capable of guilt and those which are not,—between living and dead things; but he will also see that no difficulty was felt in treating animals as guilty.

Take next an early passage of the English law, a report of what was laid down by one of the English judges. In 1333 it was stated for law, that, "if my dog kills your sheep, and I, freshly after the fact, tender you the dog, you are without recovery against me." /1/ More than three centuries later, in 1676, it was said by Twisden, J. that, "if one hath kept a tame fox, which gets loose and grows wild, he that hath kept him before shall not answer for the damage the fox doth after he hath lost him, and he hath resumed his wild nature." /2/ It is at least doubtful whether that sentence ever would have been written but for the lingering influence of the notion that the ground of the owner's liability was his ownership of the offending: thing and his failure to surrender it. When the fox escaped, by another principle of law the ownership was at an end. In fact, that very consideration was seriously pressed in England as late as 1846, with regard to a monkey which escaped and bit the plaintiff, /3/ So it seems to be a reasonable conjecture, that it was this way of thinking which led Lord Holt, near the beginning of the last century, to intimate that one ground on which a man is bound at his peril to restrain cattle from trespassing is that he has valuable property in such animals, whereas he has not dogs, for which his responsibility is less. /4/ To this day, in fact, cautious judges state the law as to cattle to be, that, "if I am the owner of an animal in which by law the right of property can exist, I am bound to take care that it does not stray into the land of my neighbor." /1/

I do not mean that our modern law on this subject is only a survival, and that the only change from primitive notions was to substitute the owner for the offending animal. For although it is probable that the early law was one of the causes which led to the modern doctrine, there has been too much good sense in every stage of our law to adopt any such sweeping consequences as would follow from the wholesale transfer of liability supposed. An owner is not bound at his peril to keep his cattle from harming his neighbor's person. /2/ And in some of the earliest instances of personal liability, even for trespass on a neighbor's land, the ground seems to have been the owner's negligence. /3/

It is the nature of those animals which the common law recognizes as the subject of ownership to stray, and when straying to do damage by trampling down and eating crops. At the same time it is usual and easy to restrain them. On the other hand, a dog, which is not the subject of property, does no harm by simply crossing the land of others than its owner. Hence to this extent the new law might have followed the old. The right of property in the offending animal, which was the ancient ground of responsibility, might have been adopted safely enough as the test of a liability based on the fault of the owner. But the responsibility for damage of a kind not to be expected from such animals is determined on grounds of policy comparatively little disturbed by tradition. The development of personal liability for fierce wild animals at Rome has been explained. Our law seems to have followed the Roman.

We will now follow the history of that branch of the primitive notion which was least likely to survive,—the liability of inanimate things.

It will be remembered that King Alfred ordained the surrender of a tree, but that the later Scotch law refused it because a dead thing could not have guilt. It will be remembered, also, that the animals which the Scotch law forfeited were escheat to the king. The same thing has remained true in England until well into this century, with regard even to inanimate objects. As long ago as Bracton, /1/ in case a man was slain, the coroner was to value the object causing the death, and that was to be forfeited sa deodand "pro rege." It was to be given to God, that is to say to the Church, for the king, to be expended for the good of his soul. A man's death had ceased to be the private affair of his friends as in the time of the barbarian folk-laws. The king, who furnished the court, now sued for the penalty. He supplanted the family in the claim on the guilty thing, and the Church supplanted him.

In Edward the First's time some of the cases remind of the barbarian laws at their rudest stage. If a man fell from a tree, the tree was deodand. /2/ If he drowned in a well, the well was to be filled up. /1/ It did not matter that the forfeited instrument belonged to an innocent person. "Where a man killeth another with the sword of John at Stile, the sword shall be forfeit as deodand, and yet no default is in the owner." /2/ That is from a book written in the reign of Henry VIII., about 1530. And it has been repeated from Queen Elizabeth's time /3/ to within one hundred years, /4/ that if my horse strikes a man, and afterwards I sell my horse, and after that the man dies, the horse shall be forfeited. Hence it is, that, in all indictments for homicide, until very lately it has been necessary to state the instrument causing the death and its value, as that the stroke was given by a certain penknife, value sixpence, so as to secure the forfeiture. It is said that a steam-engine has been forfeited in this way.

I now come to what I regard as the most remarkable transformation of this principle, and one which is a most important factor in our law as it is today. I must for the moment leave the common law and take up the doctrines of the Admiralty. In the early books which have just been referred to, and long afterwards, the fact of motion is adverted to as of much importance. A maxim of Henry Spigurnel, a judge in the time of Edward I, is reported, that "where a man is killed by a cart, or by the fall of a house, or in other like manner, and the thing in motion is the cause of the death, it shall be deodand." /5/ So it was said in the next reign that "oinne illud quod mover cum eo quod occidit homines deodandum domino Regi erit, vel feodo clerici." /1/ The reader sees how motion gives life to the object forfeited.

The most striking example of this sort is a ship. And accordingly the old books say that, if a man falls from a ship and is drowned, the motion of the ship must be taken to cause the death, and the ship is forfeited,—provided, however, that this happens in fresh water. /2/ For if the death took place on the high seas, that was outside the ordinary jurisdiction. This proviso has been supposed to mean that ships at sea were not forfeited; /3/ but there is a long series of petitions to the king in Parliament that such forfeitures may be done away with, which tell a different story. /4/ The truth seems to be that the forfeiture took place, but in a different court. A manuscript of the reign of Henry VI., only recently printed, discloses the fact that, if a man was killed or drowned at sea by the motion of the ship, the vessel was forfeited to the admiral upon a proceeding in the admiral's court, and subject to release by favor of the admiral or the king. /5/

A ship is the most living of inanimate things. Servants sometimes say "she" of a clock, but every one gives a gender to vessels. And we need not be surprised, therefore, to find a mode of dealing which has shown such extraordinary vitality in the criminal law applied with even more striking thoroughness in the Admiralty. It is only by supposing the ship to have been treated as if endowed with personality, that the arbitrary seeming peculiarities of the maritime law can be made intelligible, and on that supposition they at once become consistent and logical.

By way of seeing what those peculiarities are, take first a case of collision at sea. A collision takes place between two vessels, the Ticonderoga and the Melampus, through the fault of the Ticonderoga alone. That ship is under a lease at the time, the lessee has his own master in charge, and the owner of the vessel has no manner of control over it. The owner, therefore, is not to blame, and he cannot even be charged on the ground that the damage was done by his servants. He is free from personal liability on elementary principles. Yet it is perfectly settled that there is a lien on his vessel for the amount of the damage done, /1/ and this means that that vessel may be arrested and sold to pay the loss in any admiralty court whose process will reach her. If a livery-stable keeper lets a horse and wagon to a customer, who runs a man down by careless driving, no one would think of claiming a right to seize the horse and wagon. It would be seen that the only property which could be sold to pay for a wrong was the property of the wrong-doer.

But, again, suppose that the vessel, instead of being under lease, is in charge of a pilot whose employment is made compulsory by the laws of the port which she is just entering. The Supreme Court of the United States holds the ship liable in this instance also. /2/ The English courts would probably have decided otherwise, and the matter is settled in England by legislation. But there the court of appeal, the Privy Council, has been largely composed of common-law lawyers, and it has shown a marked tendency to assimilate common-law doctrine. At common law one who could not impose a personal liability on the owner could not bind a particular chattel to answer for a wrong of which it had been the instrument. But our Supreme Court has long recognized that a person may bind a ship, when he could not bind the owners personally, because he was not the agent.

It may be admitted that, if this doctrine were not supported by an appearance of good sense, it would not have survived. The ship is the only security available in dealing with foreigners, and rather than send one's own citizens to search for a remedy abroad in strange courts, it is easy to seize the vessel and satisfy the claim at home, leaving the foreign owners to get their indemnity as they may be able. I dare say some such thought has helped to keep the practice alive, but I believe the true historic foundation is elsewhere. The ship no doubt, like a sword would have been forfeited for causing death, in whosesoever hands it might have been. So, if the master and mariners of a ship, furnished with letters of reprisal, committed piracy against a friend of the king, the owner lost his ship by the admiralty law, although the crime was committed without his knowledge or assent. /2/ It seems most likely that the principle by which the ship was forfeited to the king for causing death, or for piracy, was the same as that by which it was bound to private sufferers for other damage, in whose hands soever it might have been when it did the harm.

If we should say to an uneducated man today, "She did it and she ought to pay for it," it may be doubted whether he would see the fallacy, or be ready to explain that the ship was only property, and that to say, "The ship has to pay for it," /1/ was simply a dramatic way of saying that somebody's property was to be sold, and the proceeds applied to pay for a wrong committed by somebody else.

It would seem that a similar form of words has been enough to satisfy the minds of great lawyers. The following is a passage from a judgment by Chief Justice Marshall, which is quoted with approval by Judge Story in giving the opinion of the Supreme Court of the United States: "This is not a proceeding against the owner; it is a proceeding against the vessel for an offence committed by the vessel; which is not the less an offence, and does not the less subject her to forfeiture, because it was committed without the authority and against the will of the owner. It is true that inanimate matter can commit no offence. But this body is animated and put in action by the crew, who are guided by the master. The vessel acts and speaks by the master. She reports herself by the master. It is, therefore, not unreasonable that the vessel should be affected by this report." And again Judge Story quotes from another case: "The thing is here primarily considered as the offender, or rather the offence is primarily attached to the thing." /2/

In other words, those great judges, although of course aware that a ship is no more alive than a mill-wheel, thought that not only the law did in fact deal with it as if it were alive, but that it was reasonable that the law should do so. The reader will observe that they do not say simply that it is reasonable on grounds of policy to sacrifice justice to the owner to security for somebody else but that it is reasonable to deal with the vessel as an offending thing. Whatever the hidden ground of policy may be, their thought still clothes itself in personifying language.

Let us now go on to follow the peculiarities of the maritime law in other directions. For the cases which have been stated are only parts of a larger whole.

By the maritime law of the Middle Ages the ship was not only the source, but the limit, of liability. The rule already prevailed, which has been borrowed and adopted by the English statutes and by our own act of Congress of 1851, according to which the owner is discharged from responsibility for wrongful acts of a master appointed by himself upon surrendering his interest in the vessel and the freight which she had earned. By the doctrines of agency he would be personally liable for the whole damage. If the origin of the system of limited liability which is believed to be so essential to modern commerce is to be attributed to those considerations of public policy on which it would now be sustained, that system has nothing to do with the law of collision. But if the limit of liability here stands on the same ground as the noxoe deditio, confirms the explanation already given of the liability of the ship for wrongs done by it while out of the owner's hands, and conversely existence of that liability confirms the argument here.

Let us now take another rule, for which, as usual, there is a plausible explanation of policy. Freight, it is said, the mother of wages; for, we are told, "if the ship perished, if the mariners were to have their wages in such cases, they would not use their endeavors, nor hazard their lives, for the safety of the ship." /1/ The best commentary on this reasoning is, that the law has recently been changed by statute. But even by the old law there was an exception inconsistent with the supposed reason. In case of shipwreck, which was the usual case of a failure to earn freight, so long as any portion of the ship was saved, the lien of the mariners remained. I suppose it would have been said, because it was sound policy to encourage them to save all they could. If we consider that the sailors were regarded as employed by the ship, we shall understand very readily both the rule and the exception. "The ship is the debtor," as was said in arguing a case decided in the time of William III. /2/ If the debtor perished, there was an end of the matter. If a part came ashore, that might be proceeded against.

Even the rule in its modern form, that freight is the mother of wages, is shown by the explanation commonly given to have reference to the question whether the ship is lost or arrive safe. In the most ancient source of the maritime law now extant, which has anything about the matter, so far as I have been able to discover, the statement is that the mariners will lose their wages when the ship is lost. /3/ In like manner, in what is said by its English editor, Sir Travers Twiss, to be the oldest part of the Consulate of the Sea, /1/ we read that "whoever the freighter may be who runs away or dies, the ship is bound to pay: the mariners." /2/ I think we may assume that the vessel was bound by the contract with the sailors, much in the same way as it was by the wrongs for which it was answerable, just as the debtor's body was answerable for his debts, as well as for his crimes, under the ancient law of Rome.

The same thing is true of other maritime dealings with the vessel, whether by way of contract or otherwise. If salvage service is rendered to a vessel, the admiralty court will hold the vessel, although it has been doubted whether an action of contract would lie, if the owners were sued at law. So the ship is bound by the master's contract to carry cargo, just as in case of collision, although she was under lease at the time. In such cases, also, according to our Supreme Court, the master may bind the vessel when he cannot bind the general owners. /4/ "By custom the ship is bound to the merchandise, and the merchandise to the ship." /5/ "By the maritime law every contract of the master implies an hypothecation." /6/ It might be urged, no doubt, with force, that, so far as the usual maritime contracts are concerned, the dealing must be on the security of the ship or merchandise in many cases, and therefore that it is policy to give this security in all cases; that the risk to which it subjects ship-owners is calculable, and that they must take it into account when they let their vessels. Again, in many cases, when a party asserts a maritime lien by way of contract, he has improved the condition of the thing upon which the lien is claimed, and this has been recognized as a ground for such a lien in some systems. But this is not true universally, nor in the most important cases. It must be left to the reader to decide whether ground has not been shown for believing that the same metaphysical confusion which naturally arose as to the ship's wrongful acts, affected the way of thinking as to her contracts. The whole manner of dealing with vessels obviously took the form which prevailed in the eases first mentioned. Pardessus, a high authority, says that the lien for freight prevails even against the owner of stolen goods, "as the master deals less with the person than the thing." /2/ So it was said in the argument of a famous English case, that "the ship is instead of the owner, and therefore is answerable." /3/ In many cases of contract, as well as tort, the vessel was not only the security for the debt, but the limit of the owner's liability.

The principles of the admiralty are embodied in its form of procedure. A suit may be brought there against a vessel by name, any person interested in it being at liberty to come in and defend, but the suit, if successful, ending in a sale of the vessel and a payment of the plaintiff's claim out of the proceeds. As long ago as the time of James I. it was said that "the libel ought to be only against the ship and goods, and not against the party." /1/ And authority for the statement was cited from the reign of Henry VI., the same reign when, as we have seen, the Admiral claimed a forfeiture of ships for causing death. I am bound to say, however, that I cannot find such an authority of that date.

We have now followed the development of the chief forms of liability in modern law for anything other than the immediate and manifest consequences of a man's own acts. We have seen the parallel course of events in the two parents,—the Roman law and the German customs, and in the offspring of those two on English soil with regard to servants, animals, and inanimate things. We have seen a single germ multiplying and branching into products as different from each other as the flower from the root. It hardly remains to ask what that germ was. We have seen that it was the desire of retaliation against the offending thing itself. Undoubtedly, it might be argued that many of the rules stated were derived from a seizure of the offending thing as security for reparation, at first, perhaps, outside the law. That explanation, as well as the one offered here; would show that modern views of responsibility had not yet been attained, as the owner of the thing might very well not have been the person in fault. But such has not been the view of those most competent to judge. A consideration of the earliest instances will show, as might have been expected, that vengeance, not compensation, and vengeance on the offending thing, was the original object. The ox in Exodus was to be stoned. The axe in the Athenian law was to be banished. The tree, in Mr. Tylor's instance, was to be chopped to pieces. The slave under all the systems was to be surrendered to the relatives of the slain man, that they might do with him what they liked. /1/ The deodand was an accursed thing. The original limitation of liability to surrender, when the owner was before the court, could not be accounted for if it was his liability, and not that of his property, which was in question. Even where, as in some of the cases, expiation seems to be intended rather than vengeance, the object is equally remote from an extrajudicial distress.

The foregoing history, apart from the purposes for which it has been given, well illustrates the paradox of form and substance in the development of law. In form its growth is logical. The official theory is that each new decision follows syllogistically from existing precedents. But just as the clavicle in the cat only tells of the existence of some earlier creature to which a collar-bone was useful, precedents survive in the law long after the use they once served is at an end and the reason for them has been forgotten. The result of following them must often be failure and confusion from the merely logical point of view.

On the other hand, in substance the growth of the law is legislative. And this in a deeper sense than that what the courts declare to have always been the law is in fact new. It is legislative in its grounds. The very considerations which judges most rarely mention, and always with an apology, are the secret root from which the law draws all the juices of life. I mean, of course, considerations of what is expedient for the community concerned. Every important principle which is developed by litigation is in fact and at bottom the result of more or less definitely understood views of public policy; most generally, to be sure, under our practice and traditions, the unconscious result of instinctive preferences and inarticulate convictions, but none the less traceable to views of public policy in the last analysis. And as the law is administered by able and experienced men, who know too much to sacrifice good sense to a syllogism, it will be found that, when ancient rules maintain themselves in the way that has been and will be shown in this book, new reasons more fitted to the time have been found for them, and that they gradually receive a new content, and at last a new form, from the grounds to which they have been transplanted.

But hitherto this process has been largely unconscious. It is important, on that account, to bring to mind what the actual course of events has been. If it were only to insist on a more conscious recognition of the legislative function of the courts, as just explained, it would be useful, as we shall see more clearly further on. /1/

What has been said will explain the failure of all theories which consider the law only from its formal side; whether they attempt to deduce the corpus from a priori postulates, or fall into the humbler error of supposing the science of the law to reside in the elegantia juris, or logical cohesion of part with part. The truth is, that the law always approaching, and never reaching, consistency. It is forever adopting new principles from life at one end, and it always retains old ones from history at the other, which have not yet been absorbed or sloughed off. It will become entirely consistent only when it ceases to grow.

The study upon which we have been engaged is necessary both for the knowledge and for the revision of the law. However much we may codify the law into a series of seemingly self-sufficient propositions, those propositions will be but a phase in a continuous growth. To understand their scope fully, to know how they will be dealt with by judges trained in the past which the law embodies, we must ourselves know something of that past. The history of what the law has been is necessary to the knowledge of what the law is.

Again, the process which I have described has involved the attempt to follow precedents, as well as to give a good reason for them. When we find that in large and important branches of the law the various grounds of policy on which the various rules have been justified are later inventions to account for what are in fact survivals from more primitive times, we have a right to reconsider the popular reasons, and, taking a broader view of the field, to decide anew whether those reasons are satisfactory. They may be, notwithstanding the manner of their appearance. If truth were not often suggested by error, if old implements could not be adjusted to new uses, human progress would be slow. But scrutiny and revision are justified.

But none of the foregoing considerations, nor the purpose of showing the materials for anthropology contained in the history of the law, are the immediate object here. My aim and purpose have been to show that the various forms of liability known to modern law spring from the common ground of revenge. In the sphere of contract the fact will hardly be material outside the cases which have been stated in this Lecture. But in the criminal law and the law of torts it is of the first importance. It shows that they have started from a moral basis, from the thought that some one was to blame.

It remains to be proved that, while the terminology of morals is still retained, and while the law does still and always, in a certain sense, measure legal liability by moral standards, it nevertheless, by the very necessity of its nature, is continually transmuting those moral standards into external or objective ones, from which the actual guilt of the party concerned is wholly eliminated.

CHAPTER 2 QUESTIONS

1. Justice Oliver Wendell Holmes tells us at the beginning of his first lecture that "The life of the law has not been logic; it has been experience." What does he mean?
2. Oliver Wendell Holmes tells us that students of history know that rules persist over time. What changes?
3. In your own words, give a definition of liability. Why do you think that Holmes chose to begin his lectures with this area of law?
4. In the Bible's Book of Exodus, if a man's oxen gored another man, how was justice administered? What example does Holmes give to show that Greek law was similar?

5. Describe the liability of the owner of a ferocious wild animal in Greek and Roman law. How is it different from liability today?
6. Holmes tells us that Aquilian Law assigned liability to shipowners and innkeepers for hiring "bad men." What is this the first example of, according to Holmes?
7. Did Teutonic (German) liability law develop in a similar or dissimilar way to Greek, Roman and later English and American liability law, according to Holmes? What are some parallels?
8. Justice Holmes provides a lengthy discussion of maritime law and liability. Do you think that this hurts or helps his argument?
9. What is the paradox of form and substance?

Chapter 3

Do You Really Want to Be an Attorney?

I SUSPECT THAT MANY OF YOU WANT to be attorneys. We of course make fun of attorneys and tell lawyer jokes. Regardless, Americans have also historically held attorneys in high esteem. Many of the founding fathers were attorneys, as are their contemporaries in the US Congress.

I imagine that some of you like to argue. You most likely take an interest in politics. Perhaps you feel strongly about an issue and want to contribute to a cause. You might also believe that your language skills are much stronger than your mathematical skills, so becoming an attorney would be a better fit than, let's say, an aeronautical engineer or a scientist.

Often, we think more about achieving a personal goal rather than what happens after one achieves it. This happens to attorneys, too. They channel their energies into finishing college and law school successfully, only to discover that practicing law is not what they imagined it to be.

When we think about attorneys, we often imagine people who are highly educated professionals who earn at least enough money to be part of the middle class. Not being attorneys ourselves, we don't see the challenges that they face and what it is like to be an attorney—and the picture in our minds is often much rosier than the reality.

Those who study the courts give much attention to the actors, in particular judges and attorneys. One important observation about lawyers that scholars have made is called the *Two Hemispheres of Law*. Lawyers, as it turns out, are not all the same.

Those attorneys who occupy the top hemisphere work for large firms. These firms are typically found in large cities and employ hundreds of attorneys. These firms have cultivated relationships with corporations and other well-heeled, often deep-pocketed clients. These firms generally accept only lawyers who attended the most prestigious law schools and held clerkships with important judges. The attorneys are paid very well.

In the bottom hemisphere are the attorneys who graduated law school and passed the state bar examinations. These attorneys work for themselves as solo practitioners or have joined small firms. These lawyers generally work for individuals rather than corporations. They handle divorce work, insurance claims, and criminal defense. As they often work alone, solo practitioners often report being professionally isolated and personally lonely.

The attorneys in the two hemispheres work almost entirely independently of each other. There exists little to no communication between the attorneys occupying each of the hemispheres. These attorneys are also unlikely to participate in cases together.

Scholars first described the legal stratification in the 1950s. Sociologist Dan C. Lortie (1959) put into words what was quietly known. He found in his study of Chicago attorneys that their career paths were largely determined by the law schools that they attended. He also found that the most desirable work was held by white, Protestant males.

In his study of 90 solo practitioners, Jerome E. Carlin (2011) reached a similar conclusion, observing that solo practitioners in Chicago endured professional isolation and personal financial struggle. Subsequent studies by Carlin and other scholars have found that the attorneys who work for themselves or small firms struggle the most (Carlin 1970; Ladinsky 1963).

Heinz and Laumann coined the phrase "Two Hemispheres of Law" in their 1982 book *Chicago Lawyers: The Social Structure of the Bar.*

Newer scholarship has found that attorneys in the lower hemisphere are increasingly specializing. Historically, these attorneys were generalists, accepting work in different areas of law. Today, there is a move toward specialization. These specialist attorneys have a rosier outlook and professional pride (Seron 1996; Van Hoy 1997)

Carlin published his original findings about solo practitioners in Chicago in *Lawyers on Their Own* (2011). In the book, he describes the day-to-day lives of the attorneys at the bottom of the legal pecking order and the challenges that they faced.

Their challenges were primarily financial, as these attorneys had to scrape together work that often did not pay very much. They were also personal, as the attorneys often were not given the attention or professional development that they needed to grow. Carlin also finds that these attorneys were more likely to violate professional norms. For example, they were more likely to give money to court clerks in exchange for favors.

Achieving a job in corporate law is often difficult, as is the life of an attorney practicing law on their own, as Carlin explores. Winning the coveted position of Supreme Court justice is even more challenging and unlikely.

The scholarship suggests that the selection process for justices is heavily influenced by the same elitism of the selection of corporate lawyers. In Reading 3.3, law professor Patrick J. Glen examines the proportion of justices on the US Supreme Court who graduated from either Harvard or Yale University, beginning with Justice Oliver Wendell Holmes in 1902 and continuing until 2010.

He observes that graduates of Harvard Law School have held at least one appointment to the Supreme Court for the entire period that he studied. However, he notes, perhaps unexpectedly, that the proportion of graduates from these two elite schools on the Supreme Court has grown dramatically, particularly in the most recent years of his study. Glen writes that "Kagan's confirmation represents the penultimate change to the Court in replacing Justice Stevens, leaving Ginsburg as the lone non-Harvard, non-Yale graduate" (137).

Glen writes that many view the growing dominance of Harvard and Yale law school graduates as to be expected. These schools have won reputations as the best schools and consequently attract the best applicants.

Nonetheless, Glen is not satisfied with this explanation. He observes that Jonathan Turley (2010) and Judge Louis Pollak (2009) found little or no difference between the quality of education at these schools and others. Timothy O'Neill posits that US presidents appoint graduates of Harvard and Yale because they are "above reproach" and the Senate is more likely to confirm them. O'Neill dismisses this explanation for the same reason, as these nominees are no more qualified than the graduates of other law schools (2007).

Glen's study ended in 2010. Since then, US Presidents Donald Trump and Joe Biden have appointed four new Supreme Court justices. The appointments have followed Glen's observation that Harvard and Yale disproportionately and perhaps unfairly dominate Supreme Court appointments. The only recent appointee from another law school is Justice Amy Coney Barret, a graduate of Notre Dame Law School.

It is also interesting to consider the perspective that the Supreme Court—now with four women and three justices who are not white—is more inclusive than ever. They all graduated from an increasingly small number of schools where they had similar experiences unlike those of most Americans.

As you read Carlin's *Lawyers on Their Own*, consider also who became attorneys in his study and their life trajectories. Why did they decide to become attorneys? What were their family backgrounds? How were they educated? Did their educations prepare them adequately for the legal profession? Were these attorneys happy?

We can also think more broadly about the two-tier legal system and society. Clearly, this system is not fair to most attorneys when one's future success is cemented by an admission letter to a top law school rather than the talent and hard work that comes after passing the bar exam.

Reading 3.1

The Road to Individual Practice

Jerome E. Carlin

THE INDIVIDUAL PRACTITIONER OF LAW IN Chicago is a self-made man who came up the hard way from poor, immigrant surroundings. His father, generally an immigrant from Eastern Europe with little or no formal education, was in most cases the proprietor of a small business.1 The one burning ambition of the son was to escape from the ghetto, to rise above his father, to become a professional man. Again and again, in answer to the question of what led them to become lawyers, respondents revealed this strong drive for professional status:

> I never had any visions of glamour or glory, but a profession, honorable, making a living. My uncle [a lawyer] was living comfortably and had standing in the

---

1 The ethnic composition of the sample of 84 lawyers [...] is as follows:

TABLE 3.2.1

Nationality Background	Per Cent
Northwestern Europe: Britain, Scandinavia, France	8
Ireland	11
Central Europe: Germany, Austria, Czechoslovakia	15
Eastern Europe: Russia, Poland, Lithuania, Romania	53
Southeastern Europe: Italy, Greece, Yugoslavia	5
Africa (Negro)	8
Total	100
Number of cases	(84)

TABLE 3.2.2

Religion	Per Cent
Protestant	24
Catholic	21
Jewish	55
Total	100
Number of cases	(84)

community. I came from poor circumstances, my father was ill many years, and my brother and I had to support the family. We became professional men [his brother is also {4} a lawyer] ... a tremendous thing, especially during the depression. (11) [*A number in parentheses is the author's identification of the respondent. A number in brackets { } references the original page number of the earlier editions.*]

TABLE 3.2.3

Generation	Per Cent
Foreign born	6
Second generation (at least one parent born abroad)	68
Third generation	13
Fourth or more	13
Total	100
Number of cases	(84)

{25} Class background:

The class background of the sample is as follows:

TABLE 3.2.4

Father's Occupation	Per Cent	
Professional		6
Proprietor		63
Manufacturer, processor, wholesaler, jobber	10	
Broker, agent, dealer, independent contractor	20	
Retailer	33	
White-collar (lower managerial, salaried employees, clerical)		19
Blue-collar		12
Total		100
Number of cases		(84)

TABLE 3.2.5

Father's Education	Per Cent
College graduate	7
High school graduate	8
Grammar school graduate	25
Some grammar school	17
None, no formal education	43
Total	100
Number of cases	(84)

I was in a big family of 13 children. When I was 12 I quit school—after two years of high school—to go to work. I was going to make a living for the family. I was doing fairly well, a shipping clerk, $15 a week. I was promised a dollar a week more if I would stay and not go back to school. But I decided to go back to school, in 1923. I decided to have a specific profession, I had no idea of any other profession. (94)

I wanted to be a lawyer, and the family wanted me to be one—although since then I've realized that monetarily you can do a lot better in business. Jewish people think it's very important to be a professional, and I was always a big talker. (35)

Principally it was a question of going into some pursuit that involved respect, dignity. Among Jewish people professions are very important. And with my parents, they had little or no education, their children should have professions. There was a certain amount of appeal. Professional men were looked up to then. At one time in former years, the almighty dollar was not as important as it is today. (64)

Well over half the lawyers interviewed claimed they had no specific intention of becoming lawyers. Most of them confessed that they came to the law by default, having abandoned the idea of going into medicine, engineering, or one of a variety of other professional pursuits because they found them to be too expensive, academically too demanding, or because they saw themselves barred by discrimination. {5}

I had been taking all sorts of courses at Crane [Junior College], I didn't know what I was going to be. When I put 'em together I had sufficient for pre-law. That's how I studied law instead of medicine. I wanted to be a doctor but I was too lazy—not that I wasn't a good student, I just didn't get around to it. I'm a pretty fair student. (30)

I decided the day I entered law school. I was thinking of medicine, dentistry, or even pharmacy. Through high school and college I had a narrow education, I couldn't go anywhere on it, except into sales. I didn't get into medical school or dental school. Law was my third choice. (25)

Interviewer: When did you decide to become a lawyer?

Respondent: I suppose in 1933, when I entered law school. I considered engineering, but funds were not available for engineering.

Interviewer: Did you want to be a lawyer?

Respondent: Not particularly. I preferred engineering.
Interviewer: Did you have any idea of the kind of work lawyers did or the kind of work you might be doing?
Respondent: Not at all, not the remotest idea. (82)

A Negro lawyer said engineering had been his first choice also:

> I wanted to be an engineer, but I would have had to go to Argentina to cash in on it, so I went into law as a second choice. (75)

A similar experience was reported by a Jewish lawyer:

> I wanted to be a chemical engineer but my college professors said it was no place for a Jew.
>
> *Interviewer:* Why did you decide on the law?
> *Respondent:* Family, I guess. {6}
> *Interviewer:* Are there any lawyers in your family?
> *Respondent:* My brother was a lawyer.
> *Interviewer:* Did you want to be a lawyer, or was it something you fell into?
> *Respondent:* A combination, both; I gravitated. (14)

The individual practitioner in Chicago has in most cases received his professional training in one of the "proprietary" or Catholic night law schools.[2] Although most of those who

2 The law school background of the sample is as follows:

TABLE 3.2.6

Type of Law School	Per Cent
Full-time University (principally Univ. of Chicago, Univ. of Illinois, and Northwestern Univ.)	33
Part-time and Mixed	
Catholic (DePaul and Loyola)	36
Proprietary (principally Chicago-Kent, John Marshall, and Chicago Law School)	31
Total	100
Number of cases	(84)

{26} The two Catholic law schools are affiliated with Catholic universities, and both have offered a mixed—a morning (full-time) as well as an evening (part-time)—program since the twenties.

The proprietary law schools have no university affiliations and prior to World War II offered only an evening (part-time) program. Chicago-Kent added a morning division in the mid-forties, and

went on to a night law school had only a year or two of college credit (if that) from either a downtown night extension school or a local junior college,[3] they encountered little difficulty in gaining admission into the notoriously low-standard night law schools and faced relatively few obstacles in getting through them.

Requirements for admission to the night law school during the twenties and thirties (when two out of three of the respondents entered law school) were practically nonexistent. The general rule in such institutions was to accept any person with a high school diploma or "its equivalent," which frequently meant accepting someone with fewer than four years of high school.[4] The concern of many such schools of that period was not in keeping out the unqualified student but in recruiting as many students as possible regardless of qualifications.

Scholastic standards suffered not only from the absence of any definite rule on exclusions but also from an unwillingness to fail a poor student. Courses of instruction were limited to subjects covered by the state bar examinations, and the instructors, most of whom conducted a full-time law practice during the day, rarely had the time or the inclination to prepare for their classes.

No better summary of the character and quality of the night law school at this time can be found than in an {7} address given in 1933 at the thirty-first annual meeting of the

---

John Marshall followed suit in the early fifties. Although most are today incorporated as not-for-profit organizations, these schools have been designated as proprietary since they were generally founded as private profit-making institutions.

Hereafter the term "night law school" will be used to refer to both part-time and mixed law schools.

3 Number of years of college training for respondents from the three types of law schools:

TABLE 3.2.7

	Type of Law School			
Years in College	**Full-time University**	**Catholic**	**Proprietary**	**Total**
None	4%	0%	31%	11%
One-Two	7	54	35	32
Three	4	13	23	13
Four	85	33	11	44
Total	100%	100%	100%	100%
Number of cases	(28)	(30)	(26)	(84)

4 From the following table (3.2.8), it can be seen that in 1923, 4 out of 5 of the night law schools required at best only a high school diploma for admission. Not until the middle thirties did this proportion drop to less than half, and by the early forties to less than 15%. Even as late as 1942, however, there were only 3 night law schools that required more than 2 years of college training for admission. {27}

Association of American Law Schools in Chicago by Will Shafroth, an indefatigable crusader in the field of legal education:

> Here indeed [in the area of legal training] we find a wilderness, and if we look around it, what do we see? A veritable host of degree-conferring law schools, less than 40 per cent of them wearing the ribbon of merit which membership in the Association of American Law Schools confers, and only eight more, or a total of 84 ... out of 194, being on the American Bar Association's roll of honor. Last year [1932] the attendance in these approved schools was 46 per cent of the total law school attendance. In other words, we are obliged to admit that more than half of our law students [93 per cent of whom were in night law schools[5]] are getting the kind of training which the leaders in the teaching profession ... regard as inadequate.
>
> Isn't that statement in itself astounding? We rail about the character of the bar, at the difficulties in securing law reform, at ambulance chasing and lack of ethics, at professional incompetence, and yet we expect improvement while we are fostering, in the great majority of the states of the Union, schools which exploit their students for their own financial gain, and send them to the bar inadequately prepared, giving to the bar examiners the impossible task of turning back time after time those who are not qualified.

TABLE 3.2.8

Number of College Years Required for Admission	**Year**					
	1923	**1925**	**1927**	**1934**	**1937**	**1942**
None	80%	68%	58%	55%	34%	14%
One	9	14	15	1	3	0
Two	10	17	26	43	60	82
Three	1	1	1	1	1	1
Four	0	0	0	0	2	3
Total	100%	100%	100%	100%	100%	100%
Number of Night Law Schools	80	92	94	115	99	72

Source: *Annual Review of Legal Education for 1924* (1926, 1928, 1935, 1938), published by the Carnegie Foundation for the Advancement of Teaching (1925–1928), published by the Section of Legal Education and Admission to the Bar of the American Bar Association (1938). See pp. 21, 25, 30, 33, 34–63 of the respective issues. For 1942 figures, *Law School and Bar Admissions Requirements in the U. S. Review of Legal Education.* (Chicago: American Bar Association, Section of Legal Education and Admissions to the Bar, 1942), pp. 3–10.

5 The distribution of law students and law schools by type of law school and whether or not approved by the Council on Legal Education of the American Bar Association for 1932 was as follows:

It may be that our judgment of what is and what is not proper preparation for the bar is at fault. Arbitrary standards are never perfect in their discriminative functions. But what can we say of those schools which ignore all the rules of experience, which admit students who have had only a high school education or what they claim for an equivalent, and which have a course of three years or less {8} of evening sessions, or less than three years of full-time work. There are 38 of these schools which confer degrees scattered over the country, and some 15 others which do not. [Most were night law schools.[6]] Every one of them is a commercial school, designed first to make a profit, and, only secondarily, and in such ways as will not interfere with that profit, to teach law. I have never seen a school in that category, that is, failing in both entrance requirements and length of course as viewed from our standards, which I regarded as a fit place for a man to study law. ... The fact that these law schools continue to exist and turn out their yearly grist is nothing short of a tragedy.[7]

TABLE 3.2.9

Type of Law School	Approved	Not Approved	Total
Full-time			
Students	13,716	1,270	14,986
Schools	73	11	84
Night			
Students	3,989	18,414	22,403
Schools	9	92	101
Total			
Students	17,705	19,684	37,389
Schools	82	103	185

Source: *Annual Review of Legal Education for 1932* (Carnegie Foundation for the Advancement of Teaching, 1933), p. 32.

{28}

6 *Annual Review of Legal Education for 1933*, p. 35.

7 Will Shafroth, "Can the Law Schools Lead Us Out of the Wilderness?" *The American Law School Review* (St. Paul, Minn.: West Publishing Co., 1934), VII, 1027–1029. Shafroth had only recently completed a survey of California law schools based on first-hand observation and knew whereof he spoke. See *Report of the California Survey Committee* (Sacramento: State Bar of California, 1933) for a strikingly candid, detailed, and indeed shattering picture of the California night law schools in the thirties. With respect to the selection of students, Shafroth noted:

> A practice analogous to ambulance chasing has grown up where commissions are paid to law students for each new victim they may bring to the school and where solicitors

are not only regularly paid to hunt out and sign up prospects but are further compensated as long as their students stay in school. Instances were found where a dean was engaged for a school and was paid a certain amount for each student whom he brought with him or induced to come over from another school (p. 3).

The general character of a substantial proportion of the metropolitan night law schools of that period was well summarized by Shafroth in the same report:

> The weakest type [of law school] is a one-man institution, dominated by a single individual who makes the important decisions and, as a rule, does a large part of the teaching. This kind of school at best has as its highest ambition mere preparation to pass the bar examinations and at its worst the collection of as much money as possible from its students. Usually it is without financial resources, admits any kind of student, whatever his qualifications or lack of them, graduates practically all who remain the required length of time and pay up regularly for their tuition and books, and has only the lowest standards of scholarship. ... None of them have passed an average of half of their men in the different bar examinations since January, 1929. In some of these institutions the average of success for those taking the bar examinations for the first time has run as low as 20 per cent (p. 2). {page 29 follows}

For an excellent summary of law school conditions prior to the thirties see Alfred Z. Reed, *Training for the Public Profession of the Law* (New York: Bulletin No. 15 of the Carnegie Foundation for the Advancement of Teaching, 1921), and *Present Day Law Schools in the United States and Canada* (New York: Carnegie Foundation for the Advancement of Teaching, 1928). Reed, who along with Shafroth had alerted the profession to the serious shortcomings of a large proportion of American law schools, was editor of the *Annual Review of Legal Education* which published not only annual statistical data on law schools but also highly informative articles on various phases of legal education.

A follow-up survey of California law schools was published in 1949 under the title *Legal Education and Admissions to the Bar of California* (Sacramento: State Bar of California, 1949). This later study suggests that, while some improvement had been made in the Catholic law schools, the proprietary night law schools remained relatively unchanged. Note the following comment with respect to one of the schools of the latter type:

> This school is deficient as an educational institution, whether judged by entrance requirements, scholastic standards, faculty, administration, physical plant, library or the success of its graduates in the California bar examinations (35.2% successes for graduates of the school taking the exam for the first time between 1932 and 1949). However well intentioned and sincere its dean and faculty, the school is not providing legal education of a quality to justify its tuition fees. It should not continue in operation on its present basis, nor is there any reasonable probability of such improvement as would justify its continuance (p. 223).

Ironically, in spite of the poor showing of the night law school graduates in the bar examination almost all were eventually admitted to practice. Thus, for example, of all the candidates who took the bar examination in the years 1922 through 1924 in New York, Pennsylvania, Illinois, and California, 83 to 95 per cent had passed the bar examination by 1932, although less than half had passed on the first try. "The persistent candidate," it has been noted, "by cramming for the examination, by taking quiz courses and by coming back again and again will eventually succeed."[8]

In general, the individual practitioner works for another lawyer as a kind of apprentice during his first few years out of law school.[9] These are usually temporary positions—rarely lasting more than a year or two—paying little or, in the case of the space-for-service

---

That these deplorable conditions continue to exist in many law schools across the country is critically noted in the following articles: Elliott E. Cheatham, "The Law Schools of Tennessee," *Tennessee Law Review,* Vol. XXI (April, 1950); John G. Hervey, "The Decline of Professionalism in the Law: An Exploration into Some Causes," *New York Law Forum,* Vol. Ill, No. 4 (October, 1957); and John W. Morland, "Legal Education in Georgia," *Mercer Law Review,* Vol. II, No. 2 (Spring, 1951). The Cheatham and Morland articles report {30} on studies conducted for the Survey of the Legal Profession. Substantially better conditions were found in the Pennsylvania law schools in a study conducted for the Survey by Lon Fuller. See Lon L. Fuller, "Legal Education and Admissions to the Bar of Pennsylvania," *Temple Law Quarterly,* XXV, No. 25 (January, 1952).

In this general area, see also Albert J. Harno, *Legal Education in the United States* (San Francisco: Bancroft-Whitney Co., 1952); Joseph T. Tinelly, *Part-Time Legal Education* (Brooklyn, N.Y.: The Foundation Press, 1957); and Lowell S. Nicholson, *The Law Schools of the United States* (Baltimore: Lord Baltimore Press, Inc., 1958). Esther L. Brown, *Lawyers and the Promotion of Justice* (New York: Russell Sage Foundation, 1938) and James Willard Hurst, *The Growth of American Law* (Boston: Little, Brown and Company, 1950) contain valuable sections on legal education, and the findings of the Survey of the Legal Profession with respect to legal education are summarized in Albert P. Blaustein and Charles O. Porter, *The American Lawyer* (Chicago: University of Chicago Press, 1954).

8 *Report of the California Survey Committee* (Sacramento: State Bar of California, 1933), p. 143.

9 Fifty-six per cent of the respondents started out working for other individual or small firm lawyers; two out of three have worked or are now working for such lawyers—better than three out of four, if we include those who clerked for other lawyers while in law school. For a systematic account of the different types of beginning careers followed by young lawyers in Chicago, and the problems which these lawyers face in their first years in practice, see Dan C. Lortie, "The Striving Young Lawyer: A Study of Early Career Differentiation in the Chicago Bar" (unpublished Ph.D. dissertation, University of Chicago, 1958), and "Laymen to Lawmen: Law School, Careers, and Professional Socialization," *Harvard Educational Review,* XXIX, No. 4 (1959), 352–369.

arrangement, no salary, the assumption being that the young lawyer will be building up his own practice on the side.[10] The employers—in nearly all cases either individual or small firm lawyers—appear to be primarily interested in getting an inexpensive {9} legman, someone to run their errands in the clerks' offices, to make perfunctory court appearances, to help prepare their routine papers and documents, and occasionally to do some research. The young lawyer, on the other hand, becomes acquainted with the courts and local agencies; he gets to know his way around—whom to see and how to approach them. In other words, he gets an initiation into the workings of the lower-level judicial and administrative bureaucracies.

> As a law clerk I got no particular attention from them [his employers], but I learned from them.
>
> *Interviewer:* You mean your way around the courts?
> *Respondent:* Yes, but law too, pleadings and depositions. The big important thing, when you go around and see—at Christmastime it's traditional in Chicago to pass out $25 in envelopes to the clerks of court, the clerks in other offices, the bailiffs. If you don't, you're out of it. (25)
>
> I worked with ______ and ______, older men. I followed them around. I did legwork; I was the clerk in the firm. I got experience, contact with the courts. I was helped by coming here. You can't do it by yourself. You must associate yourself with men who have experience. Fifty per cent of your value in Chicago depends on who you know across the street [City Hall and County Buildings]. If you absorb it from someone who knows it, that's 50 per cent of the battle. If you associate yourself you just find out sooner: who to go to, where and how to go. For example, one thing you don't learn [in law school] is what papers you file in lawsuits. You need forms to file, and you have to know where to file them. The same with following return days, books of entry in City Hall, trial dates—the actual, the practical. Here's a summons you get [indicating a form]—what

10 Starting salaries for those going into practice before the Depression began at about $5 a week. During the Depression (when most of the respondents were getting started) salaries ranged between $5 and $15 a week. According to one respondent, however: "Fifteen dollars was a lot of money in those days. The ______ firm had a list of 170 men who were willing to work for nothing." During World War II salaries ranged between $25 and $45 a week, and since have climbed to between $55 and $60 a week. These figures are based on reports {31} from several respondents, and are offered, in the absence of any statistics on the matter, only as an indication of the general range of salaries for these various periods.

> do you do with it? Well, you have to file an appearance. You go across the street and get a form. {10} You have to file in a certain window. Later you have to look and find who is assigned to it, and on what date. It's not difficult but you have to learn it and remember it, and that you get from actual doing. (30)

The relationship between the older lawyer and his "apprentice" is frequently less than harmonious. Many of those who worked for other lawyers reported unpleasant experiences: either that contact with their employer had led to disenchantment or, in most instances, that there had been open conflict with their employer. One lawyer who came out of law school in the midst of the Depression recalled:

> I was in a space-for-service arrangement in an office with four attorneys. I had a sad experience—one that influenced me adversely. These three, or four, attorneys were former politicians. They had all held jobs under Republican regimes and they were sitting and waiting for the Republicans to get back in power in Chicago. One had been with the Sanitary District (and there had been a scandal). The other one ran unsuccessfully for Municipal Court judge. They were waiting to get back to the lush days. It was a disappointment to me, being a youngster out of law school with strong ambitions about law practice and some mistaken notions about it. This was my first contact with active lawyers on a business basis. These fellows were frustrated individuals, lawyers for many years but it still was a struggle—worrying about the rent and so on. That would be discouraging to all but the very strong-ambitioned individuals. Here these men with nothing, still struggling—but that was in '36 and '38 when the law practice was at a low ebb.
>
> *Interviewer:* What were your mistaken ideas about law practice? {11}
> *Respondent:* I thought that most lawyers were successful. (59)

Several reported conflicts over salary or over financial arrangements in general. One said that he felt he hadn't been paid enough for his services and that he had little chance for advancement within the small firm that employed him. After four years he finally decided to quit:

> My bosses were cheap bastards. ... I had no chance to grow; I would never be more than I was. And they weren't giving anything away. When there was a big fee—I worked on one that brought in a $20,000 fee—they never gave us an extra bonus. (60)

Another, who worked for an active promoter in the local tax field—handling most of the paper work while his boss did the promoting—when asked why he left, stated:

> I was very dissatisfied. I collected in fees the second year I was there over $600,000 and I got $25 a week. It was unfair. I quit without having another job. When I told him I was going to leave he said, "Aren't you happy here?" I said: "No." "Why," he said, "is it the money?" "Almost nothing else," I said. "How much are you making?" he asked. I told him $25 a week and that I couldn't manage on that. Well, he went up to $50, $75, even $100 but I said *no.* (6)

Another had been clerk for a firm of eight lawyers for five years when he decided to quit:

> *Interviewer:* Why did you leave the firm?
> *Respondent:* There was a financial argument. I wanted {12} more money—at least that was part of it. The head of the firm had a theory you could always hire talent, and if you didn't bring in business there was a limit to what he would pay. I couldn't bring in business, and what I did bring in, there was a question of who got the fees. (14)

Another lawyer who had been dissatisfied with his work (he found that he was handling only eviction cases) and with his employers ("one boss knew less than I did; today he's a millionaire"), when asked why he finally left, replied:

> There was a disagreement. One of the bosses thought I was holding back [the respondent was supposed to turn over 35 per cent of the fees he brought in from his own practice], which I wasn't, and I told him to go to hell. (19)

While these clerkships do not always end in conflict and mutual recrimination, there seem to be very strong pressures leading in that direction. In large measure these pressures arise from the part-time, temporary character of the position. In most instances the young lawyer will have some practice of his own which he is attempting to expand, and he usually finds it difficult to draw the line between his own time and the time he should give to his employer—and unless he devotes himself wholly to his employer, the situation can only grow less certain, requiring frequent redefinition of the terms of employment. The employer is often more than happy to permit his clerk to develop his own practice (up to a point), since this justifies a low salary. This arrangement, however, soon places the clerk in a potentially competitive relationship with his employer, particularly in view of the fact that whatever gap {13} there may be between older and younger lawyer in terms of competence and business-getting ability is, at this level of the bar, relatively quickly bridged.

For most individual practitioners, getting started on their own was a hard, uphill struggle. Their work in the early years consisted generally of the dregs of legal practice and their income was correspondingly meager. The matters they handled were with few exceptions the least desirable from every point of view: the marginal cases, the cases no one else wanted, the cases involving the least return and the most aggravation.

> *Interviewer:* What were the problems of getting started on your own?
> *Respondent:* Getting clients that were paying clients. There are enough that float around from lawyer to lawyer who just want to check up on another lawyer—the junk. (35)
>
> The main problem was development of a clientele, and then obtaining lucrative business. A young lawyer is always recommended for small collections, dead judgments, and so on. (94)
>
> There's a lot of business around that it don't pay to handle. After a while you get independent. A lot of people want you to handle their business at your expense. (64)

Collection matters, evictions, rent cases, "dead" judgments, along with some personal injury, criminal, and divorce cases are the kinds of work most frequently handled in the early years in practice. The most distinguishing feature of such cases is their petty character—the small amount of money involved, the tenuousness of {14} the claim (or its nonexistence)—and the inordinate amount of time required to make any headway at all. In short, such practice constitutes the dirty work, the "crap," the "junk" that no one else will handle, but which the younger lawyer will often have to take if he wants any business at all.

The indications are that income in the early years barely reaches a subsistence level. One lawyer reported an average of $2,500 his first two years out of law school; several said that they averaged less than $3,000 over the first four or five years, and many earned less than $100 a month the first six or eight months in practice. In many instances, of course, these lawyers had additional sources of income, but the notion of starving through the first few years is probably not far from the truth.

The kinds of work most young lawyers get when they first start out, the sources of their business, and the problems they have in making ends meet is well illustrated by the case of a young respondent just going into his second year of practice. Let us call him Ronald.

Ronald was admitted to practice in 1956 and over a period of the next eighteen months he had three jobs working for other lawyers. Before coming to his present position he had an informal arrangement with some friends that he hoped would lead to a partnership, but one of them backed down because he didn't want to share some of his "lucrative matters."

At present Ronald is in a space-for-service arrangement in a downtown office with two other lawyers, one of whom is rarely in the office. About a fifth of his time is devoted to doing legwork for the active lawyer in the office and another six or seven hours a week are given to a lawyer outside the office who pays him on an hourly basis. The rest of his time is his own to build up his own practice. {15}

Interviewer: What is the nature of your practice?

Respondent: [Looking through his clients' file folders piled on top of his desk and in the drawers] I do all the subrogation work for an insurance company. I have 300 files in the drawer. There's supposed to be $3,000 worth of claims there; a third is mine, but most are uncollectable. It's a lot of work for the income involved.

Interviewer: How did you get these cases?

Respondent: My brother-in-law's brother knows an attorney who has a half interest in the insurance company. [Continuing through his files:]

Hardware store—collections.

A real estate deal for my milkman.

A will and trust matter for my sister-in-law's neighbor's mother.

My sister-in-law's aunt—personal injury.

This is for my sister-in-law's mother. I will do some estate planning—draw up a will and have some shares of stock transferred.

A case for ______ [lawyer for whom he works in the office]. The owner of a trailer claims a faulty installation, a suit for damages.

______ [other lawyer in the office] was in an auto accident.

My brother-in-law was in an auto accident.

I bought a washer and dryer at an appliance store. I asked them if they had any work for me. They gave me a few matters. I hope to get them for a retainer client. If only I had a few small retainers then I'd be okay. Otherwise, it's very sporadic.

Personal injury for my wife's aunt—auto accident.

Personal injury for a friend.

Personal injury for a friend—adulterated food.

Here's my star client—I've thrown her out a hundred times. I'm handling a bunch of things for her. She's not {16} satisfied with a tuck-pointing job in one of her buildings; I called him up and got him to agree to a compromise. Personal

> property tax for a shoe store she owns. Default judgment against a shoe store; I'll have that vacated. Her son and daughter-in-law got sick from a bad pizza. A precinct captain broke a window in her building; I know him and he'll fix it. I haven't got any fees from her yet. They'll start coming in soon, though.
>
> An immigration matter—I referred it to another attorney and I'm splitting a fee on it.
>
> That's the extent of my practice now.

In his first year out of law school Ronald earned $3,000 from the practice of law. In addition, he made a little over $1,000 as a telephone solicitor for a storm window concern. The first month of the second year he made $50, and in the second, $400. He has a wife and two children, and is having difficulty paying his bills.

> It's really touch and go. I don't know whether I'll make it. I may have to give up the practice. ... I could make a lot more doing something else. I was offered $10,000 at the lumber yard, and I had a $7,500 offer from the Illinois Commerce Commission.
>
> *Interviewer:* Why haven't you taken either of them?
>
> *Respondent:* I don't know. I ask myself that. That's what we talk about—my friends and I—three of my cronies and I—we have coffee every morning and talk about our practice and our problems. If you're a salesman, it doesn't sound so good. It's a matter of pride or ego. I like the law, but it's not a burning thing in my life—I *must* be a lawyer. If I quit now I'd be admitting defeat. I'd be ashamed. ... It's a nice profession, nice clean work, a respected profession. If I could get some income it would be a good life. You can get away when you want to play golf, and you're {17} your own boss, that appeals to me. And if people ask you what you're doing it's nice to tell them I'm a lawyer, and not a clerk in a store. And my dad gets satisfaction from the fact that I'm a lawyer. (2)

One cannot fully understand the nature of individual practice without first recognizing where and how the individual practitioner fits into the wider structure of the metropolitan bar.

Although half the lawyers in Chicago, as in practically all the other cities of the United States, are individual practitioners,[11] they constitute something like a lower class of the metropolitan bar. The elite of the metropolitan bar is composed of lawyers in the larger firms. These firms have a virtual monopoly of the largest, most lucrative clients—the large

11 See Table 3.2.10:

corporations whose legal needs they are geared to serve—and of the best qualified lawyers. In hiring lawyers they aspire to the ideal of the giant Wall Street firms of selecting only the top graduates of Harvard, Yale, and Columbia law schools and of bringing them into the firm as soon after they graduate as possible.[12] In Chicago, New York, Boston, Philadelphia, Cleveland, San Francisco, and Los Angeles, for example, at least one out of four lawyers in

TABLE 3.2.10 Distribution of Lawyers in the United States by Status in Practice and City Size, 1958

	City Size				
Status in Practice	**Over 500,000**	**200,000–500,000**	**50,000–200,000**	**Under 50,000**	**Total U.S.**
Individual practitioners	52%	48%	48%	56%	52%
Lawyers in firms	26	24	32	28	28
Lawyers not in private practice (house counsel, govt. legal dept., etc.)	22	28	20	16	20
Total	100%	100%	100%	100%	100%
Number of lawyers	(91,239)	(33,001)	(38,607)	(72,936)	(235,783)

Source: 1958 Supplement to *Lawyers in the United States: Distribution and Income* (Chicago: American Bar Foundation, 1959), pp. 54–55.

Between 1940 and 1958 there was only a 7 per cent decline in the proportion of individual practitioners in the Chicago bar: 60 per cent of the lawyers listed in *Martindale-Hubbell Law Directory* in 1940 were individual practitioners; 60% in 1949; and 53% in 1958.

12 How close the biggest New York firms have come to realizing this ideal may be gathered from the fact that in two of the most prominent New York firms—Cravath, Swain and Moore, and Sullivan and Cromwell—roughly 90% of the partners are Harvard, Yale, or Columbia Law School graduates. It is not true, however, that in hiring young associates these firms take only the graduates of these three schools, but graduates of other law schools are only rarely made partners. Thus, of the associates who entered the Cravath firm between 1931 and 1948, 45% were *not* graduates of Harvard, Yale, or Columbia, and 10% were graduates of night law schools; of those who {32} subsequently became partners, however, none were from the night schools and close to 70% were Ivy League law school graduates, i.e., of Harvard, Yale, and Columbia. Statistics on the Cravath firm drawn from biographical sketches in Robert T. Swaine, *The Cravath Firm* (New York: Ad Press, Ltd., 1948), Vol. III. Statistics on the Sullivan and Cromwell firm are from Arthur H. Dean, *William Nelson Cromwell* (New York: Ad Press, Ltd., 1957). For a general discussion of the hiring policies of the large New York law firms see Erwin O. Smigel, "The Impact of Recruitment on the Organization of the Large Law Firm," *American Sociological Review*, XXV, No. 1 (1960), 55–66.

That academic achievement is also a prime consideration in the selection of recruits to the large New York firms is supported by the following statistics reported by Smigel:

firms with over 25 lawyers is a Harvard, Yale, or Columbia Law School graduate (principally Harvard), and almost all the others are graduates of the top local university law schools.[13]

The practice of most metropolitan individual practitioners is consequently confined to those residual matters (and clients) that the large firms have not pre-empted: (1) matters not large enough or remunerative enough for the large firms to handle—most general work for small to medium-sized businesses and corporations, the smaller real estate {18} transactions (for individuals or small businesses), and estate matters for middle-income families; (2) the undesirable cases, the dirty work, those areas of practice that have associated with them an aura of influencing and fixing and that involve arrangements with clients and others that are felt by the large firms to be professionally damaging. The latter category includes local tax, municipal, personal injury, divorce, and criminal matters.

> The breakdown of the job activities since graduation of the Yale Law School graduating classes for 1955, 1956, and 1957 ... reveal that 53 per cent of the Yale men the large firms [with 50 or more lawyers] in New York City employed came from the top quarter of their classes, and that 27 per cent were from the first decile (p. 56).

13 The law school background of lawyers in firms with over 25 lawyers in these seven cities is as follows:

TABLE 3.2.11

Law School	Chicago	New York	Boston	Philadelphia	Cleveland	San Francisco	Los Angeles
Ivy League:							
Harvard	21%	32%	82%	20%	32%	29%	28%
Yale	3	16	4	3	11	5	8
Columbia	1	26	1	1	3	2	1
Total	25	74*	87*	24	46	36	37
Other full-time university	60	12	8	64	51	54	54
Night	15	14	5	12	3	10	9
Total	100%	100%	100%	100%	100%	100%	100%
No. of lawyers	(581)	(70)	(232)	(361)	(244)	(167)	(166)
No. of firms	16	..	7	10	5	5	4

* The top local law school in this city is an Ivy League law school.

Source: *Martindale-Hubbell Law Directory* (Summit, N.J.: Martindale-Hubbell, Inc., 1958), Vols. I and II. For all cities except New York, figures are based on total listings in biographical section. Since similar listings are not available for the larger New York City firms, these figures are based on information obtained in my current survey of New York City lawyers (based upon a random sample drawn from the alphabetical listings in the 1960 *Martindale* directory).

{33}

Individual practitioners come off second best not only with respect to type of practice but also in terms of quality of training and academic achievement. In Chicago, as we have seen, the majority of individual practitioners have had less than two years of undergraduate training, and two out of three are graduates of night law schools. This pattern seems to prevail in other large cities as well. In New York, Boston, Philadelphia, Cleveland, San Francisco, and Los Angeles 40 to 70 per cent of the individual practitioners are night law school graduates—compared with less than 15 per cent of the lawyers in firms of over 25 lawyers in these same cities.[14]

The rigidity of the class structure of the metropolitan bar is evidenced by the fact that those who start out as individual practitioners rarely become associates or partners in the larger firms. Moreover, most lawyers who are at present individual practitioners entered the profession as such (or as employees of such lawyers) and have remained at that level of practice.[15]

Between the big firm elite and the mass of individual practitioners is a stratum composed of lawyers in small to medium-sized firms. While it is difficult to distinguish the majority of these lawyers from individual practitioners in terms of social background, training, and type of practice, it is likely that the middle-sized firms, at any rate, may {19} constitute something like a middle class of the metropolitan bar.[16]

---

14 The law school background of individual practitioners in these seven cities is as follows:

TABLE 3.2.12

Law School	Chicago	New York	Boston	Philadelphia	Cleveland	San Francisco	Los Angeles
Ivy League	2%	27%	35%	5%	4%	3%	8%
Other full-time universities	29	3	23	45	54	59	42
Night	69	70	42	50	42	38	50
Total	100%	100%	100%	100%	100%	100%	100%
No. of lawyers	(109)	(103)	(79)	(75)	(70)	(65)	(119)

Source: Same as for Table 3.2.11 in note 3.2.13. Figures for all cities based on random samples drawn from the alphabetical listings in the directory.

15 In Chicago only 10% of the respondents had been an associate in a large firm, held a fairly responsible house counsel or government post, or some combination of these positions.

16 The following table (3.2.13) showing the relationship between size of firm and type of law school attended for lawyers in Chicago in private practice suggests that at least as to recruitment there is a fairly distinct middle segment of the metropolitan bar comprised of lawyers in firms with 10 to

The sharp class-like divisions in the metropolitan bar have come about as the result of historical developments beginning around the turn of the century. A factor of major importance has been the emergence of the large law firm as the principal form of organization for the leading purveyors of legal services to the business elite. Until the end of the nineteenth century there were probably no firms with more than half a dozen lawyers.[17] The period from the turn of the century to World War I witnessed the first substantial growth of law firms, with some firms in the larger East Coast cities expanding to as many as 20 or 30 lawyers. But the large firm as we know it today did not appear until the twenties, when metropolitan lawyers in increasing numbers were being called upon to shape the legal framework of the emerging economy of the giant corporation. The increased magnitude and complexity of the legal and general business advice required for the operation of these new giants necessitated

---

25 lawyers. It should be noted also that even {34} in the small firms lawyers from full-time university law schools begin to outnumber those from night law schools.

TABLE 3.2.13

		Lawyers in Firms Size of Firm				
		Small			Middle	Large
Type of Law School	**Individual Practitioners**	**2**	**3**	**4–9**	**10–25**	**26+**
Ivy League	1%	3%	5%	3%	18%	31%
Other full-time university	32	39	45	50	55	54
Night	67	58	50	47	27	15
Total	100%	100%	100%	100%	100%	100%
No. of lawyers	(84)	(38)	(20)	(34)	(74)	(383)

Source: Figures for individual practitioners based on sample in this study; for lawyers in firms of 2 to 9 lawyers, a random sample drawn from *Sullivan's Law Directory for the State of Illinois* (Chicago: Sullivan's Law Directory, 1956), and checked against *Martindale*, 1956, for law school attended; for lawyers in firms of 10 to 25 lawyers, a random sample from *Martindale*, 1956, biographical section; for lawyers in firms of 26 and more lawyers, all lawyers listed in biographical section of *Martindale*, 1956.

17 Hurst characterizes the law firm of the nineteenth century in the following terms:

> From the first quarter of the nineteenth century on, there were partnerships. But no firms of large membership appeared, even in the great cities, until the end of the century. The typical partnership was a two-man affair; it usually had its "office" member and its "court" member; and it ordinarily operated without a formal agreement of partnership, or under an agreement of the simplest kind (James Willard Hurst, op. cit., p. 306).

Koegel reports that in 1872 only one law firm in New York City was listed in *Hubbell's Legal Directory* with as many as 6 partners; and in 1900 only 2 with as many as 9 partners. Otto E. Koegel, *Walter S. Carter, Collector of Young Masters* (Great Neck, N.Y.: Round Table Press, 1955), p. 7.

a degree of specialization and concentration of legal talent that could be realized only in a very large firm. During the twenties, in New York, Chicago, and the other major cities of the country, law firms previously of 10 or 20 lawyers grew in size to 40, 50, and in some cases to as many as 70 lawyers.[18] The 1929 crash may have momentarily toppled the corporate structures that the large firms had so ingeniously assisted in creating, but the Depression and the flood of governmental controls and regulations that it brought about cemented further the interdependence between the large firm and big business and lent additional assurance to the permanence and importance of the big firm.

The establishment of the elite segment of the metropolitan {20} bar in the newly emerging large firms ensured its monopoly of the largest and most influential business and commercial clients, largely because the smaller firms with their limited resources found it more and more difficult to compete for this kind of business. Furthermore, with the initiation of hiring policies that virtually required certain kinds of legal education for admission to the large firm, entry into the ranks of the elite became increasingly restricted. Thus, from their inception at the turn of the century, the largest firms have placed considerable weight on law school background and performance in selecting associates and partners.[19] Since 1895,

---

18 Some indication of the rapid growth of the large firm after the {35} turn of the century may be had from the histories of the New York law firms of Cravath, Swaine and Moore, Sullivan and Cromwell, and Cadwalader, Wickersham and Taft. From 1819 (when the first of a line of firms leading to the present firm was organized) to 1898, none of the predecessor firms of the present Cravath firm had more than five lawyers. During the following eight or ten years the number of lawyers increased to about 30. Thereafter the size of the firm remained relatively constant until 1920. Between 1920 and 1930 the number of lawyers more than doubled (34 to 77) and between 1930 and 1940 there was better than a 50% increase (77 to 118) (Robert T. Swaine, *op. cit.*, Vol. III.) Prior to 1920 the Sullivan and Cromwell firm increased at a more even rate than the Cravath firm (from 5 lawyers in 1880 to 7 in 1890, 14 in 1900, 21 in 1910, and 32 in 1920); then, like the Cravath firm, it almost doubled in size during the twenties (from 32 to 60 lawyers). Since 1930, however, the Sullivan firm has increased at a slower pace than Cravath (76 lawyers in 1940 and 90 in 1950) (Arthur H. Dean, *op. cit.*). Data on the Cadwalader firm is less complete but the same pattern of growth was in evidence. The predecessor firm of Strong and Cadwalader started with 6 lawyers in 1878, and when the present firm was constituted in 1914 had increased to 23 lawyers. The next figure which we have, 62 lawyers in 1938, suggests a similar rapid rise during the twenties. Henry W. Taft, *A Century and a Half at the New York Bar* (New York: Privately printed, 1938).

19 "When Cravath entered [the Seward firm] as a partner in 1899 he brought to the firm a philosophy of organization quite different from that which had previously prevailed in the Blatchford and Seward firms [predecessors of the present Cravath firm]. That philosophy, of which he himself was

for example, practically all the partners in the New York firm of Cravath, Swaine and Moore have been graduates of either Harvard, Yale, or Columbia Law School and roughly two out of three of their associates over the years have been from the same schools.[20] In the Sullivan and Cromwell firm only one partner from the date of its inception to 1920 was not a graduate of either Harvard or Columbia Law School. In a foreword to the history of the firm John Foster Dulles, whose law degree was from George Washington University, recalled the difficulties he encountered in trying to get into a prominent firm.

> I went to New York armed with letters of introduction from my grandfather, John W. Foster, to the heads of certain New York law firms whom he had come to know through his own wide experience in diplomacy and international affairs. These letters served to give me a courteous reception, but not a job. A degree from Princeton was an acceptable credential so far as concerned undergraduate work. But collegiate honors counted for little. The Sorbonne counted for nothing and George Washington Law School was unknown to New York. Law degrees from {21} Harvard or Columbia were, at that time, the requirement for admission to the eminent law firms of New York.[21]

The increasing emphasis that the large firms were placing on type and quality of professional training in the selection of partners and associates was undoubtedly facilitated by the change-over, around the turn of the century, from law office apprenticeship to formal law school training for the bar.[22] It was obviously much simpler to discriminate among recruits

---

a product, had been developed by Walter S. Carter, whose office Cravath had entered when he graduated from Columbia Law School. It was Carter's practice to seek, annually, one or more of the best graduates of the leading law schools, principally Columbia, and train them through a clerkship of several years" (Robert T. Swaine, *op. cit.*, I, 3). According to Swaine, the high scholastic standards of the "Cravath system" were, in 1899, "regarded as somewhat eccentric—not to say stuffy." It could not have taken too many years, however, before such standards were adopted by most newly emerging larger firms, many of the leading members of which, like Cravath, had been "graduates" of the Carter office (see Koegel, *op. cit.*, pp. 102–111).

{36}

20 Robert T. Swaine, *op. cit.*, Vol. III.

21 Arthur H. Dean, *op. cit.*, p. i.

22 Practically to the end of the nineteenth century most lawyers entered the practice of law (in the larger as well as the smaller cities) after a period of apprenticeship in an older lawyer's office. By 1920 this system of law office apprenticeship had been virtually replaced by a formal period of training in

in terms of the law school they had attended than the type of law office in which they had apprenticed. In addition, the law schools provided a convenient measure of competence in their ratings of students by academic achievement.

Mobility into the elite stratum of the metropolitan bar was further limited during this period by a shift in the central focus of law practice from the courtroom to the conference and negotiation room, a development that accompanied the growth of large-scale corporate enterprise and the expansion of government control and regulation of business. As a result of this shift, the ambitious young lawyer of humble origin lost what had once been the most accessible and effective forum for demonstrating his ability to prospective clients of prestige and wealth. Thereafter courtroom demonstrations of ability for the most part led to prominence only in the less respected areas of practice that had been either discarded or passed over by the larger firms. Prominence in the respectable areas of practice and access to important clients were more and more to be gained only through association with the large firm.

During this period of the consolidation of the big firm elite, changes of the greatest importance were also taking place at the lower level of the metropolitan bar. The first {22} was the changeover from law office apprenticeship to night law school training for members of this part of the bar.[23] The second was a spectacular increase in the number of such lawyers.

---

a law school. Thus of the 22,859 persons who took the New York State bar examination in the decade from 1922 to 1931 (inclusive) only 193 were law office trained, or less than 1%. Philip J. Wickser, "Law Schools, Bar Examiners, and Bar Associations—Cooperation vs. Insulation," *American Law School Review*, VII (1933), 729. While further research is needed to document the exact period when this change occurred, it appears that the principal shift took place between 1890 and 1910.

23 Two factors in particular were responsible for this sudden transformation in professional training. The first was the introduction of formal written examinations in the 1890's as part of a general effort at tightening bar admissions requirements. This reform was apparently effected in a single decade: "Before 1890 only four states had boards of bar examiners, and in no more than half a dozen had written examinations been used. However, when the leading law schools began to use the written examinations, this encouraged adoption of the practice in the states, where it became the invariable method of examination after 1900" (Hurst, *op. cit.*, p. 283). That the introduction of written bar examinations did not contribute to raising educational standards was regretfully conceded by Reed in 1921: "... there can be little question but that, in spite of all recent efforts to raise bar examination standards, more incompetents are today admitted to the bar than when, under laxer formal requirements for admission and a smaller development of good law schools than we now possess, the generality of actual applicants nevertheless received a sound training in the office of an old fashioned practitioner" (*Training for the Public Profession of Law*, p. 59). What Reed failed to recognize was

During the twenties, the period of maximum growth in this century of the profession as a whole,[24] the size of the bar in the ten largest cities increased by well over 50 per cent.[25] This

---

that there were more incompetents very likely *because* of the efforts to raise bar examination standards in so far as this stimulated the development of the night law school. Whatever the educational advantages of a law office apprenticeship, systematic preparation for an academic examination was certainly not one of them. The night law school, on the other hand, whatever its educational disadvantages, {37} did hold out the promise of—and had as its principal aim—preparation for the state bar examination. Ironically, then, one may in part attribute the rise of the night law school with its notoriously low educational standards to a reform movement that had as its goal the raising of educational standards for admission to practice.

The second factor that contributed to the rise of the night law school was the advent (also around the turn of the century) of the typewriter, which led to the substitution of the "stenographer for the longhand copyist ... [which in turn] brought a gradual, but in the long run, very substantial decrease in the law offices' demand for student clerks" (Hurst, *op. cit.*, p. 257). Another invention, the electric light, should probably also be included in this list of factors: "... with improvements in methods of artificial illumination it became possible finally to hold sessions in the evening, thereby extending the opportunities to secure a legal education to a still wider element of the population" (Reed, *Training for the Public Profession of Law*, p. 56).

24 See Table 3.2.14:

TABLE 3.2.14 Changes in the Lawyer Population of the United States, 1900–1958

Year	Number of Lawyers	Per Cent Increase Over Previous Date
1900	109,140	. .
1910	114,704	6
1920	122,519	8
1930	160,605	31
1940	180,483	12
1950	204,111	13
1958	235,783	15

Source: U.S. Census, *Statistical Abstract of the United States for 1900–1950*; 1958 Supplement to Lawyers in the United States: *Distribution and Income*, for 1958 figure.

25 In 1920 there were 25,120 lawyers in the ten largest cities (New York, Chicago, Philadelphia, Detroit, Cleveland, St. Louis, Boston, Baltimore, Pittsburgh, and Los Angeles); in 1930 there were 38,596. These statistics were compiled from Fourteenth Census of the U.S., Vol. IV, *Population*, 1930, and Fifteenth Census of the U.S., Vol. IV, *Population*, 1930.

{38}

marked expansion was effected largely by the influx into the ranks of the individual practitioners of the graduates from the rapidly expanding night law schools.[26]

A third development was the shift in the ethnic composition of this part of the bar from lawyers of predominantly German and Irish to Eastern European—largely Jewish—origin.[27] This continuation of the process of ethnic succession, with newer immigrant groups moving into the lower stratum of the bar, was apparently facilitated by the change-over to night law

26 Between 1920 and 1929 the number of law students enrolled in law schools located in cities of 200,000 or more population more than doubled (114% increase). Most of this increase was accounted for by the night law schools, which increased 142% compared to 47% for the full-time law schools (*Annual Review of Legal Education for* 1921–1930). In 1928, the year of peak law school enrollment prior to World War II, 4 out of 5 law students in cities with over a half million population were in night law schools, and 1 out of 3 of *all* law students in the United States were located in just 10 night law schools situated in or near Boston and New York (*Annual Review of Legal Education for* 1932, pp. 29–33). That most of these graduates became individual practitioners is evident from Table 3.2.11 in note 13.

27 Some indication of this shift may be had from the following statistics for the New York City bar:
(1) In 1900, of all foreign-born and second-generation lawyers (most of whom presumably were individual practitioners) in New York City, approximately 65% were of Irish or Central European origin (Twelfth Census of the United States, Vol. IV, *Population*, 1900), compared to about 25% today (Columbia University Metropolitan Law Office Study, in progress).
(2) The proportion of Jewish lawyers entering the New York City bar from the turn of the century to the mid-thirties increased from 26% to 80%:

TABLE 3.2.15 Proportion of Jewish Lawyers Entering the New York City Bar, 1900–1934

Lawyers Admitted to Practice	Per Cent Jewish	Number of Cases
1900–1910	26	(623)
1911–1917	36	(491)
1918–1923	40	(566)
1924–1929	56	(1,501)
1930–1934	80	(1,382)

Source: Compiled from figures presented in Melvin J. Fagen, "The Status of Jewish Lawyers in New York City," *Jewish Social Studies*, I, 1939, 73–104.

{39}
The increase in the proportion of foreign-born and second-generation lawyers in the metropolitan bar apparently occurred at a somewhat slower rate. In New York City, for example, 47% of the bar was first or second generation in 1900, 53% in 1910, 55% in 1920, and 69% today (Twelfth-Fourteenth Census of the United States, Vol. IV, *Population*, 1900–1920; Metropolitan Law Office Study).

school training for the bar. It was doubtless easier for the sons of these more recent immigrants to gain admission to a night law school, the only requirement for which was the tuition fee, than to find a preceptor in a law office that more than likely was controlled by lawyers of Irish or German descent, or by "old Americans."[28]

Finally, there was the emergence of the automobile accident injury field after World War I. This new type of law business fell primarily into the hands of the metropolitan individual practitioner and soon became one of the most lucrative staples of his practice. Aside from its economic significance, this business had an important impact on the character of the individual lawyer's practice as well. The contingent fee probably first came into prominence with the rise of personal injury practice, and organized solicitation has very likely reached today's dimensions principally {23} because of its use in the personal injury field. Furthermore, the increasing importance of this new field of practice, occurring about the same time the larger firms were taking more and more of the better corporation business matters away from the average practitioner, only widened the gulf between the practice of the elite and the lower-class members of the metropolitan bar.

In comparison with the highly stratified metropolitan bar, the smaller city bar has over the years remained a fairly homogeneous professional community. In social background, professional training,[29] and type of practice, there has been a considerably more limited range of variation among lawyers in the smaller than in the larger city bars. A major reason

28 Indirect support for this conclusion may be found in Fuller's assessment of the Pennsylvania preceptorship system under which a prospective law student must obtain an "acceptable preceptor before he begins his law studies." Lon Fuller (*op. cit.*, pp. 289–290) notes:

When the system of preceptorships was installed in 1928, some students for a time had difficulty in obtaining preceptors. ... Shortly after the system was announced there was a large meeting of Jewish lawyers in Philadelphia who pledged themselves that no worthy and able Jewish student should be denied registration as a law student because of inability to obtain a preceptor. ... The incident tends to show that under the Pennsylvania system elements of discrimination manifest themselves ... before the student has even entered law school. Naturally at this point tendencies to discrimination are likely to be at their height. There is nothing to counteract them. The prospective employer who can only guess at the legal ability of his prospective clerk will tend to prefer those of a religious and cultural background similar to his own.

29 In five cities in Iowa with populations of 45,000 to 178,000, 93% of the lawyers are full-time university law school graduates, over 70% from just two law schools, the State University of Iowa and Drake University. In five cities in Illinois, with populations of 40,000 to 100,000, 70% are graduates of full-time university law schools, 35% from the University of Illinois (compiled from *Martindale*, Vol. I, 1958). In the northeastern states, because of the proximity of both Ivy League and night law

for this is that the changes we have just been considering, which had the effect of further widening existing class divisions within the metropolitan bar, had considerably less impact on the bar of the smaller cities. Thus there are still no large firms to speak of in these smaller cities;[30] and if there are elites, they apparently have not established exclusive access to the most desirable clients and practice, nor have they restricted entry into their own ranks anywhere near to the same extent as their counterparts have done in the larger cities.

Having considered briefly the route that the individual practitioner takes into the metropolitan bar and the position he occupies in that professional community, we shall now turn to an examination of his work.

Bibliography

References from the main volume, its endnotes, and general sources.

Books

Blaustein, Albert P., and Charles O. Porter. *The American Lawyer.* Chicago: University of Chicago Press, 1954.

Brown, Esther L. *Lawyers and the Promotion of Justice.* New York: Russell Sage Foundation, 1938.

Dean, Arthur H. *William Nelson Cromwell.* New York: Ad Press, Ltd., 1957.

Drinker, Henry S. *Legal Ethics.* New York: Columbia University Press, 1953.

Harno, Albert J. *Legal Education in the United States.* San Francisco: Bancroft-Whitney Co., 1952.

Hunting, Roger B., and Gloria S. Neuwirth. *Who Sues in New York City?* New York: Columbia University Press, 1962.

Hurst, James Willard. *The Growth of American Law.* Boston: Little, Brown and Co., 1950.

Koegel, Otto E. *Walter S. Carter, Collector of Young Masters.* Great Neck, N.Y.: Round Table Press, Inc., 1955.

Mills, C. Wright. *White Collar.* New York: Oxford University Press, 1953.

Nicholson, Lionell S. *The Law Schools of the United States.* Baltimore: Lord Baltimore Press, Inc., 1958.

---

schools and the absence of any state university law schools, we find more variation in law school background among lawyers in the smaller cities.

30 In an examination of *Martindale* (Vol. I, 1958), I found no firms with as many as 15 lawyers in cities of less than 200,000 population, and very few with more than 5 or 6 lawyers. In Des Moines, Iowa, for example, with a population of approximately 178,000, and {40} a bar of 623 lawyers, the largest firm has only 10 lawyers, and there are only 8 firms with over 6 lawyers. In Rockford, Ill., with a population of approximately 105,000 and a bar of 157 lawyers, the largest firm has only 7 lawyers, and there are only 4 firms with more than 4 lawyers.

Pound, Roscoe. *The Lawyer from Antiquity to Modern Times.* St. Paul: West Publishing Co., 1953.
Reed, Alfred Z. *Present Day Law Schools in the United States and Canada.* New York: Carnegie Foundation for the Advancement of Teaching, 1928.
———. *Training for the Public Profession of the Law. New York: Carnegie Foundation for the Advancement of Teaching, 1921.*
Swaine, Robert T. *The Cravath Firm.* 3 vols. New York: Ad Press, Ltd., 1946–1948.
Taft, Henry W. *A Century and a Half at the New York Bar.* New York: Privately printed, 1938.
Tinelly, Joseph T. *Part-Time Legal Education.* Brooklyn: The Foundation Press, 1957.
Warren, Charles. *A History of the American Bar.* Boston: Little, Brown and Co., 1911.
Zeisel, Hans, Harry Kalven, Jr., and Bernard Buchholz. *Delay in the Court.* Boston: Little, Brown and Co., 1959.

Articles and Reports

Annual Review of Legal Education for 1911. From 1911 to 1934 published by the Carnegie Foundation for the Advancement of Teaching in New York. From 1935 published by the Section on Legal Education and Admission to the Bar of the American Bar Association in Chicago. Since 1942 under the title, *Law School and Bar Admissions Requirements in the United States.*
Banks, Louis. "The Crisis in the Courts," *Fortune* (December, 1961).
Buckner, George, II. "What Your Clients Think of You," *Journal of the Missouri Bar,* Vol. 17, 1961.
Cheatham, Elliott E. "The Law Schools of Tennessee," *Tennessee Law Review,* Vol. XXI (April, 1950).
Chicago Bar Association. *Annual Reports Submitted by Committees in the Association* (1955–1956, 1956–1957, 1957–1958).
Dodge, Emily P. "Evolution of a City Law Office," *Wisconsin Law Review,* Vol. XXXV (January, 1956).
Fagen, Melvin J. "The Status of Jewish Lawyers in New York City," *Jewish Social Studies,* Vol. I, 1939.
Franklin, Marc, Robert Chanin, and Irving Mark. "Accidents, Money and the Law: A Study of the Economics of Personal Injury Litigation," *Columbia Law Review,* Vol. 61, 1961.
Fuller, Lon L. "Legal Education and Admissions to the Bar of Pennsylvania," *Temple Law Quarterly,* Vol. XXV, No. 25 (January, 1952).
Hamilton, Fowler. "The Lawyers and Business," *Fortune* (October, 1948).
Hervey, John G. "The Decline of Professionalism in the Law: An Exploration into Some Causes," *New York Law Forum,* Vol. III, No. 4 (October, 1957).
Johnstone, Quintin. "Title Insurance," *Yale Law Journal,* Vol. LXVI, No. 4 (February, 1957).
———. "The Unauthorized Practice Controversy," *The Kansas Law Review,* Vol. IV, No. 1 (October, 1955).
Kafogolis, Milton. *Economic Condition of the Legal Profession in Ohio.* Prepared under the auspices of the Professional Economics Committee of the Ohio State Bar Association, 1955.
Klaw, S. "Wall Street Lawyers," *Fortune* (February, 1958).

Koos, Earl L. "The Family and the Law." Rochester: National Legal Aid Society, 1949. (A pamphlet.)

Lawyers in the United States: Distribution and Income. Part I: Distribution, 1956; Part II: Income, 1958. Chicago: American Bar Foundation. Also: 1958 Distribution Supplement.

"Lawyers Looking at You," *Fortune* (January, 1931).

Legal Education and Admissions to the Bar of California. Sacramento: State Bar of California, 1949.

Liebenberg, Maurice. "Income of Lawyers in the Postwar Period," *Survey of Current Business,* Washington: U.S. Department of Commerce, 1956.

Llewellyn, Karl N. "The Bar's Troubles, and Poultices—and Cures?" *Law and Contemporary Problems,* Vol. V, No. 1, 1938.

Lortie, Dan C. "Laymen to Lawmen: Law School, Careers, and Professional Socialization," *Harvard Educational Review,* Vol. 29, No. 4, 1959.

Morland, John W. "Legal Education in Georgia," *Mercer Law Review,* Vol. II, No. 2 (Spring, 1951).

Parsons, Talcott. "A Sociologist Views the Legal Profession," *Conference on the Profession of Law and Legal Education,* Series No. 11. Chicago: University of Chicago Law School, 1952. Also published in *Essays in Sociological Theory.* Rev. ed. Glencoe, Ill.: Free Press, 1954.

Report of the California Survey Committee. Sacramento: State Bar of California, 1933.

Report of the Committee of Censors to the Law Association of Philadelphia, in re Contingent Fee Accident Litigation. Committee of Censors. Philadelphia: Law Associates, 1928.

Riesman, David. "Toward an Anthropological Science of Law and the Legal Profession," *American Journal of Sociology,* Vol. LVII, 1951.

Rosenberg, Maurice, and Michael I. Sovern. "Delay and the Dynamics of Personal Injury Litigation," *Columbia Law Review,* Vol. 59, 1959.

Shafroth, Will. "Can the Law Schools Lead Us Out of the Wilderness?" *The American Law School Review* (St. Paul, Minnesota, West Publishing Co.), Volume 7, 1934.

Sharswood, George. "An Essay on Professional Ethics," *Reports of the American Bar Association,* Vol. XXXII. Philadelphia: reprinted by the American Bar Association, 1907.

Smigel, Erwin O. "The Impact of Recruitment on the Organization of the Large Law Firm," *American Sociological Review,* Vol. 25, No. 1 (February, 1960).

Stone, Harlan F. "The Public Influence of the Bar," *Harvard Law Review,* Vol. XLVIII, 1934.

Swaine, Robert T. "Impact of Big Business on the Profession: An Answer to the Critics of the Modern Bar," *American Bar Association Journal,* Vol. XXXV (February, 1949).

Weinfield, William. "Income of Lawyers, 1929–1948," *Survey of Current Business,* Washington: U.S. Department of Commerce, 1949.

Wickser, Philip J. "Law Schools, Bar Examiners, and Bar Associations—Co-operation vs. Insulation," *The American Law School Review,* Vol. 7, 1933.

Unpublished Material

Hale, William H. "The Career Development of the Negro Lawyer." Unpublished Ph.D. dissertation, Department of Sociology, University of Chicago, 1949.

Harris, George B. "Ethics of the Legal Profession, 1836–1908." Unpublished essay, Chicago, American Bar Foundation, 1955.

Kent, Leonard. "Economic Status of the Legal Profession in Chicago." Unpublished Ph.D. dissertation, Business School, University of Chicago, 1950. Lortie, Dan C. "The Striving Young Lawyer: A Study of Early Career Differentiation in the Chicago Bar." Unpublished Ph.D. dissertation, Department of Sociology, University of Chicago, 1958.

McKinnon, Frederick B. "Study of the Ethical Problems of Lawyers in Private Practice." Harvard Law School project in progress.

O'Gorman, Hubert J. "Lawyers in Matrimonial Cases," Unpublished Ph.D. dissertation, Columbia University, 1961.

Thielens, Wagner P., Jr. "Socialization Processes Among Law Students." Unpublished Ph.D. dissertation in progress, Columbia University.

Wood, Arthur L. "The Criminal Lawyer." Chicago: American Bar Foundation. Unpublished report prepared for the Survey of the Legal Profession, 1955.

Directories

American Bar Association Directory, 1955–1956. Summit, N.J.: Martindale-Hubbell, Inc., 1956.

Martindale-Hubbell Law Directory. Vols. I, II. Summit, N.J.: Martindale-Hubbell, Inc., 1956, 1957, 1958.

Sullivan's Law Directory for the State of Illinois, 1956–1957. Chicago: Sullivan's Law Directory, 1956.

Statutes

Smith-Hurd, Illinois Annotated Statutes: Chapter 32 (Illinois Business Corporation Act of 1933), Chapter 120 (Revenue Act of 1939).

Census Materials

Twelfth, Thirteenth, and Fourteenth Census of the United States, Vol. IV, Population, 1900, 1910, 1920.

Statistical Abstract of the United States for 1900–1950.

Reading 3.2

The Ethical Dilemmas of Individual Practice

Jerome E. Carlin

BETWEEN THE OFFICIAL REQUIREMENTS OF THE Canons of Professional Ethics and the practical demands of individual practice there is often sharp conflict.[1] This conflict is apparent not only in the area of getting business, but also in dealings with courts and other official agencies and in relations with clients.

The solicitation problem. The conflict between the Canons on business-getting[2] and the realities of metropolitan practice have probably never been more forcefully or more clearly summarized than they were by Karl Llewellyn:

---

1 Citations to the Canons in this chapter are made with reference to the Canons of Professional Ethics of the American Bar Association as adopted at the 31st annual meeting of the ABA on August 27, 1908, with later additions and amendments. For an outstanding commentary on the Canons, see Henry S. Drinker, *Legal Ethics* (New York: Columbia Univ. Press, 1953).

2 Prohibitions against solicitation are contained principally in Canons 27 and 28. They read in part as follows:

> *Canon* 27. Advertising, Direct or Indirect
>
> It is unprofessional to solicit professional employment by circulars, advertisements, through touters or by personal communication or interviews not warranted by personal relations. Indirect advertisements for professional employment such as furnishing or inspiring newspaper comments, or procuring his photograph to be published in connection with causes in which the lawyer has been or is engaged or concerning the manner of their conduct, the magnitude of the interest involved, the importance of the lawyer's position, and all other like self-laudation, offend the traditions and lower the tone of our profession and are reprehensible; but the customary use of simple professional cards is not improper [as amended in 1937 and 1940].
>
> *Canon* 28. Stirring Up Litigation, Directly or Through Agents
>
> It is unprofessional for a lawyer to volunteer advice to bring a law suit. ... Stirring up strife is not only unprofessional, but it is indictable at common law. It is disreputable to hunt up defects in titles or other causes of action and inform thereof in order to be employed to bring suit or collect judgement, or to breed litigation by seeking out those

The canons of ethics on business-getting are still built in terms of a town of twenty-five thousand (or, much more dubiously, even fifty thousand)—a town where reputation speaks itself from mouth to mouth, even on the other side of the railroad track; and reputation not only of the {156} oldster, but of the youngster. The youngster is watched when he hangs out his shingle; watched if he be a home-town boy, watched doubly if he be not. Word of law's work passes the time of day, along with sidetaking as between the Mathematics teacher and the High School principal. All the lawyers are known, and people who have legal work to do are moderately aware of it; and they have little difficulty in finding a lawyer of whose character, abilities, experience, yes, and fees, they can get some fair inkling ahead of time. And—no little item—where reputation works and counts, the overhead becomes materially less. "Front" that socially and personally is waste is peculiarly a privilege and an expense of the metropolitan lawyer.

Turn these same canons loose on a great city, and the results are devastating in proportion to its size. If a small client does not know to whom to go, he does his pondering through his brain—they over-reach, they over-charge, they are not even to be trusted. This means, in result, undone legal business. A-plenty. Or it means turning to some non-lawyer who undertakes to help out. Or it means chancing it. If the client chances it, he very truly chances it: the conditions of legal business make it no simple thing to reach into the grab-bag and pull out a lawyer who is able, experienced in the case at hand, not too taken up with other matters, and also reasonable in fee.[3]

The model for the present American Bar Association Canons of Ethics was the Code of Ethics adopted by the Alabama Bar Association in 1887, which was largely based upon Judge

---

with claims for personal injuries or those having any other grounds of action in order to secure them as clients, or to employ agents or runners for like {166} purposes, or to pay or reward, directly or indirectly, those who bring or influence the bringing of such cases to his office, or to remunerate policemen, court or prison officials, physicians, hospital *attachés* or others who may succeed, under the guise of giving disinterested friendly advice, in influencing the criminal, the sick and the injured, the ignorant or others, to seek his professional services. A duty to the public and to the profession devolves upon every member of the Bar having knowledge of such practices upon the part of any practitioner immediately to inform thereof, to the end that the offender may be disbarred [as amended in 1928].

3 Karl N. Llewellyn, *Law and Contemporary Problems*, pp. 115–116.

Sharswood's essay on professional ethics published in 1854.[4] Although those responsible for drafting the early Canons were not totally unaware of the special problems created by the large metropolitan environment, the image of the profession that is unmistakably conveyed by the Canons is of the small-town bar, consisting of lawyers {157} who are highly visible not only to one another but to their prospective clientele, and who are capable, therefore, of attracting clients by establishing a reputation in the community as competent practitioners. These conditions, of course, do not exist today in the large metropolitan centers. The individual practitioner frequently finds himself in what we have termed an invisible market for legal services, and a market, furthermore, which is controlled to a large extent by encroaching lay agencies and business brokers. The nearly universal problem of gaining visibility, or of establishing contact with someone or some agency that has it, leads, as we have seen, to a skeptical, if not cynical view of the passive attitude toward business-getting implicit in the Canons. A large number of those in the sample, particularly in the early years although by no means confined to that stage in their careers, have assumed an aggressive attitude toward business-getting in violation of the spirit and frequently the letter of the Canons.

The problem of pay-offs and political influence. The use of personal influence and the trading or buying of favors in the courts or administrative agencies in order to obtain special treatment for a client is frowned upon by the Canons.[5] These prohibitions, however, make

---

4 George Sharswood, "An Essay on Professional Ethics" (Philadelphia: Reprinted by the ABA in Vol. XXXII of the *Reports of the American Bar Association*, 1907). Interestingly enough, the Alabama Code was somewhat more permissive on the matter of advertising than the present ABA Canons, declaring: "Newspaper advertisements, circulars, and business cards, tendering professional services to the general public are proper," but the Alabama Code went on to add that, "special solicitation to particular individuals to become clients ought to be avoided" (Rule 16, Code of Ethics, Alabama Bar Association, adopted Dec. 14, 1887). Furthermore, George W. Warvelle, in a treatise entitled "Legal Ethics," argued as long ago as 1902 that, although advertising was not necessary in a small town, it was nevertheless needed in the larger cities, "but he opposed any but modest advertisements and severely condemned lawyers advertising their talents 'like shopkeepers' wares'" (George B. Harris, "Ethics of the Legal Profession, 1836–1908," unpublished essay, 1955).

5 See particularly Canons 3 and 32, which read in part as follows:

> *Canon* 3. Attempts to Exert Personal Influence on the Court
>
> Marked attention and unusual hospitality on the part of a lawyer to a Judge, uncalled for by the personal relations of the parties, subject both the Judge and the lawyer to misconstructions of motive and should be avoided. A lawyer should not communicate or argue privately with the Judge as to the merits of a pending case, and he deserves rebuke and denunciation for any device or attempt to gain from a Judge personal consideration or favor. {167}

certain assumptions about the operation and personnel of the courts and administrative agencies and about the law that, like the rules restricting advertising and solicitation, appear to be at odds with actual metropolitan conditions. For a variety of reasons, the use of personal influence and the trading or buying of favors become an almost indispensable part of the individual lawyer's job, especially for those lawyers with more than occasional contact with the courts and administrative agencies.

In the course of handling clients' matters, there appear {158} to be two principal areas in which these problems are most acute. The first involves the routine processing of matters by clerks of the local courts and administrative offices. Here the lawyer is concerned with filing or checking through various documents, with having certain papers or documents certified or issued, with setting dates for hearings or appearances, or with having these dates changed. In order to secure prompt and efficient processing of these matters or to get a case or matter advanced or called ahead, to get a file in a hurry, or for minor conveniences or accommodations, the lawyer *must* take care of the clerk. Better than two out of three lawyers interviewed candidly admitted purchasing favors from clerks. In most instances, this meant giving a few dollars in the form of a tip or gratuity; almost a third also mentioned giving Christmas presents—box of cigars, carton of cigarettes, bottle of whisky—and several said they occasionally had to buy tickets of one kind or another. The lawyers with primarily a real estate or business-corporate practice, and who therefore have least contact with courts, account for most of those not mentioning the necessity for currying favor with the clerks. Several of these people pointed out specifically that such, however, had been their practice:

> I have no problem now as I did at the County Building. At Christmastime I had to hand out ten-dollar bills and boxes of cigars. (68)
>
> When I did a lot of court work I certainly gave gifts. (15)
>
> Years ago in the courts, when I was more active, I used to have more title work; around Christmastime, half a dozen to ten people would get gifts at the Chicago Title and Trust, and in the courts, about a dozen. But I've discontinued that. (85) {159}

Canon 32. The Lawyer's Duty in Its Last Analysis

No client, corporate or individual, however powerful, nor any cause, civil or political, however important, is entitled to receive nor should any lawyer render any service or advice involving disloyalty to the law whose ministers we are, or disrespect of the judicial office, which we are bound to uphold, or corruption of any person or persons exercising a public office or private trust, or deception or betrayal of the public. When rendering any such improper service or advice, the lawyer invites and merits stern and just condemnation.

One lawyer who has drifted out of practice, giving most of his time now to his own investments, recalled the situation as it existed when he was more active in the courts:

> I don't do it any more. If it's hard to serve someone with a summons you give a few dollars to the bailiff; a few bucks to get a file to the clerk. ... You can't get too much done without doing it. A clerk in the Municipal Court in the thirties got $1,800 a year—he has a little education, he has to be a high school graduate—$1,800 a year! Well, if you want something done in a hurry, he'll do it. (40)

Several lawyers more actively engaged in practice made some rather strong comments about the situation:

> Those officials are underpaid. Everybody's in there for what they can get. (11)
>
> It is essential to give money to get work done efficiently. (1)
>
> I maybe give them a buck to get on the docket earlier. I'm not naive, but it doesn't sit well with me. Some lawyers carry dollar bills on them when they go into these offices. (8)
>
> *Interviewer*: Do you get favors from clerks?
> *Respondent*: If we do, we pay.
> *Interviewer*: At Christmastime too?
> *Respondent*: Any time. That's one of the vicious things about the practice. Not everyone does it, but those who don't, get lost. It's a difficult situation to overcome. (82)
>
> A clerk will call me ahead once in a while, help me with papers.
>
> *Interviewer*: Do you have to give them a couple of dollars?
> *Respondent*: A hell of a lot more than that, five, ten dollars. {160}
> *Interviewer*: You give them a gift at Christmas?
> *Respondent*: Christmas is all year round. (37)
>
> They all have their hands out, all the time. Jesus Christ, twenty-five, fifty dollars each time, clerks or bailiffs. Sometimes clerks can delay you for a month. (49)
>
> I give breaks on _____ [product sold in his store]—not free. For everybody I come in contact with, even clients. It's very important. It's the reason I don't have a tough time others have. I must give away _____ by the thousands. Not money—that's a small amount. The other guy like me has to pay for these things.

... The lawyer is a fawning specimen to begin with, he is continually asking for something, a beggar to begin with—he wants service from a clerk, a lowly clerk, and he begs for consideration from the court, he "prays" the court. (30)

The wide currency of such practices results in part from the sheer inefficiency characteristic of most of these offices, which are generally understaffed and invariably plagued with a large backlog of matters. Probably more significant, however, is the fact that almost all the personnel of these offices are political appointees grown accustomed to the favor system. And, finally, there is the tendency of a good many individual lawyers to compensate for their apparent insecurity, sense of inadequacy, and lack of confidence by acting like bigshots, passing out large tips and presents in order to ensure their being known by the clerks and other officials.

The pay-off and influence problem also arises from the application of certain local statutes and ordinances that are often grossly unrealistic, practically unenforceable, and inevitably coupled with a wide range of administrative discretion. These include most of the local tax laws {161} (statutes dealing with tax foreclosure, personal property tax, real property tax), a large segment of municipal law (zoning ordinances, licensing statutes), and the divorce law (artificial limitations on or definition of the legal grounds for divorce). Under these conditions it is the lawyer who knows somebody in the State's Attorney's Office, in the Board of Zoning or Tax Appeals, in the Board of County Commissioners, or in a variety of other agencies and offices, or who is known by the judges, who will receive the more favorable interpretation or treatment, can expect a more advantageous adjustment or compromise, or will have his matter pushed through more expeditiously. Partly this is just a matter of paying off the right people and partly, because most of these officials are political appointees, of having the right political connections.

The fiduciary problem. A central requirement of the Canons is that the lawyer should adopt a trust or fiduciary relationship with his client, whose best interests he is supposed to promote, and that he deal directly and personally with the client without the intrusion of lay intermediaries.[6] From what we know of the nature of individual practice, however, there

---

6 In Canon 32, "fidelity to private trust" is declared to be one of the principal duties of the lawyer. This requirement of fiduciary self-restraint, of representing the client with "undivided fidelity," includes the obligation not to divulge confidences of a client (neither for the "personal benefit or gain" of the lawyer nor to the disadvantage of the client—see Canons 11 and 37) and the prohibition against representing conflicting interests (see Canon 6). Canon 35, which deals with intermediaries, reads in part:

Canon 35. Intermediaries

appear to be strong pressures forcing the lawyer-client relationship into two deviant forms in conflict with the requirements indicated above.

1. "Clients are expendable." In the case of those lawyers specializing in personal injury, local tax, collections, criminal, and to some extent divorce work, the relationship with the client, as we have seen, is generally mediated by a broker or business supplier who may be either another lawyer or a layman. In these fields of practice the lawyer is principally concerned with pleasing the broker or of winning his approval, more so than he is with satisfying the individual client. The source of business generally counts {162} for more than the client, especially where the client is unlikely to return or to send in other clients. The client is then expendable; he can be exploited to the full. Under these conditions, when a lawyer receives a client from a layman or a referring lawyer, he has not so much gained a client as a piece of business, and his attitude is often that of handling a particular piece of merchandise or of developing a volume of a certain kind of merchandise. If, for example, as sometimes happens, a client who was originally referred by another lawyer returns, the question that arises is not what obligation this lawyer owes in a professional sense to the client or to the lawyer who initially referred him, but how important the referring lawyer is as a source of business. Where there is an opportunity or prospect of getting more referrals, the lawyer will follow the rule of notifying the referring lawyer (and offering him part of the fee—generally a third) as an inducement to keep sending him matters, otherwise he will not. Some lawyers even extend this policy of notifying the referring lawyer to the situation where the client refers another client, in which case both the referring client and the lawyer may get a cut:

> An ex-client referred me someone. He came [the ex-client] from a certain lawyer. Well, that lawyer still appears on the file—that's my incentive to that lawyer, otherwise he'd be afraid of the repeat. A referral fee goes to the lawyer, and maybe also some to the client who referred it. (27)

Others won't go this far:

> If the client recommends someone else, then it's my client—I won't call the other lawyer. (8) {163}

The professional services of a lawyer should not be controlled or exploited by any lay agency, personal or corporate, which intervenes between client and lawyer. A lawyer's responsibilities and qualifications are individual. He should avoid all relations which direct the performance of his duties by or in the interest of such intermediary. A lawyer's relation to his client should be personal, and the responsibility should be direct to the client [as amended in 1933].

One reason for the different approach of these two lawyers is that the first is a specialist in personal injury, while the second is a general practitioner and less dependent on other lawyers for business. One young lawyer refused to do any more work for an older lawyer in his suite because where the repeat business was lucrative, the older lawyer insisted on taking complete charge of the matter.

> I used to get some referrals when I came in [to the office], but I asked him to stop—I didn't like the arrangement; they were still his clients and he charged only very small fees. I'd see the client, but he'd set small fees. He used it as an accommodation to his clients to get personal injury cases, so they'd feel warm to him and send him personal injury cases. I made peanuts, but if they came back and referred another case to me, that was to be his client and his business. (28)

In some cases the client will not even know who his lawyer is, that is to say, who is actually doing the work for him. This happens when the referring lawyer does not want the client to know that he has farmed out the matter (e.g., to a "ghost brief writer") because of the risk of losing the client to the other lawyer. As one respondent remarked:

> Usually I'll let my client know I'm referring it, but it's not always wise; you can lose clients that way. (16)

A close, trust relationship is probably rarely achieved in the type of practice to which we have just been referring, not only because of the volume-merchandising phenomenon and the importance of the broker but also because most such matters are handled on a contingency basis that {164} gives the lawyer a direct financial stake in the matter. For this reason the client often becomes, literally, a piece of business.

2. "Clients are partners." Unlike the lawyers discussed above, the upper-level real estate and business-corporate lawyers frequently have a close, intimate relationship with their business clients, so much so in fact that many become merged with their clients on something like a business partnership basis. Well over half go in on deals with clients, principally in the area of real estate, and several are officers or on the board of directors of their clients' corporations. Under these conditions it would appear to be difficult to maintain a fiduciary relationship with the client or to adopt toward him an attitude of disinterestedness. A number of respondents recognize the dangers involved in becoming "partners" of their clients, but, nevertheless, they feel that this is the only way to "make it" financially in the law practice.

> They told us in law school to stick to the law business and it will take care of you—don't go into business with your clients, no deals or arrangements, you lose your perspective, you really become a partner of your client. But this is baloney. If you're invited to go in, go in by all means; it's the only way to get any financial independence—it's the only way to make it. You can't do it practicing law, you can't get any financial security that way. Ninety per cent of the lawyers can't make it—I haven't to date. (6)

Bibliography

References from the main volume, its endnotes, and general sources.

Books

Blaustein, Albert P., and Charles O. Porter. *The American Lawyer.* Chicago: University of Chicago Press, 1954.

Brown, Esther L. *Lawyers and the Promotion of Justice.* New York: Russell Sage Foundation, 1938.

Dean, Arthur H. *William Nelson Cromwell.* New York: Ad Press, Ltd., 1957.

Drinker, Henry S. *Legal Ethics.* New York: Columbia University Press, 1953.

Harno, Albert J. *Legal Education in the United States.* San Francisco: Bancroft-Whitney Co., 1952.

Hunting, Roger B., and Gloria S. Neuwirth. *Who Sues in New York City?* New York: Columbia University Press, 1962.

Hurst, James Willard. *The Growth of American Law.* Boston: Little, Brown and Co., 1950.

Koegel, Otto E. *Walter S. Carter, Collector of Young Masters.* Great Neck, N.Y.: Round Table Press, Inc., 1955.

Mills, C. Wright. *White Collar.* New York: Oxford University Press, 1953.

Nicholson, Lionell S. *The Law Schools of the United States.* Baltimore: Lord Baltimore Press, Inc., 1958.

Pound, Roscoe. *The Lawyer from Antiquity to Modern Times.* St. Paul: West Publishing Co., 1953.

Reed, Alfred Z. *Present Day Law Schools in the United States and Canada.* New York: Carnegie Foundation for the Advancement of Teaching, 1928.

———. *Training for the Public Profession of the Law. New York: Carnegie Foundation for the Advancement of Teaching, 1921.*

Swaine, Robert T. *The Cravath Firm.* 3 vols. New York: Ad Press, Ltd., 1946–1948.

Taft, Henry W. *A Century and a Half at the New York Bar.* New York: Privately printed, 1938.

Tinelly, Joseph T. *Part-Time Legal Education.* Brooklyn: The Foundation Press, 1957.

Warren, Charles. *A History of the American Bar.* Boston: Little, Brown and Co., 1911.

Zeisel, Hans, Harry Kalven, Jr., and Bernard Buchholz. *Delay in the Court.* Boston: Little, Brown and Co., 1959.

Articles and Reports

Annual Review of Legal Education for 1911. From 1911 to 1934 published by the Carnegie Foundation for the Advancement of Teaching in New York. From 1935 published by the Section on Legal Education and Admission to the Bar of the American Bar Association in Chicago. Since 1942 under the title, *Law School and Bar Admissions Requirements in the United States.*

Banks, Louis. "The Crisis in the Courts," *Fortune* (December, 1961).

Buckner, George, II. "What Your Clients Think of You," *Journal of the Missouri Bar*, Vol. 17, 1961.

Cheatham, Elliott E. "The Law Schools of Tennessee," *Tennessee Law Review*, Vol. XXI (April, 1950).

Chicago Bar Association. *Annual Reports Submitted by Committees in the Association* (1955–1956, 1956–1957, 1957–1958).

Dodge, Emily P. "Evolution of a City Law Office," *Wisconsin Law Review*, Vol. XXXV (January, 1956).

Fagen, Melvin J. "The Status of Jewish Lawyers in New York City," *Jewish Social Studies*, Vol. I, 1939.

Franklin, Marc, Robert Chanin, and Irving Mark. "Accidents, Money and the Law: A Study of the Economics of Personal Injury Litigation," *Columbia Law Review*, Vol. 61, 1961.

Fuller, Lon L. "Legal Education and Admissions to the Bar of Pennsylvania," *Temple Law Quarterly*, Vol. XXV, No. 25 (January, 1952).

Hamilton, Fowler. "The Lawyers and Business," *Fortune* (October, 1948).

Hervey, John G. "The Decline of Professionalism in the Law: An Exploration into Some Causes," *New York Law Forum*, Vol. III, No. 4 (October, 1957).

Johnstone, Quintin. "Title Insurance," *Yale Law Journal*, Vol. LXVI, No. 4 (February, 1957).

———. "The Unauthorized Practice Controversy," *The Kansas Law Review*, Vol. IV, No. 1 (October, 1955).

Kafogolis, Milton. *Economic Condition of the Legal Profession in Ohio*. Prepared under the auspices of the Professional Economics Committee of the Ohio State Bar Association, 1955.

Klaw, S. "Wall Street Lawyers," *Fortune* (February, 1958).

Koos, Earl L. "The Family and the Law." Rochester: National Legal Aid Society, 1949. (A pamphlet.)

Lawyers in the United States: Distribution and Income. Part I: Distribution, 1956; Part II: Income, 1958. Chicago: American Bar Foundation. Also: 1958 Distribution Supplement.

"Lawyers Looking at You," *Fortune* (January, 1931).

Legal Education and Admissions to the Bar of California. Sacramento: State Bar of California, 1949.

Liebenberg, Maurice. "Income of Lawyers in the Postwar Period," *Survey of Current Business*, Washington: U.S. Department of Commerce, 1956.

Llewellyn, Karl N. "The Bar's Troubles, and Poultices—and Cures?" *Law and Contemporary Problems*, Vol. V, No. 1, 1938.

Lortie, Dan C. "Laymen to Lawmen: Law School, Careers, and Professional Socialization," *Harvard Educational Review*, Vol. 29, No. 4, 1959.

Morland, John W. "Legal Education in Georgia," *Mercer Law Review*, Vol. II, No. 2 (Spring, 1951).

Parsons, Talcott. "A Sociologist Views the Legal Profession," *Conference on the Profession of Law and Legal Education,* Series No. 11. Chicago: University of Chicago Law School, 1952. Also published in *Essays in Sociological Theory.* Rev. ed. Glencoe, Ill.: Free Press, 1954.

Report of the California Survey Committee. Sacramento: State Bar of California, 1933.

Report of the Committee of Censors to the Law Association of Philadelphia, in re Contingent Fee Accident Litigation. Committee of Censors. Philadelphia: Law Associates, 1928.

Riesman, David. "Toward an Anthropological Science of Law and the Legal Profession," *American Journal of Sociology,* Vol. LVII, 1951.

Rosenberg, Maurice, and Michael I. Sovern. "Delay and the Dynamics of Personal Injury Litigation," *Columbia Law Review,* Vol. 59, 1959.

Shafroth, Will. "Can the Law Schools Lead Us Out of the Wilderness?" *The American Law School Review* (St. Paul, Minnesota, West Publishing Co.), Volume 7, 1934.

Sharswood, George. "An Essay on Professional Ethics," *Reports of the American Bar Association,* Vol. XXXII. Philadelphia: reprinted by the American Bar Association, 1907.

Smigel, Erwin O. "The Impact of Recruitment on the Organization of the Large Law Firm," *American Sociological Review,* Vol. 25, No. 1 (February, 1960).

Stone, Harlan F. "The Public Influence of the Bar," *Harvard Law Review,* Vol. XLVIII, 1934.

Swaine, Robert T. "Impact of Big Business on the Profession: An Answer to the Critics of the Modern Bar," *American Bar Association Journal,* Vol. XXXV (February, 1949).

Weinfield, William. "Income of Lawyers, 1929–1948," *Survey of Current Business,* Washington: U.S. Department of Commerce, 1949.

Wickser, Philip J. "Law Schools, Bar Examiners, and Bar Associations—Co-operation vs. Insulation," *The American Law School Review,* Vol. 7, 1933.

Unpublished Material

Hale, William H. "The Career Development of the Negro Lawyer." Unpublished Ph.D. dissertation, Department of Sociology, University of Chicago, 1949.

Harris, George B. "Ethics of the Legal Profession, 1836–1908." Unpublished essay, Chicago, American Bar Foundation, 1955.

Kent, Leonard. "Economic Status of the Legal Profession in Chicago." Unpublished Ph.D. dissertation, Business School, University of Chicago, 1950. Lortie, Dan C. "The Striving Young Lawyer: A Study of Early Career Differentiation in the Chicago Bar." Unpublished Ph.D. dissertation, Department of Sociology, University of Chicago, 1958.

McKinnon, Frederick B. "Study of the Ethical Problems of Lawyers in Private Practice." Harvard Law School project in progress.

O'Gorman, Hubert J. "Lawyers in Matrimonial Cases," Unpublished Ph.D. dissertation, Columbia University, 1961.

Thielens, Wagner P., Jr. "Socialization Processes Among Law Students." Unpublished Ph.D. dissertation in progress, Columbia University.
Wood, Arthur L. "The Criminal Lawyer." Chicago: American Bar Foundation. Unpublished report prepared for the Survey of the Legal Profession, 1955.

Directories

American Bar Association Directory, 1955–1956. Summit, N.J.: Martindale-Hubbell, Inc., 1956.
Martindale-Hubbell Law Directory. Vols. I, II. Summit, N.J.: Martindale-Hubbell, Inc., 1956, 1957, 1958.
Sullivan's Law Directory for the State of Illinois, 1956–1957. Chicago: Sullivan's Law Directory, 1956.

Statutes

Smith-Hurd, Illinois Annotated Statutes: Chapter 32 (Illinois Business Corporation Act of 1933), Chapter 120 (Revenue Act of 1939).

Census Materials

Twelfth, Thirteenth, and Fourteenth Census of the United States, Vol. IV, Population, 1900, 1910, 1920.
Statistical Abstract of the United States for 1900–1950.

Reading 3.3

Harvard and Yale Ascendant: The Legal Education of the Justices From Holmes to Kagan

*Patrick J. Glen**

With the confirmation of Elena Kagan as a justice of the U.S. Supreme Court, eight of the nine sitting justices have graduated from only two law schools—Harvard and Yale. This Article frames this development in the historical context of the legal education of the justices confirmed between 1902 and 2010. What this historical review makes clear is that the Ivy League dominance of the Supreme Court is a relatively recent occurrence whose beginnings can be traced to Antonin Scalia's 1986 confirmation. Prior to that time, although Harvard and Yale were consistently represented among the justices, they did not constitute a majority of sitting members. In addition to this strictly historical assessment of the justices' education, this Article also attempts to ascertain why the Harvard-Yale trend has arisen and whether this trend may have deleterious effects on the future of the Court. In concluding, the Article recommends that when the next vacancy arises, the president should look outside the confines of Harvard and Yale for a qualified nominee.

Introduction

The rote and maddening repetition of the phrase "judicial monastery"[1] by Senator Patrick Leahy in his press conference reacting to the nomination of Solicitor General Elena Kagan to

---

* Adjunct Professor of Law, Georgetown University Law Center. The author would like to thank the editors and staff of the UCLA Law Review for their time and effort in bringing this article to print, especially Helen Hwang, Wesley Montalvo, Darcy Pottle, and Alyssa Simon.

1 By "judicial monastery," Leahy specifically means the federal courts of appeals, where all eight of the other sitting justices had served prior to their confirmations. The term is meant derisively, and is supposed to highlight the lack of experiential diversity that sitting judges brings to the U.S. Supreme Court and their purported aloofness from the cares and concerns of contemporary America. *See* David

the Supreme Court, in which he focused on the experiential diversity she would allegedly bring to the high court, obfuscated Justice Kagan's educational similarity with the sitting justices.[2] The nomination may not have gone to an alumnus of a federal appellate court, but it was bestowed on an Ivy League law graduate for the tenth consecutive time, dating back to Justice Scalia's 1986 confirmation. Even this phrase hides more than it clarifies, as out of these ten nominations, nine have been Harvard or Yale law graduates, while Justice Ginsburg attended Harvard Law School before transferring to, and graduating from, Columbia Law School.[3] The confirmation of Justice Kagan now marks the first time in the history of the Supreme Court that all nine sitting justices have been graduates of Ivy League law schools.[4] In fact, as seen from this angle, it is fitting that Justice Kagan has taken the place not only of the last remaining Protestant on the Court, but also of its last non–Ivy League holdout: Justice Stevens, a graduate of Northwestern Law School in Chicago.[5]

Despite Senator Leahy's focus on noneducational bases for asserting that Kagan represents diversity, other legal commentators had noted the step that Kagan's confirmation would represent to the Supreme Court.[6] Yet these observations are not new—similar comments were made at the time of the nominations of Chief Justice Roberts and Associate Justice Alito, Harvard and Yale Law School graduates, respectively.[7] What is new is the Ivy League predominance in the nomination of Supreme Court justices, especially the predominance

---

Ingram, *Leahy on Managing the Kagan Hearing*, Nat'l L.J., June 28, 2010, at 6, *available at* http://www.law.com/jsp/article.jsp?id=1202463059568.

2 For the audio of Senator Leahy's press conference, see Patrick Leahy, *Press Conference on Supreme Court Nominee Elena Kagan*, Leahy.Senate.gov (May 10, 2010), http://leahy.senate.gov/press/multimedia/?id=cef9d187-6713-4d96-bc99-c286e87681a5. For an edited transcript of his remarks, see Patrick Leahy, *Comment on the President's Nomination of Elena Kagan to Be an Associate Justice of the United States Supreme Court*, Leahy.Senate.gov (May 10, 2010), http://leahy.senate.gov/press/press_releases/release/?id=eb9a962b-17f3-46a9-99fe-ac6b5fa7768d.

3 *See* Timothy L. Hall, Supreme Court Justices: A Biographical Dictionary 425 (2001).

4 In fact, at the time of Holmes's 1902 confirmation, only two justices had graduated from Harvard Law School, Horace Gary and Benjamin Curtis, while none had graduated from Yale Law School. *See generally id.* at 1–234 (recounting biographical information for all the justices through Holmes).

5 *See* Evan Thomas, *Twilight of the WASPs*, Newswk., May 31, 2010, at 34.

6 *See* Christopher Edley, Jr., *The Elite, No Apology Needed*, Wash. Post, May 16, 2010, at B1; Jonathan Turley, Op-Ed., *It's Their Private Court*, L.A. Times, May 12, 2010, at A17; Larry Abramson, *The Harvard-Yalification of the Supreme Court*, NPR (May 16, 2010), http://www.npr.org/templates/story/story.php?storyId=126802460.

7 *See* Richard Cohen, *Ivy-Covered Court*, Wash. Post, Nov. 15, 2005, at A21.

of Harvard and Yale graduates to the exclusion of nearly all others.[8] In essence, candidates who received their legal education in a locale other than Cambridge or New Haven should lower their aspirations.[9] They may very well attain a seat on a federal appellate court, or perhaps a state supreme court, but if past is prologue, they have no hope of setting up an office in the Marble Palace.

The purpose of this [reading] is simple—to explore the trends in the legal education of the Supreme Court justices from the beginning of the twentieth century through the latest nomination. Part I analyzes these trends through a number of different comparisons, including broad trends in the 110 years under observation, the number of Ivy League law graduates as a percentage of total nominees in the relevant time frames, and the increasing predominance of Ivy League law graduates as an absolute function of the composition of the Court. These comparisons make clear that the Ivy League is not continuing any historical pattern of predominance but is in fact only recently ascendant. The trend towards Harvard and Yale law graduates is very new in the context of the 110 years surveyed here, commencing only with the 1986 nomination of Antonin Scalia. Part II offers several explanations for why this is the case. In concluding, this Article concurs with the opinion of many in academia and the profession that when the next vacancy on the Court occurs, the president should seek a qualified candidate educated somewhere other than Harvard or Yale.

I. Legal Education of the Justices: 1902–2010[10]

A number of preliminary issues must be addressed prior to assessing the trends in the legal education of those justices confirmed in this and the last century. The first is the relevant time frame. For the purposes of this Article, the analysis begins with the first confirmation in the twentieth century, that of Oliver Wendell Holmes, Jr., in 1902. The reason for setting this as the relevant starting point of the instant investigation is that the law school as an educational entity only began to gain traction in the latter third of the nineteenth century.[11] Prior to that, and even for a significant part of the twentieth century, "reading law," that is,

---

8 *See id.*

9 *See* Karen Sloan, *For High Court, Harvard or Yale Degree Is a Virtual Prerequisite*, Legal Intelligencer, May 12, 2010, at 4.

10 Part I of this Article is based on the information compiled in the Appendix pertaining to where the justices received their legal educations. An explanation and attribution of the sources used is included as a preface to the Appendix's table listing the educational backgrounds of the justices.

11 *See* Melvin I. Urofsky, *Louis D. Brandeis: His Days at Harvard Law School*, Experience, No. 2, 2010, at 13.

apprenticing with an already-barred attorney, was the far more common way of entering the legal profession.[12] Beginning the current assessment at the dawn of the twentieth century is then the most obvious place to begin an analysis of legal education, as increasingly the justices confirmed since 1902 were graduates of law schools. A corollary to this issue is that this Article is concerned only with law school *graduates*. As the law school gained traction, some studied for short periods of time, left law school and apprenticed with a lawyer without graduating, and then entered the bar via the apprenticeship. This hybrid education is disregarded for present purposes, and only those who actually graduated from a law school are counted towards that law school's presence as a function of absolute composition on the Court. Additionally, this Article confines itself to the initial legal education, the juris doctorate or LL.B (bachelor of laws). It is only the school from which a justice earned his or her basic law degree that is counted as relevant. For instance, Justices Lewis Powell and Sherman Minton earned graduate degrees in law from Harvard and Yale, respectively, but their juris doctorates were from Washington and Lee University and Indiana University.[13] It is the latter degrees, rather than the Ivy League LL.M.s, that are the focus here. Finally, the comparisons in Subparts A and B focus on Harvard and Yale graduates rather than on Ivy League graduates generally because it is graduates from these two schools that have come to predominate, rather than the Ivy League law schools generally. No Cornell law graduate has been nominated to the Court in the relevant time frame, and the only University of Pennsylvania graduate is Justice Owen Roberts, confirmed in 1930. Columbia may seem like an obvious choice for inclusion, as the sole non–Harvard or Yale graduate on the current Court is a Columbia alumnus, yet Justice Ginsburg was the first Columbia law graduate to be appointed since William Douglas's 1939 confirmation. As this Article is concerned with recent trends and how they will play out into the future, Columbia graduates do not provide a modern basis for comparison.

With these preliminaries in hand, this Part proceeds in the following manner. Subpart A compares the percentages of Harvard and Yale graduates as a function of the total number of confirmed justices over the course of the eleven decades spanning 1902 through 2010. Subpart B compares the percentages of Harvard and Yale justices as a function of the composition of the sitting Court over the same metrics. The results of Subparts A and B are obviously interrelated and make clear that the preference for Harvard and Yale graduates is

---

12 *See, e.g.*, Melvin I. Urofsky, Louis D. Brandeis: A Life 25 (2009); John H. Wilkerson, Jr., *Milestones and Memories of Jones School of Law: From Reading Law to Accredited Law School*, 71 Ala. Law. 138, 138 (2010).

13 *See* Hall, *supra* note 3, at 393 (regarding Justice Powell), 346 (regarding Justice Minton).

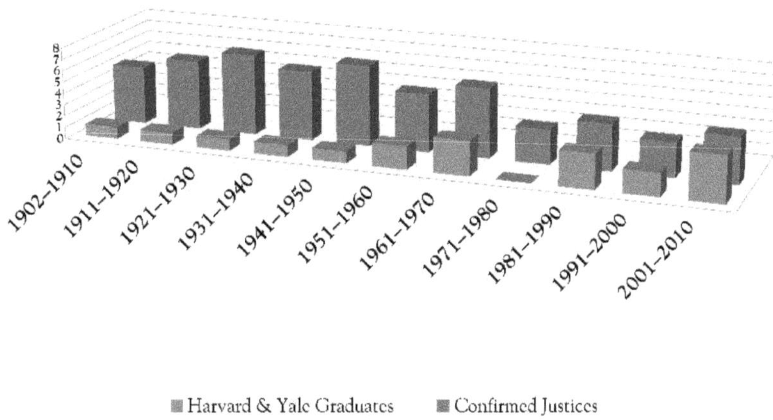

FIGURE 3.3.1 Harvard & Yale Graduates as a Percentage of Confirmed Justices: 1902–2010

of recent vintage, and that over the past thirty years, the Court has increasingly become a bastion of such graduates to the exclusion of other elite law school graduates.

A. Harvard & Yale Confirmees

Although the focus of this Article is on Harvard and Yale law graduates confirmed as justices of the Supreme Court, these two schools have only recently shared this connection. The fortunes of these two law schools in placing graduates on the High Court have not always been as closely linked in the Court's history as they are at present. Before addressing the distinct fortunes of these two elite institutions, however, it is worth noting that nominations from these schools as a percentage of total nominations have increased dramatically in just the past three decades.

Figure 3.3.1 is a decade-by-decade comparison of the total confirmations in that decade and the number of Harvard and Yale graduates confirmed as justices. In every relevant decade except for one, 1971 to 1980, at least one Harvard or Yale graduate was confirmed as a Supreme Court justice. Nonetheless, in the five decades beginning with Holmes's confirmation in 1902, only one such justice was confirmed in each relevant time period. Accordingly, between 1902 and 1950, only five Harvard graduates were included out of thirty-one confirmed justices (including chief justices). Thus, in the first half of the twentieth century, graduates from Harvard or Yale accounted for approximately 16 percent of the confirmed justices. Moreover, in no decade did Harvard or Yale graduates account for more than 20 percent of the confirmed justices in that decade. In fact, although neither Harvard nor Yale dominated the Court in this time frame, Columbia did have the sort of preeminence in placing justices that the former two schools currently enjoy. Out of the eight confirmed justices between 1925 and 1939, four were Columbia men, three of whom were graduates. The fourth Columbia justice, Benjamin Cardozo, finished the traditional two-year program of study at Columbia law but left prior to completing the newly instituted third year.[14] From 1930 through 1945, there were never less than two Columbia graduates on the Court, while there were three such graduates between 1932 and 1941. Alas, after the 1939 confirmation of William Douglas, Columbia would not have another graduate on the Court until Ginsburg's 1993 confirmation, a span of fifty-four years.

It was only in the 1950s that the fortunes of Harvard and Yale began to rise, albeit not dramatically. Between 1951 and 1960, two Harvard and Yale justices were confirmed out of five total confirmations. In the 1960s, three graduates were confirmed out of a total of six confirmations. The percentage of Harvard and Yale graduates having never previously risen above 20 percent, these two decades saw the percentage rise first to 40 percent, and then to 50 percent. The 1970s were a setback of sorts—the three justices appointed during this period were graduates of Washington & Lee University, Stanford, and Northwestern (Justices Powell, Rehnquist, and Stevens, respectively). Since 1981, however, only one justice of the eleven confirmed was not educated at an Ivy League law school, and only two of the eleven have not graduated from either Harvard or Yale. In the 1980s, Harvard and Yale accounted for 75 percent of the nominees; in the 1990s, 67 percent, and since 2000, 100 percent.

Between 1902 and 2010, fifty-six justices were confirmed to the U.S. Supreme Court. Included in this number are nineteen Harvard and Yale law graduates, accounting for a total of approximately 34 percent. Since 1980, Harvard and Yale graduates have accounted for approximately 82 percent of confirmed justices. The dominance of these institutions is thus a new development in the history of the Supreme Court, not simply a continuation of a dominance that has always existed. Although the trend in Figure 3.3.1 begins in the 1980s, there was no Ivy League confirmation in that decade until the 1986 confirmation of Scalia. Thus, it is only over the course of the past twenty-four years that these two institutions have come to dominate the Supreme Court confirmation process. Attempting to explain this result will be the subject of Part II.

It is also worth noting that the fortunes of Harvard and Yale have not always been so intertwined on the Supreme Court. Since the 1902 confirmation of Holmes, the Supreme Court has never been without at least one Harvard law graduate. Although Holmes was "alone" for fourteen years, he was joined in 1916 by Louis Brandeis and, in 1923, by Edward Terry Sanford. When Holmes left the Court in 1932, Brandeis sat alone as a Harvard graduate until his retirement in 1939, when he was replaced by Justice Frankfurter, a Harvard law legend. Without charting the entire course of Harvard's fortunes on the Supreme Court, it is simply important to note that in the 108 years since Holmes took his seat, there has never

14 Andrew L. Kaufman, Cardozo 48–49 (1998).

been a moment that the Court was without at least one Harvard graduate, and it usually has multiple graduates. Yale Law School, however, did not place a graduate on the Court until the 1958 confirmation of Potter Stewart. Nonetheless, beginning with Stewart, three of the next four confirmations were Yale law graduates, with the inclusion of Justices Byron White and Abe Fortas. From 1965 through the 1969 retirement of Fortas, the Court could boast three Yale graduates as opposed to only one Harvard graduate, Justice Brennan. Yet after Fortas's 1965 confirmation, Yale would have to wait thirty-six years before the confirmation of Justice Thomas in 1991. In all, thirteen Harvard graduates have been confirmed to the Supreme Court, spanning the entire time period between 1902 and the present, whereas six Yale graduates have been confirmed, spanning the time period between 1958 and the present. These divergent histories only began to converge as recently as the 1990s, when, between the 1991 confirmation of Justice Thomas and the 2010 nomination of Kagan, Yale matched Harvard nominee for nominee, three to three.

B. Harvard & Yale Justices as a Function of Court Composition

In addition to reviewing how Harvard and Yale graduates have fared as a percentage of confirmed justices over the course of the preceding eleven decades, it is also worth charting how this trend has altered the composition of the Court over time. It seems obvious that as Harvard and Yale graduates accounted for an increasing percentage of confirmed justices, this affected the composition of The Nine, but the following two figures are meant to graphically represent how sharp the increase in such graduates has been over the course of the preceding twenty-four years. Figure 3.3.2 plots the number of Harvard and Yale graduates

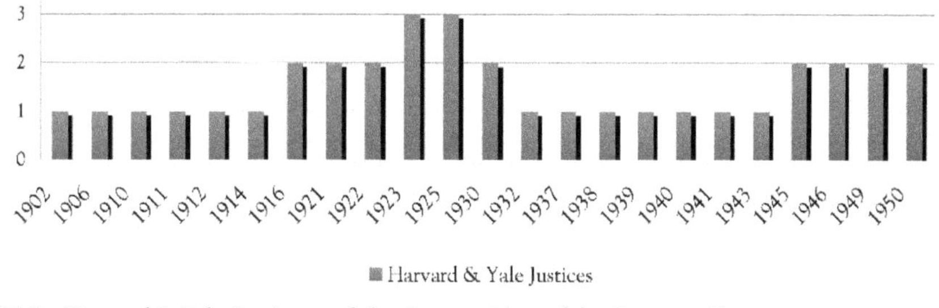

FIGURE 3.3.2 Harvard & Yale Justices and the Composition of the Supreme Court: 1901–1950

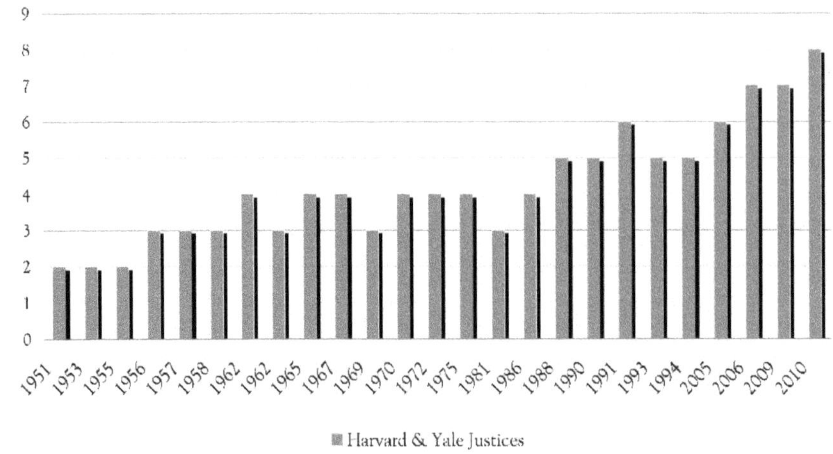

FIGURE 3.3.3 Harvard & Yale Justices and the Composition of the Supreme Court: 1951–2010

as a function of the total composition of the Court over the period of 1901 through 1950, while Figure 3.3.3 plots the same data over the period of 1951 through 2010. The *x*-axis is plotted by confirmation year, that is, a year in which one or more justices were confirmed to the Supreme Court. In all cases but one, the confirmation of multiple justices during a one-year period did not affect the plotting of the relevant information. In the one year that it did, 1962, the year is included twice, first representing the confirmation of Justice White, a Yale law graduate, and secondly representing the confirmation of Justice Goldberg, a Northwestern law graduate.

During the 1901–1950 time frame, in which no Yale law graduates were on the Court, Harvard graduates as a function of total composition peaked at 33 percent between the 1923 confirmation of Sanford and his death in 1930. Prior to Sanford's confirmation, seven years were spent with Holmes and Brandeis together on the Court, while the preceding fourteen years saw Holmes as the sole Harvard graduate. After Sanford's death, Holmes and Brandeis were again the only Harvard law graduates on the Court for two years, and following Holmes's death, Harvard enjoyed only one justice, split between Brandeis and his successor, Frankfurter, from 1932 until the 1945 confirmation of Justice Harold Burton. Harvard graduates were undoubtedly a fixture on the Court between 1901 and 1950, but they never constituted a majority of the sitting justices.

Since the 1956 appointment of William Brennan from Harvard, the Supreme Court has never had less than three Harvard or Yale graduates represented among its members. Between 1956 and 1986, the number of Harvard and Yale graduates oscillated between three and four, but not even the fallow 1970s dented their numbers, as all three non–Ivy League justices confirmed between 1972 and 1975 replaced non-Harvard and non-Yale graduates. Not until the 1988 confirmation of Anthony Kennedy did Harvard and Yale graduates represent a majority of the justices, a first in the Court's history. This majority grew to six with the confirmation of Justice Thomas from Yale in 1991, reverted to five when Columbia graduate Ginsburg took the place of the retiring Yale graduate White in 1993, and remained at five the following year when Breyer replaced Blackmun, trading Harvard for Harvard. In 2005 and 2006, the number moved from five to six to seven, as Roberts and Alito, from Harvard and Yale, respectively, replaced the departing Stanford graduates, Justices O'Connor and Rehnquist. Kagan's confirmation represents the penultimate change to the Court in replacing Justice Stevens, leaving Ginsburg as the lone non-Harvard, non-Yale graduate.

The Supreme Court with Kagan as junior justice now has eight Harvard or Yale law graduates, but as late as 1981 these graduates accounted for only three justices—33 percent of the Court—whereas even in 1986 Harvard and Yale did not yet hold, and had never before held, a majority of the justiceships. Justice Kennedy's 1988 appointment, in the wake of Scalia's trendsetting 1986 confirmation, not only created the majority, but represents an event horizon of sorts, past which Harvard and Yale graduates have become virtually the sole pool of nominees for justiceships, with the necessary result that the composition of the Court has trended dramatically in the direction of these institutions in the past two-and-a-half decades. Again, the Harvard-Yale dominance is a recent trend rather than a continuation.

II. Why The Trend, and Should Anyone Care?

If the confirmation rate of Harvard and Yale law graduates has exploded over the previous two decades, the question remains: Why has this occurred? The first potential explanation is that as the importance of a formal law school education increased, the elite law schools themselves took on an increased importance relative to other law schools. When Justice Holmes was confirmed in 1902, he joined a Court that contained only two other law school graduates, Justices John Marshall Harlan and David Brewer, who studied at the law faculty of Transylvania and Albany Law School, respectively. Not until the 1910 confirmation of Justice Horace Lurton, an alumnus of Cumberland Law School, was another justice also a law school graduate. Between the 1902 confirmation of Holmes and the 1941 confirmation of Justice Robert Jackson—the last confirmed justice who did not graduate from law school—eleven of the twenty-six confirmed justices were not law school graduates. Not until the 1957 confirmation of Charles Whittaker, who replaced the retiring Stanley Reed, was the Court composed entirely of law school graduates.

This trend towards law school education as the desired route into the legal profession initially trod local or regional lines. Harvard Law School may have been a preeminent and nationally renowned institution at the time of Justice Brandeis's attendance, but it stood alone in that category.[15] Columbia and Harvard were just beginning to gain national traction in the late nineteenth and early twentieth centuries and were still dominated by a relatively local, rather than a nationally representative, student body.[16] Justice Cardozo, who was attending Columbia Law School at this time, was decidedly equivocal about his education there.[17] Yale Law School began gaining national status only in the 1920s.[18] This increase in its reputation paid dividends with the confirmations in the late 1950s and early 1960s of three justices. Regionally elite law schools, which trained the best and brightest of the local students, filled this gap of institutions with national reputations. The Stanford of Rehnquist and O'Connor falls within this category, as does the Colorado of Wiley Rutledge, the Berkeley of Earl Warren, the Indiana of Sherman Minton, the Washington & Lee of Joseph Lamar and Lewis Powell, and the Cincinnati of Willis Van Devanter and William Howard Taft, to name just a few of the schools represented by the confirmed justices in this time period.[19] Yet as the elite institutions developed elite, nationally recognized law schools, students from across the country aspired to attend not just Harvard, but Yale and Columbia on the East Coast, as well as Stanford and Berkeley on the West Coast. As the importance of legal

---

15 *See* Urofsky, *supra* note 12, at 25–26.

16 *See id.* (regarding Harvard); James F. Simon, Independent Journey: The Life of William O. Douglas 66 (1980) (regarding Columbia).

17 *See* Kaufman, *supra* note 14, at 49. In a 1929 address to the Broome County Bar Association, Cardozo reflected on his law school experience:

> I sometimes think I might escape some of the mistakes I am sure I often make if I had had the training which is given in the law schools of today. As ill luck would have it, I went to Columbia Law School in the transition days when the old order was passing into the new, the text book system into the case one, now, we are told at times, to be in turn supplanted by something else. ... As I look back on it now, it seems as if we didn't have any instruction worthy of the name. We just grew up into lawyers, or rather into members of the bar.

Benjamin N. Cardozo, *The Bench and the Bar*, 34 N.Y. St. B.J. 444, 448 (1962).

18 *See* Robert Stevens, *History of the Yale Law School: Provenance and Perspective*, *in* History of the Yale Law School 10–16 (Anthony T. Kronman ed., 2004) (exploring the rise in Yale Law School's reputation from its founding through the 1956 appointment of Eugene Rostow as dean).

19 *See, e.g.*, Joan Biskupic, Sandra Day O'connor 24–25 (2005) (dating the beginning of Stanford's rise in national reputation to the 1946 appointment of Carl Spaeth as dean of the law school); Jim Newton, Justice for All: Earl Warren and the Nation He Made 35 (2006) (noting the relative youth of Berkeley at the time of Warren's arrival and its appeal to local, California elites); Sandra Day O'Connor, *Foreword: Fiftieth Anniversary Remarks*, 50 Stan. L. Rev. 1 (1997) ("Fifty years ago, Stanford Law School began a transformation from regional respectability to national preeminence.").

education grew, these elite institutions rose in prominence, attracting more of the best and brightest and placing them in the highest and most prestigious levels of government and private practice, from which judges and justices are often picked. Seen in this light, then, the increasing dominance of these institutions is indicative of a more general trend in the development of legal education and the legal profession in the twentieth century.

This thesis is sound in theory, but false in reality. The Supreme Court is not dominated by the graduates of elite law schools generally; it is dominated by the graduates of two elite law schools. Since the trend towards favoring Harvard and Yale commenced in the 1951 to 1960 decade in Figure 3.3.3, NYU, Penn, the University of Michigan, the University of Chicago, and the University of Virginia have had no graduates confirmed to positions on the Court, while Berkeley has had only one, Chief Justice Warren, confirmed in 1953. Harvard and Yale have dominated, with a combined fourteen graduates being confirmed, while Columbia has placed one graduate on the Court, and Stanford two, although none since 1981. Thus, the Supreme Court is not dominated by the top ten law schools but by two out of that ten.[20] Moving out of the top ten, only Northwestern is represented during this time period, with Justices Stevens and Goldberg, while Duke, Cornell, and Georgetown have not placed a graduate on the Court since 1902. Thus, the rise of the elite law schools does not itself explain the rise in the fortunes of Harvard and Yale to the exclusion of the remainder. Nor is there any basis for concluding that these two schools represent an elite within an elite from a purely educational perspective; that is, there is nothing to suggest that a Harvard and Yale education is so superior to an education at, say, Berkeley, that the former graduates should always be preferred to the latter in the context of appointments. As Jonathan Turley has written,

> [T]here is no objective basis for favoring these two schools. Annual rankings from law schools on publication or reputation or student scores show relatively small differences in the top 20 law schools. The actual scores of the small pool of students in the top tier vary by only a few points. While Harvard and Yale are routinely ranked in the top spots, the faculties and student bodies are not viewed as manifestly superior to such competitors as Stanford, Chicago, Michigan or other top schools.[21]

Judge Louis Pollak reached this same conclusion in a recent law review article, in which he offered a revised ranking of law schools by broad subgroups rather than through a strictly

20 I will not say the top two, as rankings change and are obviously hot-button topics.

21 Turley, *supra* note 6.

hierarchical ranking.[22] His ranking, based exclusively on peer assessment scores of the law schools, placed the University of Chicago, Columbia, Harvard, Stanford, and Yale together in an undifferentiated top group, followed by Berkeley, Michigan, NYU, Penn, and the University of Virginia in the second group, and finally UCLA, Cornell, Duke, Georgetown, Northwestern, and Texas in the third.[23] Without delving too far into the ranking thicket, it is also worth noting that at least one ranking of the law schools based on the number of "Super Lawyers" produced would question certain top schools' traditional rankings dominance.[24] Harvard did possess the most graduates selected for inclusion as Super Lawyers in 2009, but Yale ranked only tenth, one spot above the University of California, Hastings.[25] In short, there is no objective metric that would consistently differentiate a Harvard or Yale legal education from an education at another elite law school, and thus no objective basis for the recent turn towards graduates from these schools. Accordingly, the rise of the law school education in the twentieth century does not fully or satisfactorily explain the current dominance of Harvard and Yale graduates on the Court.

Timothy O'Neill offers a second potential explanation that fits within a more general examination of the confirmed justices over the preceding two decades. O'Neill posits that the remarkable similarity of the justices' educational and professional backgrounds, including the unifying characteristic that all were sitting and relatively uncontroversial judges on federal appellate courts, can be traced to the debacle of the Bork confirmation hearings in 1987.[26] This is a seductive thesis that approximately fits the relevant timeline—it was Scalia's 1986 confirmation, followed by the 1988 confirmation of Kennedy, the third choice to replace the retiring Lewis Powell, that proved to be the event horizon in the subsequent dominance of the Court by Harvard and Yale graduates. The more general thrust of O'Neill's argument is also seductive: that presidents wanted to nominate candidates above reproach,

---

22 Louis H. Pollak, *Why Trying to Rank Law Schools Numerically Is a Non-Productive Undertaking: An Article on the* U.S. News & World Report 2009 *List of "The Top 100 Schools"*, 1 Drexel L. Rev. 52, 61–65 (2009).

23 *Id.* at 66–67.

24 *See Rankings*, Partner's Rep. for L. Firm Owners, Aug. 2010, at 9. "Super Lawyers" is a ratings service that identifies exceptional practicing lawyers based on a variety of metrics and in approximately seventy different practice areas. *See Super Lawyers Selection Process*, Super Lawyers, http://www.superlawyers.com/about/selection_process.html (last visited Nov. 15, 2010) (explaining the selection process).

25 *Id.*

26 *See* Timothy P. O'Neill, *"The Stepford Justices": The Need for Experiential Diversity on the Roberts Court*, 60 Okla. L. Rev. 701 (2007).

which meant, among other things, that candidates have the most impressive educational backgrounds possible. Yet as convincing as O'Neill is, this explanation seems to run afoul of the same problem as the preceding explanation. To say that presidents need a nominee beyond reproach from an educational perspective is one thing; to say that this means only Harvard and Yale graduates should be nominated is quite another. Other top-ten graduates would seemingly be as much beyond reproach as the Harvard and Yale nominees actually offered, as would graduates from elite law schools outside the top ten, including the Dukes, Georgetowns, and Cornells. O'Neill's thesis makes intuitive sense but again falls upon the rough shoals of reality—it is not only elite education that presidents are seemingly looking for but education at an elite-of-two within that broader elite.

Explicit in O'Neill's argument and implicit in Senator Leahy's "judicial monastery" rhetoric, is the notion that by focusing on the courts of appeals for nominees, presidents have unduly limited the justices' experiential diversity.[27] This argument further claims that narrowly focusing on sitting appellate judges in the nomination process may restrict the diversity of the educational backgrounds of those eventually confirmed.[28] Nominees outside the courts of appeals have, of course, produced Justice Hugo Black, a senator from Alabama and a graduate of the University of Alabama School of Law,[29] and Chief Justice Earl Warren, governor of California and a Berkeley law graduate.[30] But it is not clear that a broader sweep in the nomination process by considering nonjudicial candidates would engender greater educational diversity on the Court. The only governor seriously mentioned in the past two nomination cycles was Jennifer Granholm of Michigan, a Harvard law graduate.[31] No senators have been seriously considered, and Janet Napolitano, current secretary of the Department of Homeland Security, former governor of Arizona, and University of Virginia law graduate, is the only executive branch candidate to have received any serious speculation.[32]

---

27 *See id.* at 722–24.

28 *Id.* at 724 (noting that all justices confirmed since Bork's failed nomination have been graduates of Harvard, Yale, or Columbia).

29 *See* Hall, *supra* note 3, at 304. Black was elected as a senator in 1927 and served in the Senate until his August 17, 1937 confirmation to the Supreme Court. *Id.*

30 *See id.* at 350–51. Warren was elected governor of California in 1942, reelected in 1946 and 1950, and was serving in that capacity when he was nominated to be chief justice by President Eisenhower. *Id.*

31 *See* Mark Sherman, *The I-95 Court? Five of Supreme Court's Nine Justices Hail From Boston-New York-New Jersey Corridor*, Pitt. Post-Gazette, May 9, 2010, at A8.

32 *See* Noah Schaffer, *A Quick Word With ... David A. Logan, Dean and Professor of Law, Roger Williams University School of Law, Bristol*, R.I. Law. Wkly., Apr. 26, 2010, at 3.

Accordingly, it seems the results of any broader consideration of candidates would have only mixed results in breaking the Harvard-Yale hold.

Furthermore, if Senator Leahy's and Professor O'Neill's point is more generally that sitting judges represent only narrow educational backgrounds, then the point is not valid. For instance, of the sixteen active judges on the U.S. Court of Appeals for the Sixth Circuit, which exercises federal appellate jurisdiction in the states of Kentucky, Michigan, Ohio, and Tennessee, eight law schools are represented. Although Harvard and Yale law graduates account for four of the sitting judges, this is only 25 percent of the court. Moreover, Akron law graduates account for as many judges as either Harvard or Yale, and the University of Michigan dominates the court with four graduates.[33] Even on the U.S. Court of Appeals for the District of Columbia Circuit, regarded as the second highest court in the United States and a stepping stone to the Supreme Court, Harvard and Yale graduates account for only three of the nine active judges. Other law schools represented on that court include the University of North Carolina (with two judges), the University of Chicago (two), UCLA (one), and the University of Virginia (one). These trends are generally consistent with the courts of appeals as a whole, which evidence a great deal of educational diversity in the judges' backgrounds. There are a number of reasons for this diversity, the most apparent being the influence of senators in the nomination process and the focus on qualified local candidates who are more likely to be the product of local or regional law schools. But the simple fact remains that turning to sitting judges in the Supreme Court confirmation process has not necessarily led to the Harvard-Yale duopoly.

The dominance of Harvard and Yale graduates on the Supreme Court may also be seen as simply a result of both institutions' preeminence as suppliers of the class of candidates who may be considered for future nomination.[34] These two schools dominate in sending clerks to the federal courts of appeals and the Supreme Court and have increasingly come to dominate legal academia as well.[35] These positions lead to a greater likelihood of political

---

33 In addition to the law schools mentioned, the University of Virginia, the University of Chicago, Ohio State University, Vanderbilt University, and the University of Pennsylvania all account for at least one sitting judge.

34 *Cf.* Anthony Ciolli, *The Legal Employment Market: Determinants of Elite Firm Placement and How Law Schools Stack Up*, 45 Jurimetrics 413, 430 (2005) (finding that a law school's reputation is the most significant predictor of post–law school employment).

35 *See* Sloan, *supra* note 9; *see also* Emmanuel O. Iheukwumere, *Arguing Against Elitism*, Pa. Law. July/Aug. 2010, at 48, 49 (noting that Harvard and Yale graduates accounted for approximately 50 percent of the clerks hired by the Supreme Court between 2004 and 2010); Robert J. Borthwick & Jordan R. Schau, Note, *Gatekeepers of the Profession: An Empirical Profile of the Nation's Law Professors*,

appointments, whether they are in the executive or judicial branch, which may then place the candidate squarely in the eyes of a president seeking a Supreme Court nomination. The question then becomes less why these graduates have come to form a supermajority on the Supreme Court, but why other law schools have not been as successful in placing their graduates within the range of such an appointment through clerkships, government work, or academia. In this light, it is something of a self-perpetuating dominance. Justice Scalia has often remarked that he will choose his clerks only from the very top of the top tier, half-joking that he would not have hired Jeffrey Sutton as a law clerk had he not inherited him from the retiring Lewis Powell.[36] Sutton is a "lowly" Ohio State law graduate, although he has since been confirmed as a judge on the Sixth Circuit Court of Appeals.[37] This seems the most likely explanation, but if so, it points to a cyclical nature in the confirmation process and the clear possibility that the current dominance may not be permanent. As Jeffrey Fisher, a Stanford law professor, has noted, "Stanford has had justices in the past, and I assume we will again in the future. The people who went to top law schools will get the top jobs."[38]

On the other hand, a "cultural" version of Scalia's sentiment may point to a continuation of Harvard and Yale nominees. Just as Scalia and the justices select their clerks from a small bevy of law schools, a president may believe he will have an easier time selling a nominee from Harvard or Yale based on the cultural renown that both schools share. Both names are readily recognizable by the populace at large, and in the coliseum of confirmation politics and battles, such an educational background represents at least one unimpeachable credential that can be agreed upon by all combatants. This cultural consciousness may mean that it is easier to sell a nominee to the president's constituencies if the Harvard or Yale brand is employed, even if candidates from Columbia, Penn, Michigan, and Stanford are objectively as qualified as the eventual nominee. Outside the other unquestionably elite law schools the issue is even more starkly framed, as in the case of Harriet Miers, whose legal education at Southern Methodist University served as a lightning rod for criticism over her nomination to the Court.[39] In short, the game becomes one of politics rather than qualification, and on

---

25 U. Mich. J.L. Reform 191, 27 (1991) (finding that Harvard graduates accounted for 13 percent of professors, and Yale graduates 8.3 percent).

36 *See* Abramson, *supra* note 6 ("Well, I wouldn't have hired Jeff Sutton, for God's sake, he went to Ohio State."); Turley, *supra* note 6.

37 *See Biographical Directory of Federal Judges, Sutton, Jeffrey S.*, Fed. Judicial Ctr., http://www.fjc.gov/servlet/nGetInfo?jid=3010&cid=999&ctype=na&instate=na (last visited Nov. 15, 2010).

38 Sloan, *supra* note 9.

39 *See* Mary Alice Robbins, *Applications Fall at Most Texas Law Schools*, Tex. Law., Oct. 2, 2006, at 1, *available at* http://www.law.com/jsp/article.jsp?id=900005464043 ("At the time of Miers' nomination,

some level, that has always been the case—the pool of potential nominees all have stellar credentials and qualifications, so the nomination often comes down to other factors, some of them intangible. If this is the case, the dominance of these two schools will most likely continue into the future, even if it is not quite as pronounced as it is at present.

Regardless of the reason, should anybody care that only Harvard and Yale nominees have been confirmed in recent memory if these justices are eminently qualified individuals? To begin, if Fisher is correct that the current dominance is simply a self-correcting aberration, there is nothing to be worried about as the Harvard-Yale duopoly will subside with the subsequent appointment of graduates of other elite law schools. It's not clear that this will be the case, however, as the trend has been dominant now for twenty-four years and has shown little sign of subsiding if the "short list" of candidates the Obama administration has compiled in the last two years is a realistic indication of what future nominees may look like. This is not to say that the administration would certainly go with another Harvard or Yale graduate, only that the most likely candidates have these credentials. And for the second time, with the nomination of Kagan, Obama cast aside the eminently qualified Texas Law graduate Diane Wood, a current judge on the Seventh Circuit whose legal experience and education would bring at least as much diversity to the Court as Kagan.[40] In addition, to say simply that the trend may not continue into the future is no reason not to question the current prominence of Harvard and Yale graduates on the Court.

It is also clear that the rise of the Harvard and Yale justices has not led to a period of confluence in adjudication. Justices Alito and Sotomayor share the exact same educational background yet view constitutional adjudication in remarkably different lights. Justice Thomas represents a third viewpoint, not entirely consistent with Alito's.[41] Across the

---

there was a heated, snobbish battle over her credentials that often centered around the SMU law school. Conservative commentators branded it an institution of lower learning, unworthy of birthing a Supreme Court justice.").

40 Following law school, and prior to her appointment to the Seventh Circuit, Wood clerked for Irving Goldberg on the U.S. Court of Appeals for the Fifth Circuit and Justice Blackmun on the Supreme Court, practiced law in the U.S. State Department and Covington & Burling, taught at the law schools of Georgetown University and the University of Chicago, and served in high level appointments in the Justice Department. *See Biographical Directory of Federal Judges: Wood, Diane Pamela*, Fed. Judicial Ctr., http://www.fjc.gov/servlet/nGetInfo?jid=2636&cid=999&ctype=na&instate=na (last visited Nov. 18, 2010).

41 *See generally* Stephen E. Gottlieb, The Jurisprudence of the Roberts Court (Feb. 27, 2009) (unpublished manuscript), *available at* http://ssrn.com/abstract=1393413 (exploring the different jurisprudential approaches of the justices and their voting patterns in a range of cases).

Harvard justices, Scalia represents the originalists while Brennan represents the "living Constitution" school, two antithetical visions of how the Constitution should be interpreted. Quite simply, a legal education at Harvard or Yale does not lead inexorably to one viewpoint, meaning that diversity of opinion is not necessarily compromised by the prominence of only two law schools on the Supreme Court. Life and career experience informs judicial decisions and provides a far greater point of departure than where an education was obtained. Of course, three years in New Haven or Cambridge would be remarkably different from three years in Austin, Palo Alto, or Durham, so the question is not simply whether the concentration leads only to singular viewpoints, but whether the Court would benefit from the introduction of justices whose life and educational experiences have taken them outside the purview of the Ivies.

On this point, the opinion of legal commentators seems relatively consistent that candidates outside the Ivy League schools, especially Harvard and Yale, should be examined as vacancies occur in the coming years. This opinion is shared by many graduates of Harvard and Yale in legal academia, including Giovanna Shay of the Western New England College School of Law and Mark Tushnet of Harvard Law School,[42] as well as prominent commentator and Northwestern graduate Jonathan Turley.[43] Turley went so far as to declare that "[t]he favoritism shown Harvard and Yale should be viewed not just as incestuous but as scandalous. It undermines educational institutions across the country by maintaining a clearly arbitrary and capricious basis for selection. It also runs against the grain of a nation based on meritocracy and opportunity."[44] The underlying point is that there are few, if any, objective metrics on which to favor two law schools to the exclusion of other unquestionably elite institutions.

Conclusion

When Michelle and Robert King were creating the CBS drama *The Good Wife*, they decided to make the two main characters, lawyers Alicia Florrick and Will Gardner, Georgetown law alumni. Michelle King explained the rationale behind their choice of law school: "We wanted to highlight that they were smart, highly successful people without falling into the every-bright-fictional-character-went-to-Harvard-or-Yale trap."[45] Harvard and Yale law grad-

42 *See* Sloan, *supra* note 9.

43 Turley, *supra* note 6.

44 *Id.*

45 Ann W. Parks, *It's That Georgetown Thing: CBS TV Series Features Fictional Law "Alums"*, Geo. U. L. Ctr. (Nov. 19, 2009), http://www.law.georgetown.edu/news/webstory/11.19.09.html.

uates undoubtedly represent some of the best and brightest entrants to the legal profession every year, and it has not been the purpose of this Article to question that in any way. The concluding point is, however, that an applicant pool for the Supreme Court, or any other legal position, composed entirely of Harvard and Yale law graduates does not exhaust the range of highly intelligent, competent, and driven candidates who may be able to bring significant life, educational, or professional experience to bear on issues of grave and pressing importance. When the next vacancy does occur on the Court, President Obama, or his successor, would be wise to look outside Cambridge and New Haven for a qualified candidate. There is no shortage of these in the legal profession, although this point seems to have been obscured in the past two and a half decades. Such diversity would bring a boon to schools currently unrepresented on the Court, and it would bring diversity to that very Court that has so often trumpeted how important diverse views and experiences can be.[46] Although it is impossible to quantify what would be lost if Harvard and Yale perpetuate their current hold on the Court, it is easy to see what could have been lost had such dominance pervaded the mindset of presidents in the last century. The Court may never have had a Hugo Black, John Marshall Harlan II, Thurgood Marshall, Sandra Day O'Connor, Wiley Rutledge, or John Paul Stevens. The Court and the country benefited from the service of these men and women as justices, and both can benefit again by casting a wider net in the next nomination cycle.

Appendix

The primary source utilized in compiling the educational data regarding the justices was Timothy L. Hall's *Supreme Court Justices: A Biographical Dictionary* (2001). In the table below, a page number follows the educational institution (or lack thereof) listed for each justice, which corresponds to that justice's biographical sketch in Hall's *Dictionary*. A citation is only given for the justice's first appearance in this table.

Hall's *Dictionary* does not include information for the justices confirmed after Justice Breyer. For Chief Justice Roberts and Justice Alito, the source used was the *Encyclopedia of the Supreme Court of the United States* (David Tanenhaus ed., 2008). Roberts's educational information is contained on page 261 of Volume 4, and Alito's is on page 50 of Volume 1. Educational information for both Justices Sotomayor and Kagan was included in their

---

46 *See* Grutter v. Bollinger, 539 U.S. 306, 327–43 (2003) (holding that the University of Michigan Law School's use of diversity factors in its admissions process constituted a compelling state interest on account of the many benefits that diversity may bring to the educational process); Regents of Univ. of Cal. v. Bakke, 438 U.S. 265, 315 (1978) (noting that diversity, when utilized in the proper way, may constitute a compelling interest for a race-based admissions process).

submissions to the Senate Judiciary Committee. *See Nomination of Judge Sonia Sotomayor to Be an Associate Justice of the Supreme Court: Hearings Before the S. Comm. on the Judiciary*, 111th Cong. 152 (2009); *Nomination of Elena Kagan to Be an Associate Justice of the Supreme Court: Hearings Before the S. Comm. on the Judiciary*, 111th Cong. (2010).

In addition to these specific resources, both the Federal Judicial Center and the United States Supreme Court provide information regarding the justices' educational backgrounds on their websites. *See Biographical Directory of Federal Judges*, Fed. Judicial Ctr., http://www.fjc.gov/history/home.nsf/page/judges.html (last visited Nov. 15, 2010); *Members of the Supreme Court of the United States*, Sup. Ct. U.S. http://www.supremecourt.gov/about/members.aspx (last visited Nov. 15, 2010).

Education of the Justices: Appointments Since 1900

Justice and Nomination Year	**Other Sitting Justices**							
2010 Kagan (Harvard)	Roberts (Harvard)	Scalia (Harvard)	Kennedy (Harvard)	Thomas (Yale)	Ginsburg (Columbia)	Breyer (Harvard)	Alito (Yale)	Sotomayor (Yale)
2009 Sotomayor (Yale)	Roberts (Harvard)	Stevens (Northwestern)	Scalia (Harvard)	Kennedy (Harvard)	Thomas (Yale)	Ginsburg (Columbia)	Breyer (Harvard)	Alito (Yale)
2006 Alito (Yale)	Roberts (Harvard)	Stevens (Northwestern)	Scalia (Harvard)	Kennedy (Harvard)	Souter (Harvard)	Thomas (Yale)	Ginsburg (Columbia)	Breyer (Harvard)
2005 Roberts (Harvard)	Stevens (Northwestern)	O'Connor (Stanford)	Scalia (Harvard)	Kennedy (Harvard)	Souter (Harvard)	Thomas (Yale)	Ginsburg (Columbia)	Breyer (Harvard)
1994 Breyer (Harvard, 429)	Rehnquist (Stanford)	Stevens (Northwestern)	O'Connor (Stanford)	Scalia (Harvard)	Kennedy (Harvard)	Souter (Harvard)	Thomas (Yale)	Ginsburg (Columbia)
1993 Ginsburg (Columbia, 425)	Rehnquist (Stanford)	Blackmun (Harvard)	Stevens (Northwestern)	O'Connor (Stanford)	Scalia (Harvard)	Kennedy (Harvard)	Souter (Harvard)	Thomas (Yale)
1991 Thomas (Yale, 421)	Rehnquist (Stanford)	White (Yale)	Blackmun (Harvard)	Stevens (Northwestern)	O'Connor (Stanford)	Scalia (Harvard)	Kennedy (Harvard)	Souter (Harvard)

(Continued)

Justice and Nomination Year	Other Sitting Justices							
1990 Souter (Harvard, 417)	Rehnquist (Stanford)	White (Yale)	Marshall (Howard)	Blackmun (Harvard)	Stevens (North-western)	O'Connor (Stanford)	Scalia (Harvard)	Kennedy (Harvard)
1988 Kennedy (Harvard, 413)	Rehnquist (Stanford)	Brennan (Harvard)	White (Yale)	Marshall (Howard)	Blackmun (Harvard)	Stevens (North-western)	O'Connor (Stanford)	Scalia (Harvard)
1986 Scalia (Harvard, 409)	Rehnquist (Stanford)	Brennan (Harvard)	White (Yale)	Marshall (Howard)	Blackmun (Harvard)	Powell (W&L)	Stevens (North-western)	O'Connor (Stanford)
1981 O'Connor (Stanford, 405)	Burger (St. Paul)	Brennan (Harvard)	White (Yale)	Marshall (Howard)	Blackmun (Harvard)	Powell (W&L)	Rehnquist (Stanford)	Stevens (North-western)
1975 Stevens (North-western, 401)	Burger (St. Paul)	Brennan (Harvard)	Stewart (Yale)	White (Yale)	Marshall (Howard)	Blackmun (Harvard)	Powell (W&L)	Rehnquist (Stanford)
1972 Rehnquist (Stanford, 397)	Burger (St. Paul)	Douglas (Colum-bia)	Brennan (Harvard)	Stewart (Yale)	White (Yale)	Marshall (Howard)	Blackmun (Harvard)	Powell (W&L)
1972 Powell (W&L, 393)	Burger (St. Paul)	Douglas (Colum-bia)	Brennan (Harvard)	Stewart (Yale)	White (Yale)	Marshall (Howard)	Blackmun (Harvard)	Rehnquist (Stanford)
1970 Blackmun (Harvard, 389)	Burger (St. Paul)	Black (Ala-bama)	Douglas (Colum-bia)	Harlan (NYLS)	Brennan (Harvard)	Stewart (Yale)	White (Yale)	Marshall (Howard)
1969 Burger (St. Paul, 385)	Black (Ala-bama)	Douglas (Colum-bia)	Harlan (NYLS)	Brennan (Harvard)	Stewart (Yale)	White (Yale)	Marshall (Howard)	—
1967 Marshall (Howard, 381)	Warren (Berkeley)	Black (Alabama)	Douglas (Colum-bia)	Harlan (NYLS)	Brennan (Harvard)	Stewart (Yale)	White (Yale)	Fortas (Yale)

Justice and Nomination Year	Other Sitting Justices							
1965 Fortas (Yale, 377)	Warren (Berkeley)	Black (Alabama)	Douglas (Columbia)	Clark (Texas)	Harlan (NYLS)	Brennan (Harvard)	Stewart (Yale)	White (Yale)
1962 Goldberg (Northwestern, 373)	Warren (Berkeley)	Black (Alabama)	Douglas (Columbia)	Clark (Texas)	Harlan (NYLS)	Brennan (Harvard)	Stewart (Yale)	White (Yale)
1962 White (Yale, 369)	Warren (Berkeley)	Black (Alabama)	Frankfurter (Harvard)	Douglas (Columbia)	Clark (Texas)	Harlan (NYLS)	Brennan (Harvard)	Stewart (Yale)
1958 Stewart (Yale, 366)	Warren (Berkeley)	Black (Alabama)	Frankfurter (Harvard)	Douglas (Columbia)	Clark (Texas)	Harlan (NYLS)	Brennan (Harvard)	Whittaker (Kansas City)
1957 Whittaker (Kansas City, 363)	Warren (Berkeley)	Black (Alabama)	Frankfurter (Harvard)	Douglas (Columbia)	Burton (Harvard)	Clark (Texas)	Harlan (NYLS)	Brennan (Harvard)
1956 Brennan (Harvard, 359)	Warren (Berkeley)	Black (Alabama)	Reed (N/A)	Frankfurter (Harvard)	Douglas (Columbia)	Burton (Harvard)	Clark (Texas)	Harlan (NYLS)
1955 Harlan (NYLS, 355)	Warren (Berkeley)	Black (Alabama)	Reed (N/A)	Frankfurter (Harvard)	Douglas (Columbia)	Burton (Harvard)	Clark (Texas)	Minton (Indiana)
1953 Warren (Berkeley, 350)	Black (Alabama)	Reed (N/A)	Frankfurter (Harvard)	Douglas (Columbia)	Jackson (N/A)	Burton (Harvard)	Clark (Texas)	Minton (Indiana)
1949 Minton (Indiana, 346)	Vinson (Centre)	Black (Alabama)	Reed (N/A)	Frankfurter (Harvard)	Douglas (Columbia)	Jackson (N/A)	Burton (Harvard)	Clark (Texas)
1949 Clark (Texas, 342)	Vinson (Centre)	Black (Alabama)	Reed (N/A)	Frankfurter (Harvard)	Douglas (Columbia)	Jackson (N/A)	Rutledge (Colorado)	Burton (Harvard)
1946 Vinson (Centre, 338)	Black (Alabama)	Reed (N/A)	Frankfurter (Harvard)	Douglas (Columbia)	Murphy (Michigan)	Jackson (N/A)	Rutledge (Colorado)	Burton (Harvard)

(Continued)

Justice and Nomination Year	Other Sitting Justices							
1945 Burton (Harvard, 335)	Stone (Columbia)	Black (Alabama)	Reed (N/A)	Frankfurter (Harvard)	Douglas (Columbia)	Murphy (Michigan)	Jackson (N/A)	Rutledge (Colorado)
1943 Rutledge (Colorado, 331)	Stone (Columbia)	O. Roberts (Penn)	Black (Alabama)	Reed (N/A)	Frankfurter (Harvard)	Douglas (Columbia)	Murphy (Michigan)	Jackson (N/A)
1941 Jackson (N/A, 327)	Stone (Columbia)	O. Roberts (Penn)	Black (Alabama)	Reed (N/A)	Frankfurter (Harvard)	Douglas (Columbia)	Murphy (Michigan)	Byrnes (N/A)
1941 Byrnes (N/A, 324)	Hughes (Columbia)	Stone (Columbia)	O. Roberts (Penn)	Black (Alabama)	Reed (N/A)	Frankfurter (Harvard)	Douglas (Columbia)	Murphy (Michigan)
1940 Murphy (Michigan, 320)	Hughes (Columbia)	McReynolds (UVa)	Stone (Columbia)	O. Roberts (Penn)	Black (Alabama)	Reed (N/A)	Frankfurter (Harvard)	Douglas (Columbia)
1939 Douglas (Columbia, 316)	Hughes (Columbia)	McReynolds (UVa)	Butler (N/A)	Stone (Columbia)	O. Roberts (Penn)	Black (Alabama)	Reed (N/A)	Frankfurter (Harvard)
1939 Frankfurter (Harvard, 312)	Hughes (Columbia)	McReynolds (UVa)	Butler (N/A)	Stone (Columbia)	O. Roberts (Penn)	Black (Alabama)	Reed (N/A)	—
1938 Reed (N/A, 308)	Hughes (Columbia)	McReynolds (UVa)	Brandeis (Harvard)	Butler (N/A)	Stone (Columbia)	O. Roberts (Penn)	Cardozo (N/A)	Black (Alabama)
1937 Black (Alabama, 304)	Hughes (Columbia)	McReynolds (UVa)	Brandeis (Harvard)	Sutherland (N/A)	Butler (N/A)	Stone (Columbia)	O. Roberts (Penn)	Cardozo (N/A)
1932 Cardozo (N/A, 300)	Hughes (Columbia)	Van Devanter (Cincy)	McReynolds (UVa)	Brandeis (Harvard)	Sutherland (N/A)	Butler (N/A)	Stone (Columbia)	O. Roberts (Penn)
1930 O. Roberts (Penn, 296)	Hughes (Columbia)	Holmes (Harvard)	Van Devanter (Cincy)	McReynolds (UVa)	Brandeis (Harvard)	Sutherland (N/A)	Butler (N/A)	Stone (Columbia)
1930 Hughes (Columbia, 248)	Holmes (Harvard)	Van Devanter (Cincy)	McReynolds (UVa)	Brandeis (Harvard)	Sutherland (N/A)	Butler (N/A)	Sanford (Harvard)	Stone (Columbia)

Justice and Nomination Year	Other Sitting Justices							
1925 Stone (Columbia, 291)	Taft (Cincy)	Holmes (Harvard)	Van Devanter (Cincy)	McReynolds (UVa)	Brandeis (Harvard)	Sutherland (N/A)	Butler (N/A)	Sanford (Harvard)
1923 Sanford (Harvard, 288)	Taft (Cincy)	McKenna (N/A)	Holmes (Harvard)	Van Devanter (Cincy)	McReynolds (UVa)	Brandeis (Harvard)	Sutherland (N/A)	Butler (N/A)
1923 Butler (N/A, 284)	Taft (Cincy)	McKenna (N/A)	Holmes (Harvard)	Van Devanter (Cincy)	McReynolds (UVa)	Brandeis (Harvard)	Sutherland (N/A)	—
1922 Sutherland (N/A, 280)	Taft (Cincy)	McKenna (N/A)	Holmes (Harvard)	Day (N/A)	Van Devanter (Cincy)	Pitney (N/A)	McReynolds (UVa)	Brandeis (Harvard)
1921 Taft (Cincy, 276)	McKenna (N/A)	Holmes (Harvard)	Day (N/A)	Van Devanter (Cincy)	Pitney (N/A)	McReynolds (UVa)	Brandeis (Harvard)	Clarke (N/A)
1916 Clarke (N/A, 272)	White (N/A)	McKenna (N/A)	Holmes (Harvard)	Day (N/A)	Van Devanter (Cincy)	Pitney (N/A)	McReynolds (UVa)	Brandeis (Harvard)
1916 Brandeis (Harvard, 268)	White (N/A)	McKenna (N/A)	Holmes (Harvard)	Day (N/A)	Van Devanter (Cincy)	Pitney (N/A)	McReynolds (UVa)	—
1914 McReynolds (UVa, 263)	White (N/A)	McKenna (N/A)	Holmes (Harvard)	Day (N/A)	Hughes (Columbia)	Van Devanter (Cincy)	Lamar (N/A)	Pitney (N/A)
1912 Pitney (N/A, 260)	White (N/A)	McKenna (N/A)	Holmes (Harvard)	Day (N/A)	Lurton (Cumberland)	Hughes (Columbia)	Van Devanter (Cincy)	Lamar (N/A)
1911 Lamar (N/A, 257)	White (N/A)	Harlan I (Transylvania)	McKenna (N/A)	Holmes (Harvard)	Day (N/A)	Lurton (Cumberland)	Hughes (Columbia)	Van Devanter (Cincy)
1911 Van Devanter (Cincy, 253)	White (N/A)	Harlan I (Transylvania)	McKenna (N/A)	Holmes (Harvard)	Day (N/A)	Lurton (Cumberland)	Hughes (Columbia)	Lamar (W&L)
1910 Hughes (Columbia, 248)	White (N/A)	Harlan I (Transylvania)	McKenna (N/A)	Holmes (Harvard)	Day (N/A)	Moody (N/A)	Lurton (Cumberland)	—

(Continued)

Justice and Nomination Year	Other Sitting Justices							
1910 Lurton (Cumberland, 244)	Fuller (N/A)	Harlan I (Transylvania)	Brewer (Albany)	White (N/A)	McKenna (N/A)	Holmes (Harvard)	Day (N/A)	Moody (N/A)
1906 Moody (N/A, 240)	Fuller (N/A)	Harlan I (Transylvania)	Brewer (Albany)	White (N/A)	Peckham (N/A)	McKenna (N/A)	Holmes (Harvard)	Day (N/A)
1903 Day (N/A, 236)	Fuller (N/A)	Harlan I (Transylvania)	Brewer (Albany)	Brown (N/A)	White (N/A)	Peckham (N/A)	McKenna (N/A)	Holmes (Harvard)
1902 Holmes (Harvard, 231)	Fuller (N/A, 199)	Harlan I (Transylvania, 174)	Brewer (Albany, 203)	Brown (N/A, 207)	Shiras (N/A, 211)	White (N/A, 219)	Peckham (N/A, 223)	McKenna (N/A, 227)

CHAPTER 3 QUESTIONS

1. Describe the Two Hemispheres of Law. Which hemisphere are attorneys most likely to find themselves in?
2. Describe the background of the "individual (law) practitioner from Chicago" according to Carlin. What motivated these people to become lawyers?
3. Were apprenticeships helpful or burdensome for new lawyers in Carlin's study?
4. What is the career progression of individual practitioners, according to Carlin?
5. Describe the historical evolution of corporate law firms. What changes happened concurrently at the "lower level of the metropolitan bar"?
6. Give some examples of unethical behavior that Carlin describes in his book.
7. Carlin writes that "The cannon of ethics on business-getting are still built in terms of a town of twenty-five thousand." What does he mean by this? How are large cities different from smaller ones?
8. How do payoffs work?
9. Why does the individual practitioner devalue his client?
10. Do you think that the legal profession is more or less inclusive today?

Chapter 4

Defendants and Their Attorneys

On June 3, 1961, Florida police arrested Clarence Earl Gideon. That day, a witness reported to police that they had seen him at the Bar Harbor Pool Room in Panama City at 5:30 a.m. with a wine bottle and change in his pocket. Sometime after midnight, someone had broken in, stolen cash, and damaged a cigarette machine, record player, and door.

Gideon stood trial at a Florida court for the crime of petty larceny. As he was poor, he asked the court to appoint an attorney for his defense; the court declined his request. Following his conviction, he appealed to the Florida Supreme Court and later in handwriting to the US Supreme Court.

In his appeals, Gideon argued that the Florida court had not fulfilled its obligation under the Sixth Amendment to provide him with a criminal defense. The Florida high court denied his appeal. The US Supreme Court, however, agreed with him, arguing that the Sixth and Fourteenth Amendments gave Gideon the right to the legal counsel that he could not afford.

At the time of the decision in *Gideon v. Wainwright* in 1963, much time had passed since the ratification of the US Constitution and Sixth Amendment, which required that "the accused shall ... have the Assistance of Counsel for his defense."

The states, of course, were under no obligation to follow the limitations placed on the US Congress at the time of the ratification of the Constitution. In 1868, the Fourteenth Amendment was passed. It declared that states cannot "deprive any person of life, liberty, or property, without due process of law" (US Constitution, amend. 14, sec. 1).

For criminal defendants at that time, the Fourteenth Amendment was of little help. It would take almost a century for the Supreme Court to require that states begin to provide counsel under the due process clause of the Fourteenth Amendment.

I believe that it's fair to say that Americans were not eager to extend rights to those accused of crimes.

Why was this? The Bill of Rights gives most of its attention to the rights of those accused of crimes. American law follows the tradition of presuming a defendant's innocence until guilt is proven, a tradition that can be traced to twelfth-century Continental Europe (Pennington 2003, 112). Despite this, there often exists a strong presumption of guilt for criminal defendants. This is especially true for defendants from racial minority groups (Pennington 2003; Seiff 1934).

Americans, it would seem, have not overlooked defense attorneys in giving blame for crime. They see defense attorneys as helping criminals. They are looked down upon by Americans and other attorneys. Defense attorneys are often unhappy. They are on average paid less than their contemporaries, putting in long hours in crowded courthouses (Wice 1978). Defense attorneys often get asked the question, "How can you defend those people?"

Defense attorney Barbara Babcock attempts to answer this question in her short piece "'Defending the Guilty' after 30 Years" (2013). If defense attorneys do, in fact, defend criminals, how can these people go home without guilty consciences? How can they retire from their careers feeling that they made a positive contribution to society?

It might be easy to assume that the personal moral justifications of defense attorneys are hard to come by. Babcock, nonetheless, offers a multitude of them, ranging from the philosophical and constitutional to the personal. Some defense attorneys enjoy cases that they see as more interesting and the challenge of winning them (Babcock 2013, 2–4).

Babcock continues by giving her personal answer. She then tries to communicate why she believes that her work as a defense attorney is important by telling a story about her defense of Geraldine, a 42-year-old Black woman charged with heroin possession.

After a law professor challenged her victory in the case as unethical, Babcock read the existing literature on the ethics of criminal defense. She ultimately sides with Clara Foltz, the founder of the public defender movement in the nineteenth century, who argued that the defense attorney's moral justification came from the legal presumption of innocence (9).

As you read through her account, ask yourself how robust you think our criminal defense should be. Should criminal defendants like Clarence Earl Gideon be afforded defenders as competent and capable as the prosecutors of their cases? Or is a minimal defense, perhaps even without counsel, sufficient, as Judge Richard Posner argues when he asserts that the truly innocent are highly unlikely to be convicted (10–11)?

Reading 4.1

"Defending the Guilty" After 30 Years

Barbara Babcock

In 1983, I published "Defending the Guilty,"[1] a piece that lives on in citations and classrooms. Perhaps it's the provocative title, or the story of Geraldine, the essential client, that has made the article popular. For this volume, I've spruced up the diction and added some reflections from the life of Clara Foltz, the founder of the public defender movement. The [reading] also draws on my memoir-in-progress, *Recollections of a Woman Lawyer.*

I always wanted to be a criminal defense lawyer, which was even more unusual for a woman in the early 1960s than wanting to be a lawyer at all. Reflecting back now, I have no insights on the source of my ambition. Maybe it sprang from my Christian upbringing, my innate sympathy for the underdog, my love for the Robin Hood stories. Nothing really adds up. Criminal defense was a rare goal for men too at the time, especially at elite schools like Yale. Along with this set ambition, I also had a fixed belief that lawyers had a high moral duty to defend—the more heinous the crime, the greater the duty.

In his book, *One Man's Freedom*, published while I was in law school, the famous defense lawyer Edward Bennett Williams confirmed my instincts when he wrote of taking on "difficult cases for unpopular clients ... because of the unwritten law that I might not refuse."[2]

John Ely, a classmate who went on to become a distinguished law professor, disputed the "unwritten law." He thought that only if the lawyer was the last one on earth was he obligated to represent the client he disliked or whose cause he disapproved. In the manner of law students everywhere, we argued heatedly. Fifty years later, I can still remember walking along the winter streets of New Haven, furious at John for claiming that he might refuse to defend some dreadful criminal. Who did he think he was? Defense of the defenseless, the guilty, and even the indefensible was already my religion.[3]

1 Barbara Allen Babcock, "Defending the Guilty," *Cleveland State Law Review* 32 (1983–1984). 175.

2 Edward Bennett Williams, *One Man's Freedom* (Atheneum: New York, 1962), 12–13.

3 For more on the debate between John and me, see Barbara Allen Babcock, "The Duty to Defend," *Yale Law Journal* 114 (2005): 1489.

Given my passion about defending, it seems fortuitous that *Gideon v. Wainwright*[4] should come down the year I graduated from law school. In one of its most far-reaching and important decisions, the Warren Court held that lawyers were necessities in criminal cases and that due process required an attorney even for the accused who could not pay. The most salient years of my career would be spent at the Public Defender Service, established in Washington, DC, to fulfill the mandate of *Gideon*.

My years at "the agency," as we always called it—from 1966 to 1972—were exciting and happy, including the four years I served as director. Paradoxically, they were also the most frazzled and anxious time of my life. Often I felt alone, standing between the client and powerful pneumatic forces that threatened to sweep us both away. The work was endless because there was always something more that might be done. Filing a motion, finding a witness, or stopping by the jail for a chat on a Sunday afternoon could mean the difference between victory or defeat, between freedom and prison.

A few years ago, I was remembering (in an oral history) what it felt like to be a public defender:

> I was always tired, and driven, and in a rage (that I was repressing) because it seemed that no one in power could see the injustice that was happening and the necessity of providing real defense lawyers and doing it right away ... But the thing was it was fun, there wasn't that rigid work/play distinction. I loved what I was doing, even though I was just tremendously wrought up all the time when I look back on it.[5]

One of the daily stressors was the constant question: How Can You Defend Someone You Know Is Guilty? Everyone asks it—benign old aunts, eager young students, the gardener, the grocery store clerk, and lately even the oncologist. Today, 40 years after I last appeared in court, interviewers still bring up the subject. Every defense lawyer develops an answer to keep at the ready for the inevitable, existential query. I wrote *Defending the Guilty*, with its sardonic title, on the twentieth anniversary of *Gideon*, to offer a list of responses I had used or heard.

The Garbage Collector's Answer. Yes, it is dirty work, but someone must do it. We cannot have a functioning adversary system without partisans for both sides. A defense lawyer

---

4 372 U.S. 335 (1963).

5 "Oral History of Barbara Babcock," by LaDoris Cordell, *ABA Commission on Women in the Profession*, February 8, 2006, http://www.americanbar.org/content/dam/aba/directories/women_trailblazers/babcock_interview_4.authcheckdam.pdf.

keeps the system clean by holding the police and the prosecutors to high standards. True, his methods are often unrefined and he may use rough tactics and searing cross-examination, but essentially his work is the same as that of any skilled trial lawyer, civil or criminal, who arranges, argues, and even orients the facts with only the client's interests in mind.

The Constitutionalist's Answer. It is noble work. The Right to Counsel is here invoked—to the best effect still by Anthony Lewis, speaking on the "dream of Gideon" of "a vast, diverse country in which every [person] charged with crime will be capably defended, no matter what his economic circumstances, and in which the lawyer representing him will do so proudly, without resentment."[6] Or as Clara Foltz, the founder of the public defender, put it, speaking of the duty of the government to provide counsel for the indigent, 70 years before Gideon: "Let the criminal courts be [reorganized] upon a basis of exact, equal and free justice."[7]

The Civil Libertarian's Answer. The criminally accused are the representatives of us all. When their rights are eroded, the camel's nose is under and the tent may collapse on anyone. In protecting the constitutional rights of criminal defendants, we are only protecting ourselves.

The Legal Positivist's Answer. Truth cannot be known. Facts are indeterminate, contingent, and, in criminal cases, often evanescent. A finding of guilt is not necessarily the truth, but instead is a legal conclusion arrived at after the role of the defense lawyer has been fully played.

The sophist would add that it is not the duty of the defense lawyer to act as fact finder. Were she to handle a case according to her own assessment of guilt or innocence, she would be in the role of judge rather than advocate.

The Philosopher's Answer. There is a difference between legal and moral guilt; the defense lawyer should not let her apprehension of moral guilt interfere with the analysis of legal guilt. The usual example is that of the person accused of murder who can respond successfully with a claim of self-defense. The accused may feel morally guilty but not be legally culpable. Foltz would add that all the accused are presumed innocent by sacred principles of law and should be treated accordingly until a final verdict or plea.

The Oddsmaker's Answer. It is better that ten guilty people go free than that one innocent is convicted. The risk of acquitting the guilty is the price of our societal concern for sparing the innocent.

The Political Activist's Answer. Most people who commit crimes are themselves the victims of injustice. This statement is true generally when those accused are oppressed minorities. It is also often true in the immediate case because the defendant has been battered and mistreated in the process of arrest and investigation. Moreover, the conditions of imprisonment

---

6 Anthony Lewis, *Gideon's Trumpet* (New York: Random House, 1964), 205.

7 Clara Foltz, "Public Defenders," (lecture, Congress on Jurisprudence and Law Reform, Chicago World's Fair, 1893) in *Albany Law Journal* 48 (1893).

may impose violence worse than that inflicted on the victim. A lawyer performs good work when he helps to prevent the imprisonment of the poor, the outcast, and minorities in shameful conditions.

The Social Worker's Answer. This reason is closely akin to the political activist's reason, but the emphasis is different. Those accused of crime, as the most visible representatives of the disadvantaged underclass in America, will actually be helped by having a defender, regardless of the actual outcome of their cases. Being treated as a real person in our society (almost by definition, one who has a lawyer is a real person) and accorded the full panoply of rights and the measure of concern afforded by a lawyer can promote rehabilitation. Because the accused comes from a community, the beneficial effect of giving him his due will spread to his friends and relatives, decreasing their anger and alienation.

The Humanitarian's Answer: The criminally accused are men and women in great need, and lawyers should come to their aid. That great icon of the criminal defense bar, Clarence Darrow, wrote in his autobiography:

> Strange as it may seem, I grew to like to defend men and women charged with crime. It soon came to be something more than the winning or losing of a case. I sought to learn why one goes one way and another takes an entirely different road ... I was dealing with life, with its hopes and fears, its aspirations and despairs. With me it was going to the foundation of motive and conduct and adjustments for human beings, instead of blindly talking of hatred and vengeance, and that subtle, indefinable quality that men call "justice," and of which nothing really is known.[8]

The Egotist's Answer. Defending criminal cases is more interesting than the routine and repetitive work done by most lawyers, even those engaged in what passes for litigation in civil practice. The heated facts of crime provide voyeuristic excitement. Actual court appearances, even jury trials, come earlier and more often in one's career than can be expected in any other area of law. And winning, ah winning, has great significance because the cards are stacked for the prosecutor. To win as an underdog, and to win when the victory is clear—there is no appeal from a "Not Guilty" verdict—is sweet.

My Answer. Though many of the answers overlap, many do not. For instance, one can be a successful defender without a drop of social worker in her veins, or love the work without any particular attachment to the development of the law. My point is only that, whatever the rationale, the defender, unlike most professionals, must have one. My own reason for finding

8 Clarence Darrow, *The Story of My Life* (New York: Da Capo Press, 1996), 75–76.

criminal defense work rewarding and important is an amalgam in roughly equal parts of the social worker's, the humanitarian's, and the egotist's reason and is encapsulated in a story.

I once represented a woman, I will call her Geraldine, who was accused under a draconian federal drug law of her third offense for possessing heroin. The first conviction carried a mandatory sentence of five years with no possibility of probation or parole. The second conviction carried a penalty of ten years with no probation and no parole. The third conviction carried a sentence of twenty years on the same terms. Geraldine was 42 years old, black, poor, and uneducated. During the few years of her adult life when not incarcerated by the state, she had been imprisoned by heroin addiction of the most awful sort.

But even for one as bereft as Geraldine, the general practice was to allow a guilty plea to a local drug charge, which did not carry the harsh mandatory penalties. In this case, however, the prosecutor refused the usual plea. Casting about for a defense, I sent her for a mental examination. The doctors at the public hospital reported that Geraldine had a mental disease: inadequate personality. When I inquired about the symptoms of this illness, one said: "Well, she is just the most inadequate person I've ever seen." But there it was—at least a defense—a disease or defect listed in the Diagnostic and Statistical Manual of that day.

At the trial I was fairly choking with rage and righteousness. I tried to paint a picture of the poverty and hopelessness of her life through lay witnesses and the doctors (who were a little on the inadequate side themselves). The prosecutor and I almost came to physical blows—the angriest I have ever been in court. Geraldine observed the seven days of trial with only mild interest, but when after many hours of deliberation the jury returned a verdict of "Not Guilty by Reason of Insanity," she burst into tears. Throwing her arms around me, she said: "I'm so happy for you."

Embodied in the Geraldine story, which has many other aspects but which is close to true as I have written it, are my answers to the question: "How can you defend someone you know is guilty?" By direct application of my skills, I saved a woman from spending the rest of her adult life in prison. In constructing her defense, I became intimate with a life as different from my own as could be imagined, and I learned from that experience. In ways that are not measurable, I think that Geraldine's friends and relatives who testified and talked with me were impressed by the fact that she had a "real" lawyer provided by the system. But in the last analysis, Geraldine was right. The case became my case more than hers. What I liked most was the unalloyed pleasure of the sound of "Not Guilty." There are few such pure joys in life.

The story of Geraldine is one of my urtexts—I've told it at least once or twice a year for decades, regularly in criminal procedure and sometimes in civil procedure as well. Recalling the thrill of that verdict also brings to fond memory Judge William B. Bryant. He was the first African-American judge on the US District Court in DC, as he had been the first federal prosecutor there, a job he left to become a criminal defense lawyer.

In the cold marble precincts of that court where most judges felt it beneath their dignity to preside over trials for street crimes, Judge Bryant alone fully appreciated the difficult work of a defender. His courtroom was also wonderfully civilized—he listened to both sides with sympathy and intelligence, and best of all, a certain enjoyment of the human predicament in which we were all enmeshed. His good humor leavened the irate adversary exchange in Geraldine's case. When the prosecutor asked for a recess because I had "threatened" him, Judge Bryant responded with unfeigned interest: "What on earth did she say?" (In one of many angry moments, I had said I would get him disbarred if he asked another question inviting inadmissible evidence.)

Though outside the courthouse, I had some friends who were prosecutors, in trial they were usually the enemy—even more so in this case because the prosecutor AUSA had denied the customary plea bargain. After hearing a rumor that he simply wanted the experience of a trial against me, I offered to turn the case over to another defender. But he claimed that Geraldine was a dealer who deserved a long prison sentence and refused the merciful plea.

Drawing Judge Bryant from the random assignment system was one of the few lucky things that had ever happened to Geraldine, and to her lawyer it felt like a form of insurance. I was sure the judge would avoid imposing the mandatory 20 years of hard time by taking the case from the jury and granting a judgment of acquittal. And I knew also that there would be plausible grounds for it because the government bore the ultimate burden of proving sanity beyond a reasonable doubt, a hard one to meet.

My confidence in the judge's compassion led me into an experiment in jury selection—that I once heard Edward Bennett Williams recommend. He scorned the services of jury consultants (though he hired them) and advocated putting the first 12 in the box. "If you do your job they will do theirs," he said. I had always wanted to try it and see if it would impress a jury in my client's favor to be accepted without probing inquires into their beliefs and prejudices. But I was afraid to experiment in an actual case until this golden opportunity. After the acquittal I expected from the judge, I would be able to question the jurors about their reaction to the absence of voir dire. So, as soon as 12 people were seated, I announced: "The defense accepts this jury."

The dramatic move threw the prosecutor off his game. Expecting that jury selection in an insanity case would take some hours, he had no witnesses ready and only a rough opening statement. My early tactical advantage paled during the trial, however, because this unselected jury just looked so bad. They were diverse enough, but, regardless of race or gender, they shrugged and sneered and slept as I presented the evidence of my client's horrendous childhood and of the toll on the development of her personality from many years of heroin addiction. Juror number six in particular distressed me. I can see her today—a large Germanic woman with thin lips whose hair looked like it was cut around a bowl. Every time I looked at her, she rolled her eyes and shook her head.

The only thing that sustained me during the seven dreary days of trial was the expectation that the judge would direct the verdict. But instead he sent the jury out to deliberate and told me privately to "keep the faith." When at last they announced "Not Guilty by Reason of Insanity" and Geraldine acted as if my life had been the one saved, Judge Bryant started laughing. He laughed so hard that he almost fell off his high bench.

He continued laughing when Juror number 6 joined Geraldine and me: "Well, we went out 11–1 for conviction, but I was finally able to bring them around," she declared. Singlehandedly she had led the jury to see that Geraldine should be treated and not punished. Her eye-rolls and head-shakings were indications of empathy. Since that verdict I have joined my hero, Judge Bryant, in believing in the ultimate wisdom of the jury and in its often mysterious deliberative process.[9] The Geraldine story has a number of such lessons, but the subtext is always the fun and satisfaction, the glory and goodness of defending. Perhaps its triumphal tone roused the critics who complain that it is dishonest and does not reflect the real life of defenders. Women charged with nonviolent crimes are not the usual clients, happy endings are rare, and one could spend a lifetime in the work and never have a case like Geraldine's. Some people also use the story to illustrate the insensitivity of white elites like me, charging that Geraldine was objectified, her secrets and sorrows revealed without her approval or participation. But this reported criticism does not bother me because I knew Geraldine approved of what I was doing.[10]

A more jarring censure arose some years ago when I told the story in a speech at Indiana Law School. As usual, I joked a little about the ridiculous diagnosis (inadequate personality) and its treatability (zero). But I was not implying that insanity was an illegitimate defense in Geraldine's case. Mental illness caused by profound, untreated addiction was a valid claim that I could have presented solely through lay witnesses if I had not found experts to agree. My main point in telling the story that night was the absurdity of the system and the need for a zealous creative defense lawyer to save the client from its extremities. As always I was proselytizing, trying to attract young people to the work, especially to the defense,

---

9 Barbara Babcock and Ticien Sassoubre, "Deliberation in 12 Angry Men," *Chicago-Kent Law Review* 82 (2007) (commentary on the workings of the jury).

10 Most of all, Geraldine wanted to avoid another long prison sentence. An acquittal on the grounds of insanity would mean a sentence to a mental hospital until no longer dangerous to herself or others. Since her diagnosis of inadequate personality disorder described a condition neither treatable nor dire, she was likely to be (and was) out of the hospital in months rather than years.

by showing how much intellectual and forensic enjoyment there can be in such a case and what a difference an individual lawyer can make.

To my surprise, and dismay, in the comment period, Indiana professor William Hodes compared the Geraldine defense to that in the O. J. Simpson murder trial.[11] He suggested that both Simpson's and Geraldine's defenses were fabricated by highly skilled defense lawyers going to the outer barricade of zealous representation. I had constructed an insanity defense for a guilty drug dealer, and "the dream team" (O. J's lawyers) had implied that the racist LA police had framed him for murder and demanded that the jury "send a message" to the people of the city with a not guilty verdict. Professor Hodes praised the defense performances in both cases and implied that the not guilty verdicts showed the workings of our justice system at its best.

I could not accept the compliment or comparison. To me, the trial of O. J. Simpson was a travesty and the verdict a miscarriage of justice. There is not enough space here to compile the errors and missteps on every side in the trial, but I believe that if the judge, jury, and prosecution had done their jobs, there would have been a guilty verdict.[12] To my students at the time, I explained that juries are imperfect human institutions that make mistakes. But years later, I still find it painful that the jury failed in the O. J. case so publicly.

Did the defense lawyers do anything wrong, dishonest, or unethical in putting the police on trial instead of O. J. Simpson? Attacking the police is a familiar tactic used especially by defense lawyers who view their work partly as guardians of the criminal justice system. Certainly the defense team did not commit established wrongs like suborning perjury or manufacturing evidence. On the other hand, some capable and ethical defense lawyers would not think there was sufficient connection between the racism of the police and framing Simpson for murder, enough of a foundation for the far-ranging questions allowed by the judge.

The issue of what a defense lawyer may honestly and ethically do in "defending the guilty" is subtle and inherent in the omnipresent question. Indeed, it was present at the creation of public defense. When researching the life of Clara Foltz, the nineteenth-century founder

---

11 W. William Hodes, "Rethinking the Way Law Is Taught: Can We Improve Lawyer Professionalism by Teaching Hired Guns to Aim Better?" *Kentucky Law Journal* 87 (1999): 1050 (describing the talk at Indiana on September 29, 1997).

12 See, for example, Barbara Allen Babcock, "In Defense of the Criminal Jury," in *Postmortem: The O. J. Simpson Case*, ed. Jeffrey Abramson (New York: Basic Books, 1996) (drawing on articles I wrote during the trial for the LA Times); Barbara Allen Babcock, "Protect the Jury System, Judge was the Problem," *Los Angeles Times*, October 8, 1995, http://articles.latimes.com/1995-10-08/opinion/op-54586_1_jury-system.

of the movement, I studied the authorities available to her on the subject of representing the so-called guilty client. Thomas Cooley's *Constitutional Limitations* was the best known of these.[13] He advised that a lawyer who, after he has begun his representation, becomes convinced of his client's guilt must nevertheless continue his advocacy to assure that "a conviction is not secured contrary to law."[14]

But Cooley went on to say that in this situation "how persistent counsel may be in pressing for the acquittal of his client, and to what extent he may be justified in throwing his own personal character as a weight in the scale of justice, *are questions of ethics rather than of law.*"[15] In other words, the law demands that the attorney continue his representation, but how eager and ardent he should be in the defense is entirely up to the individual lawyer. After identifying the "ethical" question, however, the great jurisprude did not even attempt an answer. He said that counsel must not use fraud or falsehood "even in a just cause" and at the same time that it was wrong to accept "the confidence of the accused, and then [betray] it by a feeble and heartless defense." Cooley implied a middle ground between these two, but locating that ground has proved difficult for academics and practitioners alike.

Clara Foltz found it in the presumption of innocence; she believed that a defense lawyer should live out the law's presumption and consider her client guiltless until the contrary was proved.[16] Monroe Freedmen and Abbe Smith [...] have been the major modern proponents of robust representation along the client-centered lines that Foltz suggested.[17] Others propose that lawyers should take into account their roles as officers of the court and citizens concerned with public justice when choosing their tactics.[18] "Defending the Guilty," published so long ago, was meant as a contribution to this discourse, although admittedly it elides the ethical issues inherent in the question of how to defend the guilty.

---

13 Barbara Allen Babcock, "Inventing the Public Defender," *American Criminal Law Review* 43 (2006); Thomas M. Cooley, *A Treatise on the Constitutional Limitations Which Rest upon the Legislative Power of the States of the American Union*, 2nd ed. (Boston: Little, Brown, and Company, 1871).

14 Cooley, *A Treatise on Constitutional Limitations*, 361–362.

15 Ibid., emphasis supplied.

16 Babcock, "Inventing the Public Defender," 1305–1307 (describing Foltz's position).

17 Monroe H. Freedman and Abbe Smith, *Understanding Lawyers' Ethics*, 4th ed. (New Providence, NJ: LexisNexis, 2010). Both have written many articles on aspects of zealous representation. Monroe Freedman's 1966 article was the first modern treatment of the issues and laid the foundation for the debate that followed. Monroe H. Freedman, "Professional Responsibility of the Criminal Defense Lawyer: The Three Hardest Questions," *Michigan Law Review* 64 (1966).

18 William H. Simon, "The Ethics of Criminal Defense," *Michigan Law Review* 91 (1993).

I elided the issues in practice as well; I managed to represent hundreds of people charged with serious crimes without confronting the harrowing moral dilemmas posited in the debates over defense ethics. For instance, not once in my practice did a client admit his guilt and then demand to testify falsely. Using techniques gleaned from what I saw when working as a paid lawyer, I did not advise the client at the outset that he must tell me the truth. Instead, I would say: "I don't want to know now from you whether you are, or feel, guilty. I intend to investigate the government's case, and talk to witnesses who might help you. Who are these? And how did you get arrested?" For my indigent clients, I would turn to collecting information to get them released pending trial.

I would investigate possible defenses, file motions to suppress, and gather favorable information generally so that we had something to bargain with beyond the client's trial right. But unless there was a decent defense, it was too risky to roll the dice at trial, hoping for an anomalous, merciful, or mistaken verdict. A judge who has heard the witnesses and the full account of the crime will tend toward a heavier sentence than one who has only the limited information presented at a guilty plea. And though it is wrong (indeed unconstitutional), some judges will penalize the accused for insisting on his trial and for presumably committing perjury if she testifies and is convicted.[19]

Most of my clients understood these things as well as I did. When we disagreed about going to trial, it was mostly in cases where I thought we had a fighting chance and that I would enjoy myself. Naturally, these were also the cases in which the prosecutors offered the best pleas—and usually the clients jumped at them. Preparing the defendant to enter a plea was soon enough for me to learn from him about his actual guilt.

In the cases that went to trial, I always managed to develop at least a reasonable doubt, coupled with the atavistic desire simply to win. Once or twice I represented clients I thought were factually innocent—but usually the prosecutor would drop such cases before trial. I enjoyed considerable success with juries, based I think on projecting my faith in my clients and my belief in the evidence and arguments. As Thomas Cooley would say, I "threw my own personal character as a weight in the scale of justice."

I didn't discuss any of this in the original "Defending the Guilty" article. Thirty years ago, I did not want to engage in the ethical quandaries of defending. I still don't want to discuss them—as if those were the important issues confronting the criminal justice system. In the 1983 article, I used a classic rhetorical gambit by arguing that the question itself was wrong. It should not be "how can you defend" but "how can you fail to defend." That is still the real question today.

---

19 Barbara Allen Babcock, "Taking the Stand," *William and Mary Law Review* 35 (1993): 1–19.

Almost 50 years after *Gideon* and more than a 100 after Clara Foltz first urged the pressing need for a public defender in 1893, the representation of the indigent accused remains woefully inadequate. Most defender offices (not all, but most) are overwhelmed with caseloads and clients they cannot serve adequately, no matter the amount of their skill or devotion.[20] Sometimes the failure of the criminal justice system to provide adequate defense services appears willfully defective.

Take Judge Richard Posner's "hardheaded" (his description) approach: after acknowledging the poor quality of much indigent criminal defense, he wrote that the lawyers nevertheless "seem to be good enough to reduce the probability of convicting an innocent person to a very low level. If they were much better, either many guilty people would be acquitted or society would have to devote much greater resources to the prosecution of criminal cases. A bare-bones system for defense of indigent criminal defendants may be optimal."[21] His premise that few innocent people are convicted seems wrong in light of the many much-publicized exonerations in recent years, and even the guilty often serve unjust sentences because of ineffective assistance of counsel.

Faced with a criminal justice system in disarray, surprisingly like that of today, Foltz believed that a public defender who was equal in skills and resources to the public prosecutor could make great changes. Her vision was one of equal adversaries, bearing each other mutual respect and regard, a fair judge, an honest jury—all engaged in the same task, to assure "exact, equal and free justice." And she promised in return "the blessings which flow from constitutional obligations conscientiously kept and government duties sacredly performed." I believe that if we can only summon the political will, the promise holds true today.

CHAPTER 4 QUESTIONS

1. What are some ways that defense attorneys answer the question "How can you represent those people?", according to Barbara Babcock?
2. What is the difference between the political activist's and social worker's answers to this question?

---

20 Norman Lefstein, *Securing Reasonable Caseloads, Ethics and Law in Public Defense* (Chicago: American Bar Association, 2011), http://www.americanbar.org/content/dam/aba/publications/books/ls_sclaid_def_securing_reasonable_caseloads.authcheckdam.pdf (documenting the dire condition of public defense, and calling the profession to action).

21 Richard A. Posner, *The Problematics of Moral and Legal Theory* (Cambridge, MA: Harvard University Press, 1999), 163–164.

3. What personal answers from her list does Babcock give for why she defends those accused of crimes?
4. Who did the Indiana University Law School professor compare the author's defense of Geraldine to? In your opinion, was this a fair comparison given what you learned about her defense?
5. When Thomas Cooley says that a defense attorney's persistence and strength of character are "questions of ethics rather than law," what does he mean?
6. How does Clara Foltz answer the ethical question that Cooley poses?
7. What does the author mean when she says that she "elided" ethical questions in her practice?
8. What is Babcock's characterization of criminal defense? Are we doing enough?
9. What do you think are Foltz's "blessings which flow from constitutional obligations consciously kept and government duties sacredly performed"?

Chapter 5

Are Americans Too Litigious?

In 1992, Stella May Liebeck bought a cup of coffee from a McDonald's drive-through in Albuquerque, New Mexico. While she was adding cream and sugar, the coffee spilled, severely burning the 79-year-old Liebeck. Her injuries required eight days in the hospital and two years of treatment. Her medical bill was more than $10,000.

Liebeck sued McDonalds, arguing that the 180–190 degrees Fahrenheit coffee was dangerously and inappropriately hot. Consequently, McDonald's had a legal responsibility to pay for her injuries and lost income from being unable to work. McDonalds offered her $800.

The story was quickly picked up by the national media. The accounts of the incident were often unsympathetic toward Liebeck, portraying the case as an example of Americans' over-litigiousness. Americans, it would seem, would go to court over something as trivial as a cup of coffee.

In American politics, claims that Americans take their disputes to the courts too often are not new. American politicians have often called for greater restrictions on Americans' ability to bring cases to the courts and on the monetary awards available.

US President George Bush is one example. He strongly advocated for tort reform during his presidency, signing the Class Action Fairness Act of 2005, which gave the federal courts greater ability to preside over class action lawsuits, as they were viewed as wasteful and unnecessary. The federal courts were seen as less sympathetic to class action claims at the time. "We've got too many darn lawsuits, too many frivolous and junk lawsuits that are affecting people," the president declared in a speech in 2004.

This popular debate over the appropriateness of litigation has not escaped those who study the courts. In their writings, some have concluded that Americans are overly litigious, while others have come to the opposite conclusion.

Lawyer Philip Howard argues that Americans' litigiousness takes away from the exercise of judgment that society requires. He gives the decision of the Appellate Committee of the House of Lords, Britain's highest court, to illustrate the direction that he wishes American law would take (2009, 15–17).

In *Tomlinson v. Congleton Borough Council* (2003), the Court declared that the law should consider the "social value" of an activity when deciding liability. The ruling overturned the decision of a lower court holding the Cheshire County Council legally responsible for a swimmer who broke his neck while diving at a lake in a county park.

For those who believe that America is overly litigious, the inability to exercise discretion is not the only social ill. Law professor Lawrence Friedman parrots the term "hyperlexis" and states that its perceived negative consequences include too much work for the courts to do an adequate job; greater costs for taxpayers, consumers, and businesses; and less trust, as people become more cautious about being taken to court (1994, 15–16).

Despite his detailed description of American litigiousness and its perceived consequences, Friedman is not convinced that there is too much. He finds that the existing data isn't very good for several reasons: First, most legal cases go through the state courts, which have not kept good records. Also, it is difficult to quantify and measure litigiousness. Finally, when one only considers the cases with outcomes in the courts, these cases were often uncontested (a divorce, for example) (1994, 17–19).

Using what he calls "the best evidence so far," Friedman finds that litigation has not risen since the 1950s. Interestingly, he also suggests that the American colonists were much more likely to have an encounter with the legal system than an American today (1994, 19).

A study by J. Mark Ramseyer and Eric B. Rasmusen (2010) discovered a similar amount of litigation to the United States in Canada and three Western European countries. The authors did find that Americans had higher amounts of certain types of cases, which they called "second order." These cases included lawsuits that sought high monetary awards from corporations.

Friedman also observes that Americans had become more likely to litigate certain types of cases. These cases often coincided with developing areas of American law. They included civil rights, class action lawsuits, and the monitoring of hospitals, prisons, and schools (1994, 20–21).

Law professor Erwin Chemerinsky adds his voice to those who argue against a tsunami of American litigation. Chemerinsky, in fact, asserts that there needs to be more of a certain type of litigation—namely, cases addressing constitutional issues.

Chemerinsky tells us that the federal courts are not deciding the number of constitutional cases that they should because the Supreme Court has restricted access to the federal courts by parties wanting them to decide cases involving constitutional issues.

The Supreme Court did this in a number of ways: For one, it imposed doctrines that limit access to the federal courts for those who seek justice for the violation of their constitutional rights. Additionally, the Court has granted greater immunity for both the government and its workers in cases involving constitutional rights. Moreover, justices have restricted legal standing and the issues that federal courts can adjudicate. Finally, the Court has curtailed the ability of the federal courts to grant a writ of habeas corpus for prisoners, including those who are innocent (2017, 4–5).

The Supreme Court, then, has ostensibly prioritized the federal government over the Constitution. This is ironic, as Justice John Marshall declared that the US Constitution takes precedence over other types of law in the Court's seminal decision in *Marbury v. Madison* (1803). Chemerinsky explains why he believes that the courts are the ideal political institution to protect constitutional rights and liberties (5–8).

As you read through Chemerinsky's argument, imagine that you could personally decide which cases get heard by the federal courts. Do you agree with completely, partially, or not at all with Chemerinsky's argument that the federal courts have a responsibility to hear all cases involving constitutional questions? Might the Court's rulings be seen as an effort to curtail expensive and unnecessary litigation? Or is litigation necessary because constitutional rights represent the foundation of our democracy?

Also consider the degree of protection from lawsuits that you think the government should have. Might unrestricted liability limit the federal government's power to act, as cautioned the Appellate Committee of the House of Lords cautioned?

Reading 5.1

Why Do We Have Federal Courts?

Erwin Chemerinsky

In 2014, the United States Court of Appeals for the District of Columbia Circuit dismissed a lawsuit brought by a dozen current and former sailors and Marines who had been severely sexually harassed or raped while in military service.[1] The Court of Appeals accepted that the plaintiffs had suffered great harms and egregious violations of their rights, but it concluded that the federal courts could provide no relief.[2] It described this resolution of the case as "easy."

Ariana Klay was one of the plaintiffs. While she was an active duty lieutenant in the U.S. Marine Corps, her fellow Marines gang-raped her at her home, a few blocks away from the Marine barracks in Washington, D.C. Apparently, one of Klay's colleagues felt that she had embarrassed him in front of a group of Junior Marines.[3] That Marine and a friend, a former Marine, showed up at Klay's house one day around 5:00 in the morning and raped her in retaliation.

Klay testified that in the months before the rape, she was constantly sexually harassed. From her first day of military service, she said that she and the other women in the barracks were treated with hostility by her fellow Marines. She described the culture in the barracks as "vile."[4] When she reported the harassment to her superior, he told her to "deal with it" and refused to take any action.

Not until Klay filed a restricted report—which gives the victim access to medical care or advocacy services—did the Marine Corps investigate the harassment. Although a restricted report is supposed to be confidential, Klay's rape was widely known soon after the report was filed and then leaked.[5] The Marine Corps investigation implied that because Klay wore skirts (which were regulation-length and part of her uniform) and makeup, and exercised in tank tops and running shorts, therefore she had invited and welcomed the harassment. During the pretrial hearing on the rape in the military court, Klay was questioned for sixteen hours, during which

---

1 *Klay v. Panetta*, 758 F.3d 369 (D.C. Cir. 2014).

2 *Id.* at 379.

3 *See* Rep. Jackie Speier, *A Woman Who Channels Pain into Solutions*, POLITICO (December 10, 2013), http://www.politico.com/story/2013/12/women-rule-jackie-speier-ariana-klay-100898.html.

4 *Id.*

5 *Id.*

she repeatedly was asked inappropriate and humiliating questions. The prosecuting attorney made no objections on Klay's behalf. The court eventually ruled, mostly on the basis of the two perpetrators' testimony, that the sex was consensual and that there had been no rape. Afterward, because she had complained about the incident, the harassment grew so severe that Klay at one point attempted suicide.

Janet Galla was another plaintiff in the lawsuit. The Court of Appeals explained what happened to her:

> Galla served in the Navy from 1999 to 2005 as a Hospital Corpsman. On June 11, 2004, after having dinner with a group of friends, Galla returned to her ship. While she was checking her email in the ship's Medical Department, a fellow Corpsman asked if he could show her something in one of the Department's operating rooms. She followed him into an operating room, where he tried to kiss her. She resisted, asked him to stop, and tried to leave the room, but he prevented her from escaping and then raped her. Galla immediately reported the rape. Although her attacker was ultimately convicted and sent to prison, Galla faced retaliation from those within her chain of command. She was not allowed to work in enclosed spaces with male colleagues, a restriction her superiors claimed was for her own protection. This limitation not only made it difficult for her to do her job, but left her feeling ostracized from her shipmates. Galla began to receive negative performance evaluations and was eventually told by her commander that it would be best for "morale" if she left the ship. She transferred to a duty station on land, but the retaliation continued when her new chain of command learned about the rape and the ongoing investigation. ... One member of her new command told her that the rape was only "five minutes of her life" and she needed to "get over it already." In the face of such harassment and ostracism, Galla accepted her superiors' offer of immediate separation from the Navy in 2005.[6]

Galla and Klay were joined by ten other plaintiffs, all of whom had suffered sexual harassment or rape. When some of them reported "being raped by their colleagues, they were labeled as 'troublemakers,'"[7] a label that eventually got them discharged or forced them to resign from the military.[8] Some of the survivors "were directed to be silent, and refrain from

6 758 F.3d. at 371.

7 Brief for Appellants at 3, *Klay v. Panetta*, 758 F.3d 369 (D.C. Cir. 2014) (No. 13-5081).

8 *Id.* at 3–4.

telling anyone about the rapes and the subsequent mistreatment."[9] All of the plaintiffs "were on active duty when they suffered these sexual assaults and retaliatory actions at the hands of other service members."[10] Further, most of the sexual assaults detailed in the plaintiffs' complaint "took place on military bases, military ships, or during foreign deployment."[11] The rest "occurred at private residences that were located off-base or in connection with social events with other service members."[12]

Although the survivors faced immediate and lifelong consequences from their assaults, the rapists suffered few repercussions. "The vast majority," the women's complaint noted, "were not prosecuted or punished in any meaningful way."[13] Those who felt any consequences at all were permitted by their superiors to "receive nonjudicial punishment and to be honorably discharged."[14]

In 2012, Klay, Galla, and the other plaintiffs filed suit in federal district court against nine defendants: the three most recent Secretaries of Defense, Secretaries of the Navy, and Commandants of the Marine Corps. They alleged that the defendants were responsible for what they suffered and for the violations of their constitutional rights. The complaint explained that the defendants were fully aware of the prevalence of sexual misconduct and retaliation in the Navy and Marine Corps and had the power to eliminate it, yet they had taken no effective steps to do so.

But the United States Court of Appeals for the District of Columbia Circuit ordered the plaintiffs' suit dismissed, saying that military officials cannot be sued in federal court for constitutional violations. The Court declared: "Their appeal is both difficult and easy. Difficult, because it involves shocking allegations that members of this nation's armed forces who put themselves at risk to protect our liberties were abused in such a vile and callous manner. Easy, because plaintiffs seek relief under a legal theory that is patently deficient." The Court did not question the plaintiffs' allegations or their assertion that the defendants, top government officials, were ultimately responsible for what occurred. But it held that the federal courts cannot provide relief to those who have suffered violations of even their most basic rights while in military service. It concluded: "In affirming the district court's dismissal, we do not take lightly the severity of plaintiffs' suffering or the harm done by sexual assault

---

9 *Id.* at 3.

10 *Klay v. Panetta*, 924 F. Supp. 2d 8, 9 (D.D.C. 2013).

11 *Id.*

12 *Id.*

13 Brief for Appellants at 4, *Klay v. Panetta*, 758 F.3d 369 (D.C. Cir. 2014) (No. 13-5081).

14 *Klay v. Panetta*, 758 F.3d 369, 372 (D.C. Cir. 2014).

and retaliation in our military. But the existence of grievous wrongs does not free the judiciary to authorize any and all suits that might seem just."[15]

The Court of Appeals accepted (as it had to at that stage of the litigation) that the women had been raped, sexually harassed, and retaliated against. But the women had absolutely no remedy. They could not sue the United States because it has sovereign immunity; that is, the United States government is completely immune from being sued unless there is a federal statute authorizing it. No such statute existed here. The victims could not sue their rapists and harassers, or anyone else in the military, because the Supreme Court has ruled that people cannot sue others in the military or its chain of command.[16] Although it agreed that female service members have a right to be free from sexual assaults and harassment, the Court concluded that federal courts cannot enforce that right or provide a remedy when it is violated.

This case is not an anomaly. Many legal doctrines fashioned by the Supreme Court over the last several decades prevent the federal courts from providing any remedy to those whose constitutional rights have been violated. The Court has expanded the immunity of government and government officials, making it difficult to sue even when there are egregious constitutional violations. The Court has restricted who has standing to sue in federal courts and limited the constitutional claims that can be adjudicated. Congress and the Supreme Court have greatly restricted the ability of federal courts to grant a writ of habeas corpus in favor of those convicted of crimes, meaning that wrongly convicted individuals are often left without recourse. In recent decisions, the Court has changed procedural doctrines to make it harder for injured plaintiffs to get into federal courts, especially with class action suits.

My purpose in this [reading] is to describe these doctrines and prescribe changes. Because they involve technical doctrines that are often about legal procedure—matters like sovereign immunity, absolute and qualified immunity for individual officers, justiciability principles such as standing and the political question doctrine, habeas corpus, and pleading—they do not make headlines. But they mean that people whose rights have been violated and who have suffered great injuries, including even fatal ones, are left without recourse. They have rights under the Constitution, but the federal courts cannot enforce them.

If the Supreme Court were to hold that the government can give unlimited amounts of money to religious schools, the decision would make the front-page headline of every newspaper in the country. But if the Court were to hold that no one has standing to challenge the government when it gives money to parochial schools, that would get far less attention.

---

15 *Id.* at 379.

16 *See, e.g., United States v. Stanley*, 483 U.S. 669 (1987) (no suits can be brought against military officers for harms suffered in the military). [...]

Yet the effect is exactly the same: if no one can challenge a government action in court, the government can do what it wants. If the Secretary of Defense announced that men are permitted to rape and sexually harass women in the Army, Navy, Air Force, and Marines, the country would be justifiably outraged. But the Court of Appeals got almost no attention when it ruled that women in military service who are raped and harassed have no remedy.

Why Do We Have Federal Courts?

This is an obvious injustice, and if the situation of Klay, Galla, and their co-plaintiffs makes you feel angry, you are not alone. It is a situation that cries out for remedy. To understand how to correct it, in a manner consistent with our constitutional values, we must start with a question at the very foundation of our judicial system: why do we have federal courts at all?

The preeminent purpose of the federal courts is to enforce the United States Constitution. Legal doctrines should be directed toward allowing the federal courts to fulfill this mission.

This position should not be controversial, yet it is so at odds with many legal doctrines that it needs to be justified. The first justification comes from *Marbury v. Madison*, the 1803 Supreme Court decision which held that federal courts have the power to review the constitutionality of federal laws and executive actions.[17] The Constitution does not expressly give the federal judiciary the authority to do this; it is silent on the subject. In *Marbury v. Madison*, the Supreme Court found this authority in the Constitution, and the power of judicial review has existed ever since.

The facts of *Marbury v. Madison* are familiar. On February 27, 1801, less than a week before the end of President John Adams's term, Congress adopted the Organic Act of the District of Columbia, which authorized the President to appoint forty-two justices of the peace. Adams had lost his reelection bid, and his and George Washington's Federalist Party was about to leave power. Adams announced his nominations on March 2. On March 3, the day before Thomas Jefferson's inauguration as President, the Senate confirmed the nominees. Immediately, the departing Secretary of State, John Marshall (who was also Chief Justice of the Supreme Court), put the seal of the United States on these commissions and set out to deliver them. A few commissions, including one for William Marbury, were not delivered before Jefferson's inauguration. President Jefferson instructed his incoming Secretary of State, James Madison, to withhold the undelivered commissions.

Marbury filed suit in the United States Supreme Court seeking a writ of mandamus—a court order—to compel Madison to deliver his commission. He claimed that the Judiciary Act of 1789 authorized the Supreme Court to grant mandamus in a proceeding filed initially

17 5 U.S. (1 Cranch) 137 (1803).

in the Supreme Court. Although Marbury's petition was filed in December 1801, the Supreme Court did not hear the case until 1803 because Congress had abolished the Court's June and December 1802 terms.

Near the beginning of his opinion, Chief Justice Marshall declared a basic principle of American government: "The very essence of civil liberty certainly consists in the right of every individual to claim the protection of the laws, whenever he receives an injury."[18] It follows that the preeminent role of the judiciary is to provide remedies to those whose rights have been violated.

The specific issue in *Marbury v. Madison* was whether the Court could give Marbury a remedy against the executive branch of government. The Court answered this by declaring that "the government of the United States has been emphatically termed a government of laws, and not of men."[19] In other words, no person—not even the President—is above the law.

Marbury's problem was that he filed his lawsuit initially in the Supreme Court under a provision of the Judiciary Act of 1789 that purportedly authorized this.[20] The Court concluded that the federal statute was unconstitutional because it expanded the Supreme Court's jurisdiction beyond what was authorized by Article III of the Constitution. Having decided that Congress had passed a law that was beyond its authority, the Court then considered the most important question: Did it nonetheless have to follow the law, or could it declare that provision unconstitutional? Marshall's decision began by stating: "The question, whether an act, repugnant to the Constitution, can become the law of the land, is a question deeply interesting to the United States; but, happily, not of an intricacy proportioned to its interest."[21] He then offered several reasons why the Court could declare federal laws unconstitutional.

Most important, he explained that the Constitution exists to impose limits on government powers, and these limits are meaningless unless subject to judicial enforcement. Borrowing from Alexander Hamilton's Federalist No. 78, Marshall wrote: "The powers of the legislature are defined and limited; and that those limits may not be mistaken or forgotten, the constitution is written."[22] And he went on, in perhaps the most frequently quoted words of the opinion: "It is emphatically the province and duty of the judicial department

---

18 *Id.* at 163.

19 *Id.*

20 For a persuasive criticism of this conclusion, and other aspects of the Court's reasoning in *Marbury v. Madison*, *see* Burt Neuborne, MADISON'S MUSIC 146–194 (2015); William Van Alstyne, *A Critical Guide to Marbury v. Madison*, DUKE L.J. 1 (1969).

21 5 U.S. at 176.

22 5 U.S. at 176. *See* THE FEDERALIST No. 78, at 446–469 (A. Hamilton) (Clinton Rossiter ed. 1961).

to say what the law is."[23] In other words, the Constitution depends on having judges with the power to enforce it.

I believe Marshall got it exactly right—and that is why *Marbury v. Madison* has been a cornerstone of American government for almost its entire history. The Constitution exists to limit government, and the limits are meaningful only if they are enforced. Enforcement often will not happen without the judiciary. Therefore, the most important role of the federal courts should be seen as enforcing the Constitution.

Of course, federal courts are not the only institution that enforces the Constitution. State courts also exist and can and do enforce the Constitution. But this in no way diminishes the importance of the federal courts doing so. State courts often have no authority over federal officers or the federal government. For example, it is firmly established that state courts cannot grant habeas corpus to federal prisoners.[24] Nor would it make sense to have state courts resolve issues of federal separation of powers, such as when there is a dispute between Congress and the President. To pick a recent example, it would not have been desirable to have a state court decide the constitutionality of a federal law requiring that the State Department allow the parents of children born in Jerusalem to have the passport indicate "Israel" as the birthplace.[25] In situations like this, when there is a constitutional impasse between the other branches of the federal government, the federal courts must act as the umpire. Also, many of the doctrines that keep federal courts from enforcing the Constitution—such as the limits on suing government entities and government officers—apply just the same way in the state courts.[26]

More generally, the very existence of federal courts reflects a particular view of how the Constitution should be enforced.[27] Under the Articles of Confederation, there were neither

---

23 5 U.S. at 177.

24 *Tarble's Case*, 80 U.S. 397, 411 (1871).

25 *Zivotofsky v. Kerry*, 135 S.Ct. 2076 (2015) (because the power to recognize foreign states resides in the President alone, Section 214(d) of the Foreign Relations Authorization Act of 2003—which directs the Secretary of State, upon request, to designate "Israel" as the place of birth on the passport of a U.S. citizen who is born in Jerusalem—infringes on the executive's consistent decision to withhold recognition with respect to Jerusalem).

26 *See, e.g.*, *Alden v. Maine*, 527 U.S. 706 (1999) (state governments have sovereign immunity and cannot be sued in state court, including on federal claims). [...]

27 There is an endless debate among academics, and even justices, as to whether there is parity between federal courts and state courts. *See, e.g.*, Burt Neuborne, *The Myth of Parity*, 90 HARV. L. REV. 1105 (1977); for a review of the literature in the debate over parity, *see* Erwin Chemerinsky, *Parity Reconsidered: Defining a Role for the Federal Judiciary*, 36 UCLA L. REV. 233 (1988). I do not need to

federal courts nor a federal judicial power. Article III of the Constitution created the Supreme Court and authorized the creation of the lower federal court because of a belief that the enforcement of federal law could not be left exclusively to the state judiciaries. Congress created the lower federal courts in 1789, and they have existed ever since, because the Supreme Court by itself does not have the capacity to review all state court decisions. Federal courts exist, above all, and have since their creation, to enforce federal law, and the most important federal law is the Constitution.

Nor can we rely on voluntary compliance from the other branches and levels of government.[28] Far too often, legislators and officials have a strong incentive not to comply with the Constitution. These situations, which often involve the most vulnerable in society, are where the federal judiciary is most needed.

Most dramatically, those without political power have nowhere to turn except the judiciary for the protection of their constitutional rights. The reality is that participants in the political process have little reason to be responsive to the constitutional rights of prisoners or criminal defendants or those who are not citizens. These individuals lack political power—they do not give money to political candidates, they generally are prohibited from voting, they are unpopular and often unsympathetic. When was the last time a legislature acted to expand the rights of prisoners or criminal defendants? In the competition for scarce dollars, legislatures have every political incentive to spend as little as possible on prisoners. Politicians compete to sound tough on crime, not to expand defendants' rights. Yet how much worse might it be if politicians and prison officials knew that no court would review the constitutionality of their actions? Admittedly, the Supreme Court has a less than stellar record of protecting these individuals' rights, but there is no doubt that judicial review has provided protections for criminal defendants and dramatically improved conditions for countless prison inmates abandoned by the political process. Although these are obvious examples, the nature of democracy is that the elected branches of government are often insensitive to the rights of those who lack political influence.

More generally, if not for the federal courts, what is to stop the Congress or the President from enacting a law that is unconstitutional but politically expedient? What, other than the drastic remedy of impeachment, is to stop the President from pursuing unconstitutional

---

take a position on this debate for purposes of this [reading]. The choice to create federal courts in 1789 reflected a view that some matters should not be left exclusively to state courts with federal court review only in the United States Supreme Court.

28 There are those who argue that this is sufficient and that judicial review should be eliminated. *See, e.g.*, James MacGregor Burns, PACKING THE COURT (2009); Mark Tushnet, TAKING THE CONSTITUTION AWAY FROM THE COURTS (1999).

policies when they are politically popular? Often there is no one, other than the courts, to deter wrongdoing and compensate those injured by constitutional violations.

This view of the federal judiciary inevitably is derived from the purpose of the Constitution itself. My agreement with *Marbury v. Madison* ultimately is based on my belief that the written Constitution exists to be the supreme law of the land and to limit what everyone in government, at all levels, can do.

Harvard Law Professor Laurence Tribe powerfully asked: "Why would a nation that rests legality on the consent of the governed choose to constitute its political life in terms of commitments to an original agreement—made by the people, binding on their children, and deliberately structured so as to be difficult to change?" It is hardly original or profound to answer this question by observing that the framers deliberately made the Constitution very difficult to change as a way of preventing tyranny of the majority and protecting the rights of the minority from oppression by social majorities. If the structure of government were placed in a statute, the urge to create dictatorial powers in times of crisis might be irresistible. If individual liberties were protected only by statutes, a tyrannical government could overrule them. If terms of office were specified in a statute rather than in the Constitution, those in power could alter the rules to remain in power.

Thus the Constitution represents society's attempt to tie its own hands, to limit its ability to fall prey to weaknesses that might harm or undermine its most cherished values. History teaches that under the passions of the moment, people may sacrifice even the most basic principles of liberty and justice. The Constitution is society's attempt to protect itself from itself. It enumerates basic values—regular elections, separation of powers, individual rights, equality—and makes departure very difficult. In large part, the decision to be governed by the Constitution is animated by fear that a political majority could gain control of government and disenfranchise and perhaps persecute the minority. Compared to all other laws, the Constitution is uniquely difficult to amend or alter, precisely to ensure that the limits it sets are not easily changed.

Accordingly, in deciding who should be the authoritative interpreter of the Constitution, the answer is the branch of government that can best enforce the Constitution's limits against the desires of political majorities. By this criterion, the federal judiciary is the obvious choice. It is the institution most insulated from political pressures. Article III of the Constitution provides that federal court judges have life tenure unless impeached, and that their salary may not be decreased during their terms of office. Unlike legislators or the President, they never face reelection.

Furthermore, the method of federal judicial selection reinforces its antimajoritarian character. Unlike the House of Representatives, whose members are elected at the same time, or the Senate, where one third of the members are chosen in each election, the Court's members are appointed one at a time, as vacancies arise. No single administration is generally able to appoint a majority of the Court or the federal judiciary. The result is that the Court reflects many political views, not just the one that dominates at a particular time.

Thus the primary reason for having federal courts—the Supreme Court and the lower federal courts—is to enforce the Constitution against the will of the majority. I do not mean to suggest that this is their only role. Twenty-five years ago, I co-authored with Professor (and later Dean) Larry Kramer an article entitled "Defining the Role of the Federal Courts," in which we identified the federal courts' functions.[29] First on the list was "enforcing the Constitution."[30] We also identified five other important functions:[31]

- protecting the interests of the federal government as a sovereign, including by providing a forum for enforcement of federal criminal law;
- serving as an umpire in interstate disputes;
- assuring uniform interpretation and application of federal law;
- developing federal common law, a body of judge-made law in the absence of statutes; and
- hearing appeals.

These categories are not mutually exclusive. There is no tension between saying that federal courts exist preeminently to enforce the Constitution and also identifying these other functions. I, of course, accept all of these as important tasks for the federal judiciary. But my focus in this [reading] is on the task we intentionally put first: enforcing the Constitution.

Why the Judiciary?

There are other reasons, too, why the judiciary is the branch of government that is best suited to enforce the Constitution.

First, the judiciary is the only institution obligated to hear the complaints of a single person. For the most part, the federal judiciary's jurisdiction is mandatory. Although the Supreme Court can choose which cases to hear, a lower federal court must (with relatively rare exceptions) rule on every case properly filed with it. Long ago, Chief Justice Marshall wrote, "It is most true that this Court will not take jurisdiction if it should not but it is

---

29 Erwin Chemerinsky and Larry Kramer, *Defining the Role of the Federal Courts*, 1990 BYU L. REV. 67.

30 *Id.* at 77.

31 *Id.* at 77–88.

equally true that it must take jurisdiction if it should. ... We have no more right to decline the exercise of jurisdiction which is given, than to usurp that which is not given."[32]

The legislature and the executive, on the other hand, are under no duty to hear any single person's complaints. An individual or small group complaining of an injustice to a legislator or the president could be easily ignored. If only a few constituents care about something, and if acting to help them would consume too much time for the number of votes it will yield, they often will be ignored. Moreover, if helping the few will hurt more constituents, the few are likely to be disregarded no matter how just their cause. To use the example mentioned above, prisoners are a constituency with little political power. In many states, felons are permanently disenfranchised from voting, meaning that elected officials need not worry about meeting their demands.[33] Providing adequate resources for prisoners—for their shelter, food, medical care, and training—requires expenditures unlikely to be popular with taxpayers, and certainly less popular than if the money were spent on almost anything else. With no constituency to pressure for their humane treatment, prisoners' rights and needs are likely to be ignored.

The courts, however, are obligated to rule on any properly filed complaint, no matter whether the litigant is rich or poor, powerful or powerless, incarcerated or not. The judiciary is much more likely than the legislature to listen to criminal defendants' claims that their rights were violated or to poor individuals' objections that they are denied equal justice—because they must at least give such claims a hearing. The Constitution's purpose of protecting the minority from the tyranny of the majority is best fulfilled by an institution obligated to listen to the minority.

Second, the judiciary is not only the branch most likely to listen to complaints, it is also most likely to respond to them. The judiciary is supposed to decide each case on its own merits, subject to the accepted norm that like cases should be treated alike. In every case where there is an allegation of a constitutional violation, the judiciary is obligated, if it has jurisdiction and if there is no way to decide the case on nonconstitutional grounds, to issue a constitutional ruling. The legislature, by contrast, need not decide each matter before it on its merits—or at all. Logrolling, vote trading, and the tabling of bills are accepted parts of the legislative process. Procedural devices like the filibuster and holds often let a minority prevent legislative action; for decades Southerners in the Senate used them to block civil rights legislation. Although legislators are forbidden by their oath of office to enact laws they believe to be unconstitutional, they are not required to provide a remedy every time someone complains that government is violating the Constitution. Only the judiciary is obligated to respond to such complaints—and this makes the courts an ideal forum for ensuring that the Constitution is upheld.

---

32 *Cohens v. Virginia*, 19 U.S. (6 Wheat.) 264, 404 (1824).

33 See *Richardson v. Ramirez*, 418 U.S. 24 (1974).

Third, as the branch most insulated from day-to-day politics, the judiciary is the branch most willing to enforce the Constitution in the face of strong pressures from political majorities. Even if the legislature and executive were to listen to all claims and respond on the merits, they are still less likely to uphold the Constitution against the intense opposition of their constituents. It is this insulation that moved Alexis de Tocqueville to remark that "the power vested in the American courts of justice of pronouncing a statute unconstitutional forms one of the most powerful barriers that have been devised against the tyranny of political assemblies."[34]

The argument is not that legislators act in bad faith and disregard their oath to uphold the Constitution, although this sometimes happens. Rather, it is that constitutional interpretation inherently requires choices as to what the Constitution should mean: how its abstract values should be applied in specific situations. These choices are best made by an institution whose primary commitment is to the Constitution, not to gaining reelection. Professor Owen Fiss observed that "legislatures are not ideologically committed or institutionally suited to search for the meaning of constitutional values, but instead see their primary function in terms of registering the actual, current preferences of the people."[35] The judiciary is much more to be trusted in deciding, for instance, whether the Constitution should protect the speech activities of a politically unpopular group like the Nazi Party. Being committed to upholding the First Amendment and not faced with intense pressure from constituents, it is in a better position to decide whether school prayer violates the Constitution or whether the right of privacy includes the right of a woman to decide whether to have an abortion.

The best institution for interpreting the Constitution is thus not the one that most reflects the majority's current preferences. Constitutional interpretation is best done by a relatively politically insulated body. Harry Wellington explains:

> If society were to design an institution which had the job of finding society's set of moral principles and determining how they bear on concrete situations, that institution would be sharply different from one charged with proposing policies. The latter institution would be constructed with the understanding that it was to respond to the people's exercise of political power. ... The former would be insulated from pressure. It would provide an environment conducive to rumination, reflection and analysis.[36]

---

34 Alexis de Toqueville, DEMOCRACY IN AMERICA, ed. Bradley 103 (1945).

35 Owen Fiss, *Foreword: The Forms of Justice*, 93 HARV. L. REV. 1, 10 (1979).

36 Harry Wellington, *Common Law Rules and Constitutional Double Standards: Some Notes on Adjudication*, 83 YALE L.J. 221, 246–247 (1973).

Constitutional interpretation is a process of deciding what values are so fundamental that they should be safeguarded from political majorities. It makes little sense to entrust these decisions to those same political majorities. The judiciary's insulation and commitment to decisions based on the merits make it far better suited for this task. Alexander Bickel remarked that "courts have certain capacities for dealing with matters of principle that legislatures and the executive do not possess. Judges have, or should have, the leisure, the training, and the insulation to follow the ways of the scholar in pursuing the ends of government. This is crucial in sorting out the enduring values of a society."[37] Constitutional interpretation requires an institution to serve as the nation's moral conscience—an institution responsible for identifying values so important that they should not be sacrificed, and reminding the country when its own most cherished values are being violated. The Supreme Court, at times, has functioned in exactly this way: as a moral conscience holding the nation to its highest values.

The legislature is to be trusted least when the question is the constitutionality of a statute it has enacted. Allowing the same body to both enact laws and determine their constitutionality is no way to protect constitutional values. Review by another branch of government creates a necessary check on the majority. The executive veto provides something of a check, but Congress can override a veto. Moreover, the President is electorally accountable, at least in his first term, and may feel the same pressures as Congress. The judiciary is most detached from both the enactment of laws and the implementation of policies.

The Court's self-interest is in enhancing its long-term powers. Certainly, the judiciary's institutional self-interest justifies fear of its deciding cases to aggrandize its own powers. I would argue, however, that in resolving specific controversies it is better to trust an institution with only long-term interests than one with immediate interests in the outcome of the matter.

In sum, once it is decided that society should be governed by a constitution in order to make certain matters less amenable to majoritarian control, judicial review is an essential mechanism for interpreting and enforcing the document's limits on majority action.

The methods of judicial decision-making also make it the best institution for constitutional interpretation. The judiciary is the only institution committed to arriving at decisions based entirely on arguments and reasoning. Executive and legislative officials frequently offer no formal explanations for their decisions, and the statements they provide usually do not purport to be comprehensive. The judicial method is a process of hearing arguments from the parties, reaching decisions based on those arguments, and justifying the results with a written opinion. Although neither the Constitution nor any statute compels a court to write and publish opinions, publicly stated reasons for these decisions are embedded in

37 Alexander Bickel, THE LEAST DANGEROUS BRANCH: THE SUPREME COURT AND THE BAR OF POLITICS (1962), 26.

the American legal system. It has long been recognized that the "traditional means of protecting the public from judicial fiat ... [are] that judges give reasons for their results."[38]

For each ruling it hands down, the Court must write an opinion demonstrating that its decision was not arbitrary. It must explain why the values it is protecting are worthy of constitutional status, how those values are embodied in legal principles, and how they are to be applied in a specific case. It must also explain why its decision is consistent with prior holdings, is legitimately distinguishable from precedents, or justifies overruling conflicting cases.

In contrast, the legislature and the executive need not follow any particular decision-making process. Neither Congress nor the President is required, by law or tradition, to state reasons for their decisions. Although Congress produces legislative histories and the President issues executive proclamations, only the judiciary is committed to reaching its decisions through logical reasoning from principles rather than via political considerations. A legislature is allowed to make arbitrary choices unsupported by a guiding principle. Even though inevitably the Supreme Court's constitutional decisions are a product of the justices' ideology and values, the Court still must justify them in legally acceptable terms. Moreover, only the judiciary is committed to following precedent.

For all of these reasons, I believe the judiciary's essential role is to enforce the Constitution, and legal doctrines must facilitate its performing this task. There are alternative conceptions of the judicial role, but I reject them.

One such alternative is that the federal courts' primary role should be to resolve disputes between litigants, and that resolving constitutional issues is a secondary function that comes into play only when they are presented in litigation. The so-called traditional model described adjudication as a process for resolving disputes among private parties that have not been privately settled.[39]

This is not an accurate depiction of the role of the federal courts; nor should it be. Almost thirty years ago, Professor Abram Chayes wrote in a famous article: "Whatever its historical validity, the traditional model is clearly invalid as a description of much current civil litigation in the federal district courts. Perhaps the dominating characteristic of modern federal litigation is that lawsuits do not arise out of disputes between private parties about private rights. Instead, the object of litigation is the vindication of constitutional or statutory policies. The shift in the legal basis of the lawsuit explains many, but not all, facets of what is going on 'in fact' in federal trial courts."[40] The traditional model focuses only on

38 G. Edward White, *The Evolution of Reasoned Elaboration: Jurisprudential Criticism and Social Change*, 59 VA. L. REV. 279, 299 (1973).

39 Abram Chayes, *The Role of the Judge in Public Law Litigation*, 89 HARV. L. REV. 1281 (1976).

40 *Id.* at 1282–1283.

private civil litigation and does not account for all of the criminal prosecutions in federal court that are brought by the federal government, or the civil cases where a government entity or officer is a party.

Moreover, the distinction between "private" and "public" adjudication is largely false. Most of the cases I describe [...] involve individuals who have suffered harm, often great harm, at the hands of the government and seek a remedy. Ariana Klay and Janet Galla sought redress for the violation of their rights that they suffered while in the military. [...O]ther people [...] were injured and could not get into federal court because of the immunity of government entities and officers or because of restrictive procedural requirements. If any of these people have a desire to vindicate the Constitution, it is secondary to their personal interests. But the public's interest in these cases is different: it has to do with the rights we all should possess. Every decision is a precedent that controls lower courts in subsequent cases and even, more or less, the Supreme Court. Every Supreme Court decision is making law that affects all of us and not simply resolving individual disputes.

Finally, if there is a choice to be made between the "private rights" and the "public law" models of adjudication, the latter should be followed to the extent that it better facilitates enforcement of the Constitution. The choice of a model for adjudication, if one needs to be made, should follow from the reasons for having federal courts. My argument is that the most important role of the federal courts should be to enforce the Constitution and thus legal doctrines should facilitate that.

A second alternative vision says that the role of the federal courts needs to be constrained by the separation of powers. In a dissenting opinion urging a narrow view of who has standing to bring a case to federal court, Justice Antonin Scalia wrote in 2015: "That doctrine of standing, that jurisdictional limitation upon our powers, does not have as its purpose (as the majority assumes) merely to assure that we will decide disputes in concrete factual contexts that enable 'realistic appreciation of the consequences of judicial action.' To the contrary. '[T]he law of Art. III standing is built on a single basic idea—the idea of separation of powers.' It keeps us minding our own business."[41] This restrictive view has been expressed many times, in regard to several doctrines that limit federal court jurisdiction [...].[42]

But such an argument begs the question of the appropriate role of the federal courts. Courts, of course, should "mind their own business." But that requires defining what their business is. The proper role of the federal courts has to be determined based on the purposes the federal judiciary should serve. If the business of the federal courts is enforcing the

41 *Arizona State Legislature v. Arizona Independent Redistricting Comm*, 135 S.Ct. 2652, 2695 (2015) (Scalia, J., dissenting), quoting *Allen v. Wright*, 468 U.S. 737, 752 (1984).

42 [...].

Constitution, that is what the doctrines defining federal court jurisdiction should facilitate. It cannot be assumed, as Justice Scalia did, that separation of powers is best served by restricting the courts' role. Less judicial review is not inherently better. Doctrines that facilitate the courts' function of enforcing the Constitution advance the courts' proper role in the system of separation of powers. Doctrines that limit its authority undermine separation of powers.

Finally, there are those who argue for a more limited role for the federal judiciary based on their concern that the courts must conserve their scarce institutional capital. This position is most frequently associated with Justice Felix Frankfurter and Professor Alexander Bickel.[43] Their view rests on several assumptions: that the judiciary's credibility is fragile; that unpopular, controversial decisions will undermine the Court's legitimacy; that if the Court comes to lack legitimacy it will be disobeyed and rendered less powerful; and that the risk of this outweighs the costs of not enforcing particular constitutional provisions.

All of these assumptions are highly questionable. History shows that judicial credibility and legitimacy are not fragile. Some of the Court's most controversial rulings—such as those desegregating schools and reapportioning state legislatures—ultimately enhanced the judiciary's stature. As John Hart Ely wrote: "The possibility of judicial emasculation by way of popular reaction against constitutional review by the courts has not in fact materialized in more than a century and a half of American experience. The warnings probably reached their peak during the Warren years; they were not heeded; yet nothing resembling destruction materialized. In fact, the Court's power continued to grow and probably never has been greater than it has been over the past two decades."[44]

There is no reason to believe that greater enforcement of the Constitution by the federal courts will undermine their credibility, lead to disobedience of judicial orders, or decrease the judiciary's power. Quite the contrary, additional enforcement of the Constitution could well enhance the Court's public esteem and credibility. At the very least, it is entirely speculative whether greater enforcement of the Constitution would have any ill effects.

Most important, even if there were such a risk, it is worth bearing in order to ensure constitutional enforcement. The Court's very reason for accumulating institutional capital is to enforce the Constitution. As Professor Laurence Tribe remarked, "The highest mission of the Supreme Court, in my view, is not to conserve judicial credibility, but in the Constitution's own phrase, 'to form a more perfect Union,' between right and rights."[45]

---

43 *See* Bickel, THE LEAST DANGEROUS BRANCH; *Baker v. Carr*, 369 U.S., 186, 267 (Frankfurter, J., dissenting).

44 John Hart Ely, DEMOCRACY AND DISTRUST 47–48 (1980).

45 Laurence H. Tribe, AMERICAN CONSTITUTIONAL LAW viii (2d ed. 1988).

Enforcing the Constitution

When I teach constitutional law and federal jurisdiction to law students, I always encourage them to focus not just on the legal rules, but also on what they mean for people's lives. Ariana Klay, Janet Galla, and the other plaintiffs in their lawsuit were sexually harassed and raped. Their constitutional rights were violated, but the federal judiciary ruled that it could not hear their case or give them any remedy. In fact, no court could. This cannot be reconciled with John Marshall's words in *Marbury v. Madison*: "The very essence of civil liberty certainly consists in the right of every individual to claim the protection of the laws, whenever he receives an injury."[46] The Court of Appeals decision in their case cannot be reconciled with *Marbury*'s declaration that no one is above the law. It cannot be reconciled with the most important reason we have federal courts: to enforce the United States Constitution.

CHAPTER 5 QUESTIONS

1. Why did the US Court of Appeals dismiss the lawsuit by the women who were raped while serving in the Marines?
2. Describe some of the ways that the government has made it more difficult for the federal courts to address grievances against it.
3. Why does Chemerinsky assert that the government can do what it wants if it cannot be challenged in the federal courts?
4. According to Chemerinsky, what is the primary responsibility of the federal courts?
5. Why do you think that President Thomas Jefferson refused to deliver William Marbury's writ of mandamus?
6. Chief Justice John Marshall stated that he was unable to deliver William Marbury's writ of mandamus. Why?
7. What is the significance of the Court's decision in *Marbury v. Madison?*
8. How does Chemerinsky think that the Court's decision in *Marbury v. Madison* speaks to limitations placed on the federal courts to address constitutional rights violations by the government?
9. Why does Chemerinsky think that federal courts have the primary responsibility to ensure that the government complies with the Constitution? Why can't the other branches of government fulfill this role?

---

46 *Id.* at 163.

Chapter 6

Law versus Society

I SUSPECT THAT YOU REMEMBER THE STORY of Wolf Lies Down from the readings in chapter 1. His horse was taken from him without his permission. While this act was against the traditions of the Cheyenne, there did not exist a formal rule, a law, against it. Nor did there exist a formal punishment. This, of course, changed when the Chiefs addressed Wolf Lies Down's complaint, publicly declaring that horses were not to be taken and those who did not return them would be whipped (Llewelyn and Hoebel 1941, 127–128).

Paul Bohannan's notion of *reinstitutionalization* (see Kidder 1983) perfectly describes what happened in the story. With the Cheyenne, there existed an informal expectation about personal behavior, a social norm. This informal expectation became formalized into law when the Chiefs declared that horses were to be returned when taken. In Bohannan's conception of the emergence of law, law begins with custom, or social norms.

It would seem, then, that law follows custom. Law is based on the customs that are rooted in both tradition and morality. It would make sense that the laws of your city, state, or country would be based on long-standing notions of right and wrong that go back millennia. I suspect that you've read stories about courthouses displaying the Ten Commandments outside their doors until very recently.

Those who study law and society have found support for the notion that law follows custom. Sumner ([1906] 2019) and Savigny ([1831] 1975) both emphasize the role of mores and folkways. Law, they argue, reflects these social norms. Dror (1959) observes that the law often takes time to catch up with an often quickly changing society (789). Case studies of areas of law also show law following custom. These include laws on homelessness (Chambliss 1964), divorce (Friedman 2005), interracial marriage (Pascoe 2009) and adultery (Rhode 2016).

Law and Society scholars have also discovered support for the opposite conclusion. Dror (1959) argues that law influences custom in two ways. First, law can directly change custom. He gives the example of a law restricting polygamy as one that changes custom. Second, law can indirectly affect custom. If a law requires that all children attend school, this creates social change. Perhaps this change comes in part from the attitudes that school instills (Schur 1965).

Students of Law and Society have identified other ways that law changes society. Mayhew (1971) argues that change happens when courts give new procedural rights. The case *Gideon v. Wainwright*, for example, greatly expanded access to an attorney for poor defendants. Friedman (2005) finds that laws create new social relationships. This can happen when laws either tear apart old relationships or create new ones. President Barrack Obama's efforts to ultimately pass the Affordable Healthcare Act in 2010, for example, changed the relationship between healthcare providers and patients.

Anthropologist Stanley Diamond contributes a unique perspective to this debate. For Diamond, law does not follow custom, and custom does not take its cues from law. Rather, the two are alienated from each other.

Diamond contends that law does not follow custom. He finds that the laws bear little resemblance to the customs that they originated from. He argues that it doesn't make sense to claim that law follows custom when the law shares so little in common with customary social norms.

Diamond also asserts that custom does not follow law. He makes the point that law ultimately takes precedence over custom. Legality becomes the same as morality. Custom does not follow law because it has been replaced by it.

To support his position, Diamond describes the historical divergence between law and custom. At first, the link between law and custom was strong in smaller society composed of families and kin groups. As these societies grew, conflicts emerged, and those who won power changed the law to serve their interests.

For Diamond, law became the enemy of custom because those with power need it to maintain their own power. "Law and order is the historical illusion; law versus order is the historical reality," Diamond writes.

While reading Diamond's piece (Reading 6.1), there are many different things that you can consider. Think about modern laws. Do you think that they are disconnected from commonly held mores and social traditions? Has modern law become something completely alien to custom? If you follow Diamond's conception that social norms become law, is there any way back?

Reading 6.1

The Rule of Law Versus the Order of Custom*

Stanley Diamond

Creon: Knowest thou the edict has forbidden this?
Antigone: I knew it well. Why not? It was proclaimed.
Creon: But thou didst dare to violate the law?
Antigone: It was not God above who framed that law,
Nor justice, whispering from the underworld,
Nor deemed I thy decrees were of such force
As to o'er ride the sanctities of heaven;
Which are not of today or yesterday.
From whom—whence they first issued, no one knows.
I was not like to scant their holy rites
And brave the even justice of the gods
For fear of someone's edict.

(Sophocles, *Antigone*)

The lowest police employee of the civilized state has more "authority" than all the organs of gentilism combined. But the mightiest prince and the greatest statesman or general of civilization may look with envy on the spontaneous and undisputed esteem that was the privilege of the least gentile sachem. The one stands in the middle of society, the other is forced to assume a position outside and above it.

(Friedrich Engels, *Origin of the Family, Private Property and the State*)

* Author's Note—This [reading], in slightly different form, appears in *The Rule of Law*, Robert Paul Wolff, ed., New York: Simon & Schuster.

There's too much due process of law. The electric chair is a cheap crime deterrent to show these criminal elements that law and order is going to triumph.

(Detective Sergeant John Heffernan, current vice-president of the International Conference of Police Associations and head of the New Jersey State Police Benevolent Association)

I

We must distinguish the rule of law from the authority of custom. In a recent effort to do so (which I shall critically examine because it is so typical), Paul Bohannan, under the *imprimatur* of the *International Encyclopedia of the Social Sciences*,[1] contends that laws result from "double" institutionalization. He means by this no more than the lending of a specific force, a cutting edge, to the functioning of "customary" institutions: marriage, the family, religion. But, he tells us, the laws so emerging assume a character and dynamic of their own. They form a structured, legal dimension of society; they do not merely reflect, but interact with given institutions. Therefore, Bohannan is led to maintain that laws are typically out of phase with society and it is this process which is both a symptom and cause of social change. The laws of marriage, to illustrate Bohannan's argument with the sort of concrete example his definition lacks, are not synonymous with the institution of marriage. They reinforce certain rights and obligations while neglecting others. Moreover, they subject partners defined as truant to intervention by an external, impersonal agency whose decisions are sanctioned by the power of the police.

Bohannan's sociological construction does have the virtue of denying the primacy of the legal order, and of implying that law is generic to unstable (or progressive) societies, but it is more or less typical of abstract efforts to define the eternal essence of the law and it begs the significant questions. Law has no such essence but a definable historical nature.

Thus if we inquire into the structure of the contemporary institutions which, according to Bohannan, stand in a primary relation to the law, we find that their customary content has drastically diminished. Paul Radin made the point as follows: "A custom is, in no sense, a part of our properly functioning culture. It belongs definitely to the past. At best, it is moribund. But customs are an integral part of the life of primitive peoples. There is no compulsive submission to them. They are not followed because the weight of tradition overwhelms a man ... a custom is obeyed there because it is intimately intertwined with a

1 Paul Bohannan, "Law," *International Encyclopedia of the Social Sciences* (New York, 1968), pp. 73–78.

vast living network of interrelations, arranged in a meticulous and ordered manner."[2] And, "What is significant in this connection," as J. G. Peristiany indicates, "is not that common values should exist, but that they should be expressed although no common political organization corresponds to them."[3]

No contemporary institution functions with the kind of autonomy that permits us to postulate a significant dialectic between law and custom. We live in a law-ridden society; law has cannibalized the institutions which it presumably reinforces or with which it interacts.

Accordingly, morality continues to be reduced to or confused with legality. In civil society we are encouraged to assume that legal behavior is the measure of moral behavior, and it is a matter of some interest that a former Chief Justice of the Supreme Court proposed, with the best of intentions, that a federal agency be established in order to advise government employees and those doing business with the government concerning the legal propriety of their behavior. Any conflict of interest not legally enjoined would thus tend to become socially or morally acceptable; morality becomes a technical question. Efforts to legislate conscience by an external political power are the antithesis of custom: customary behavior comprises precisely those aspects of social behavior which are traditional, moral, and religious, which are, in short, conventional and non-legal. Put another way, custom *is* social morality.[4] The relation between custom and law is, basically, one of contradiction, not continuity.

The customary and the legal orders are historically, not logically related. They touch coincidentally; one does not imply the other. Custom, as most anthropologists agree, is characteristic of primitive society, and laws of civilization. Robert Redfield's dichotomy between the primitive "moral" order and the civilized "legal" or "technical" order remains a classic statement of the case.

"The dispute," writes William Seagle, "whether primitive societies have law or custom, is not merely a dispute over words. Only confusion can result from treating them as interchangeable phenomena. If custom is spontaneous and automatic, law is the product of organized force. Reciprocity is in force in civilized communities too but at least nobody

---

2 Paul Radin, *The World of Primitive Man,* New York, 1953, p. 223.

3 J. G. Peristiany, *The Institutions of Primitive Society,* Glencoe, Illinois, 1956, p. 45.

In the words of V. C. Uchendu, writing about the Ibo: "... the use of force is minimal or absent; ... there are leaders rather than rulers, and ... cohesion is achieved by rules rather than by laws and by consensus rather than by dictation. In general, the Igbo have not achieved any political structure which can be called a federation, a confederacy, or a state." V. C. Uchendu, *The Igbo of Southeast Nigeria,* N.Y. 1965, p. 46.

4 Sydney P. Simpson and Julius Stone, *Law and Society in Evolution*, Book I, Saint Paul, 1942, p.2.

confuses social with formal legal relationships."[5] Parenthetically, one should note that students of primitive society who use the term "customary law" blur the issue semantically, but nonetheless recognize the distinction.

It is this overall legalization of behavior in modern society which Bohannan fails to interpret. In fascist Germany, for example, laws flourished as never before. By 1941, more edicts had been proclaimed than in all the years of the Republic and the Third Reich. At the same time, ignorance of the law inevitably increased. In a sense, the very force of the law depends upon ignorance of its specifications, which is hardly recognized as a mitigating circumstance. As Seagle states, law is not definite and certain while custom is vague and uncertain. Rather, the converse holds. Customary rules must be clearly known; they are not sanctioned by organized political force, hence serious disputes about the nature of custom would destroy the integrity of society. But laws may always be invented, and stand a good chance of being enforced: "Thus, the sanction is far more important than the rule in the legal system ... but the tendency is to minimize the sanction and to admire the rule."[6]

In fascist Germany, customs did not become laws through a process of "double institutionalization." Rather, repressive laws, conjured up in the interests of the Nazi Party and its supporters, cannibalized the institutions of German society. Even the residual customary authority of the family was assaulted: children were encouraged to become police informers, upholding the laws against their kin. "The absolute reign of law has often been synonymous with the absolute reign of lawlessness"[7]

Certainly, Germany under Hitler was a changing society, if hardly a progressive one, but it was a special case of the general process in civilization through which the organs of the state have become increasingly irresistible. It will be recalled that Bohannan takes the domination of law over custom to be symptomatic of changing societies. But the historical inadequacy of his argument lies exactly here: he does not intimate the overall direction of that change and therefore fails to clarify the actual relation between custom and law. Accordingly, the notion that social change is a function of the law, and vice versa, implies a dialectic that is out of phase with historical reality.

Plato, it deserves note, understood this well enough when he conceived the problem of civilization as primarily one of injustice, which he did not scamp by legalistic definition. His remedy was the thorough restructuring of society. Whether we admire his utopia or not, *The Republic* testifies to Plato's recognition that laws follow social change and reflect prevailing social relationship, but are the cause of neither. Curiously, this view of the relationship

---

5 William Seagle, *The History of Law, Tudor,* 1946, p. 35.

6 *Ibid.*, pp. 19–20.

7 *Ibid.*

between law and society accords with the Marxist perspective on the history of culture. Customary societies are said to precede legal societies, an idea which, semantics aside, most students of historical jurisprudence would accept. But Marxists envision the future as being without laws as we know them, as involving a return to custom, so to speak, on a higher level, since the repressive, punitive and profiteering functions of law will become superfluous. Conflicts of economic and political interest will be resolved through the equitable reordering of institutions. Law, for the Marxists and most classical students of historical jurisprudence, is the cutting edge of the state—but the former, insisting on both a historical and normative view of man, define the state as the instrument of the ruling class, anticipating its dissolution with the abolition of classes and the common ownership of the basic means of production. Whatever our view of the ultimate Marxist dynamic, law is clearly inseparable from the state. Sir Henry Maine equates the history of individual property with that of civilization: "Nobody is at liberty to attack several property and to say at the same time that he values civilization. The history of the two cannot be disentangled. Civilization is nothing more than the name for the ... order ... dissolved but perpetually re-constituting itself under a vast variety of solvent influences, of which infinitely the most powerful have been those which have, slowly, and in some parts of the world much less perfectly than others, substituted several property for collective ownership."[8] In the words of Jeremy Bentham, "Property and law are born together and die together."

Law, thus, is symptomatic of the emergence of the state; the legal sanction is not simply the cutting edge of institutions at all times and in all places. The "double institutionalization" to which Bohannan refers needs redefinition. Where it does occur, it is an historical process of unusual complexity and cannot be defined as the simple passage of custom into law. It occurs, as we shall see, in several modes. Custom—spontaneous, traditional, personal, commonly known, corporate, relatively unchanging—is the modality of primitive society; law is the instrument of civilization, of political society sanctioned by organized force, presumably above society at large, and buttressing a new set of social interests. Law and custom both involve the regulation of behavior but their characters are entirely distinct; no evolutionary balance has been struck between developing law and custom, whether traditional or emergent.

II

The simple dichotomy between primitive society and civilization does not illustrate the passage from the customary to the legal order. The most critical and revealing period in

8 Henry Maine, *Village Communities and Miscellanies,* New York, 1889, p. 230.

the evolution of law is that of *archaic societies,* the local segments of which are the cultures most often studied by anthropologists. More precisely, the earlier phases of these societies, which I call proto-states, represent a transition from the primitive kinship-based communities to the class-structured polity. In such polities, law and custom exist side by side; this gives us the opportunity to examine their connections, distinctions, and differential relationship to the society at large. The customary behavior typical of the local groups—joint families, clans, villages—maintains most of its force; the Vietnamese, for example, still say: "The customs of the village are stronger than the law of the emperor." Simultaneously, the civil power, comprising bureaucracy and sovereign, the dominant emerging class, issues a series of edicts that have the double purpose of confiscating "surplus" goods and labor for the support of those not directly engaged in production while attempting to deflect the loyalties of the local groups to the center.

These archaic societies are the great historical watershed; it is here that Sir Henry Maine and Paul Vinogradoff located the passage from status to contract, from the kinship to the territorial principle, from extended familial controls to public law. One need not be concerned with the important distinctions among archaic societies, or with the precise language or emphases of those scholars who have recognized their centrality for our understanding of the law. The significant point is that they are transitional. Particularly in their early phase they are the agencies that transmute customary forms of order into legal sanction. Here we find a form of "double institutionalization" functioning explicitly; we can witness, so to speak, what appears to be the *emergence* of a custom, in defense of the kinship principle against the assault of the state, and the subsequent shift of the customary function into its own opposite as a legal function. The following example from the archaic proto-state of Dahomey, prior to the French conquest in 1892, will make this process clear.

Traditionally, in Dahomey each person was said to have three "best" friends, in descending order of intimacy and importance. This transitional institution, a transfiguration of kin connections, of the same species as blood brotherhood, reinforced the extended family structure, which continued to exist in the early state, but was being thrown into question as a result of the political and economic demands made by the emerging civil power. So, for example, the best friend of a joint-family patriarch would serve as his testator, and, upon the latter's decease, name his successor to the assembled family. It seems that the ordinary convention of succession no longer sufficed to secure the family's integrity, since the central authority was mustering family heads as indirect rulers. In this instance, the institution of friendship was assimilated to the form and purpose of customary behavior. On the other hand, the best friend of a man charged with a civil "crime" could be seized by the king's police in his stead. However, these traditional friendships were so socially critical, so deeply held that the person charged, whether or not he had actually committed a civil breach, would typically turn himself in rather than implicate a friend in his punishment. The custom of friendship was thus given a legal edge and converted by the civil power into a means of enforcing its will. This example of "double institutionalization" has the virtue of explicitly revealing the contradiction between law and custom; but there are others in which law appears as a *reinforcement* of customary procedure.

In eleventh century Russia, for instance, Article 1 of the codified law states, "If a man kills a man ... the brother is to avenge his brother; the son, his father; or the father, his son; and the son of the brother (of the murdered man) or the son of his sister, their respective uncle. If there is no avenger (the murderer) pays 40 grivna wergeld ..."[9]

Similarly, circa A.D. 700, the law of the Visigoths states, "Whoever shall have killed a man, whether he committed a homicide intending to or not intending to (*volens aut nolens*) ... let him be handed over into the potestas of the parents or next of kin of the deceased. ..."[10] In these instances, a custom has been codified by an external agency, thus assuming legal force with *its punitive character sharpened.* Such confirmation is both the *intimation* of legal control and the antecedent of institutional change beyond the wish or conception of the family. "Whatever princes do, they seem to command," or, as Sir Henry Maine put it, "What the sovereign permits, he commands."[11] Maine had specifically in mind "the Sikh despot who permitted heads of households and village elders to prescribe rules, therefore these rules became his command and true laws, which are the solvent of local and domestic usage." Simpson and Stone explain this apparent reinforcement of custom by the civil power as follows: "Turning then to the role of law in the emergent political society ... it is true that political institutions, independent of the kin and the supernatural, had risen to power; yet these institutions were young, weak and untried. Their encroachment on the old allegiance was perforce wary and hesitating. Social cohesion still seemed based on nonpolitical elements, and these elements were therefore protected. It is this society which Pound has perceived and expressed when he says that the end of law envisaged in his period of strict law, is the maintenance of the social *status quo.* In modern terminology this means the primacy of the interest in the maintenance of antecedent social institutions." (italics added)[12]

This sort of confirmation, which betrays the structural opportunism of the early civil power, inheres in the limitations of sovereignty, and is further apparent in the sovereign's relation to the communally held clan or joint-family land. In Dahomey, for example, where the king was said to "own" all property, including land, it is plain that such ownership was a

9 George Vernadsky, *Medieval Russian Laws,* 1947, pp. 26–27.

10 Quoted by Simpson and Stone, *op. cit.,* p. 78.

11 Henry Maine, *Early History of Institutions,* 1897, p. 383.

12 Simpson and Stone, *op. cit.,* p. 177.

legal fiction and had the effect of validating the pre-existent joint-family tradition. That is, the king "permitted" the joint families, by virtue of his fictional ownership, to expand into new lands and continue transmitting their property intact, generation after generation. The civil power could not rent, alienate or sell joint-family property, nor could any member of a joint family do so.[13] This is borne out by A. I. Richards, who informs us that "in Northern Rhodesia (Zambia) the statement that 'all the land is mine' does not mean that the ruler has the right to take any piece of land he chooses for his own use ... I have never heard of a case where a chief took land that had already been occupied by a commoner."[14] The same point is made by Rattray on the Ashanti[15] and Mair on the Baganda,[16] among others. Civil validation, then, expresses the intention but not yet the reality of state control. We might more realistically formulate Maine's epigram as: What he cannot command, the sovereign permits.

Ultimately, local groups have maintained their autonomy when their traditional economies were indispensable to the functioning of the entire society. They could be hedged around by restrictions, harassed by law, or, as we have seen, they could be "legally" confirmed in their customary usage; but, so long as the central power depended on them for support, in the absence of any alternative mode or source of production, their integrity could be substantially preserved. This certainly seems the case during the early phases of state organization in the classic nuclear areas (e.g., Egypt, Babylonia, Northern India) before the introduction of large-scale irrigation and analogous public works, and it was true of precolonial Africa. But in all archaic societies, whether incipient, as in sub-Saharan Africa, florescent, as in the ancient peasant societies of the Middle East or China, or in cognate contemporary societies which probably still embrace most of the world's population, the extensive kin unit was more functional, in spite of varying degrees of autonomy, than the family in commercial and industrial civilization.

As the state develops, according to Maine, "the individual is steadily substituted for the family as the unit of which civil laws take account."[17] And in Jhering's words, "The progress of law consists in the destruction of every natural tie, in a continued process of separation and isolation."[18] That is to say, the family increasingly becomes a reflex of society at large. Hence, one might add, the legal stipulation that spouses may not testify against each other

13 Stanley Diamond, *Dahomey, a Proto-state in West Africa,* Ann Arbor, Microfilm, 1951, p. 109.

14 Quoted by Max Gluckman, "Studies in African Land Tenure," *African Studies,* Vol. III, 1944, pp. 14–21.

15 R. S. Rattray, *Ashanti, Law and Constitution,* London, 1929.

16 L. P. Mair, "Baganda Land Tenure," *Africa,* Vol. VI, 1933.

17 Henry Maine, *Ancient Law,* p. 140.

18 R. von Jhering, *Geist des Romischen Recht,* 1866, Vol. II, p. 31.

appears as one of the last formal acknowledgements of familial integrity, and the exception that proves the historical case. Clearly, the nuclear family in contemporary urban civilization, although bound by legal obligations, has minimal autonomy; obviously, the means of education, subsistence and self-defense are outside the family's competence. It is in this sense that, given the absence of mediating institutions having a clearly defined independent authority, the historical tendency of all state structures vis-à-vis the individual may be designated as totalitarian. Indeed, the state *creates* the disaffiliated individual whose bearings thus become bureaucratic or collective; the juridical "person," who may even be a corporation doing business, is merely the legal reflection of a social process. If "totalization" is *the* state process, totalitarianism cannot be confined to a particular political ideology but is, so to speak, *the* ideology, explicit or not, of political society.

This étatist tendency has its origins in archaic society; we can observe it with unusual clarity in the proto-states of sub-Saharan Africa. In East Africa, pastoralists, competing for land, and in West Africa, militaristic clans, catalyzed by the Arab, and, later, the European trade, notably in slaves, conquered horticulturalists, thereby providing the major occasions for the growth of civil power. Since the basic means of exploiting the environment in these polities remained substantially unchanged, and, to some extent, survived under colonialism, we can reconstruct through chronicles extending back for centuries and by means of contemporary field work, the structure of early state controls, which evolved in the absence of writing and the systematic codification of law. The absence of writing *should* relieve the scholar from that dependence on official records that has so thoroughly shaped our sense of European history; unfortunately, rubbing shoulders with the upper class in a non-literate state creates equivalent distortions.

In such societies, Rattray tells us, referring to Ashanti, "the small state was ever confronted with the kindred organization which was always insidiously undermining its authority by placing certain persons outside its jurisdiction. It could only hold its own, therefore, by throwing out an ever-widening circle to embrace those loyalties which were lost to it owing to the workings of the old tribal organization which has survived everywhere."[19] Further, "the old family, clan and tribal organization survived in the new regime which was ever striving to make territorial considerations, and not the incidence of kinship, the basis of state control." Rattray concludes that "corporate responsibility for every act was an established principle which survived even the advent of a powerful central public authority as the administration of public justice."[20] Nadel asserts, concerning the Islamized Nupe of the Nigerian Middle Belt, that what emerged from his analysis was "a much more subtle development and a deeper

19 Rattray, *op. cit.*, p. 80.

20 *Ibid.*, p. 286.

kind of antagonism (than interstate warfare), namely, the almost eternal antagonism of developed State versus that raw material of the Community which, always and everywhere, must form the nourishing soil from which alone the state can grow."[21] And Engels refers to the "irreconcilable opposition of gentile society to the state."[22]

I have documented this conflict in detail in a study of the Dahomean proto-state. There, as elsewhere, it is apparent that the contradictory transition from customs to specified laws, "double institutionalization," if you will, *is by no means the major source of law.* Whether the law arises latently in "confirmation" of previous usage, or through the transformation of some aspect of custom, which the law itself may have, in the first instance, provoked, as in the example of the "best friend," neither circumstance brings us to the heart of the matter. For we learn by studying intermediate societies that the laws so typical of them are *unprecedented;* they do not emerge through a process of "double institutionalization," however defined. They arise in opposition to the customary order of the antecedent kin or kin-equivalent groups; they represent a new set of social goals pursued by a new and unanticipated power in society. These goals can be reduced to a single complex imperative: the imposition of the inter-related census-tax-conscription system. The territorial thrust of the early state, along with its vertical social entrenchment, demanded conscription of labor, the mustering of an army, the levying of taxes and tribute, the maintenance of a bureaucracy, and the assessment of the extent, location, and numbers of the population being subjected. *These were the major direct or indirect occasions for the development of civil law.*

The primary purpose of a census is indicative. Census figures (in non-literate societies, pebbles, for example, would be used as counters) provided the basis on which taxes were apportioned among the conquered districts and tribute in labor exacted from the constituent kin units. The census was also essential for conscripting men into the army. This information was considered so important in Dahomey that each new king, upon his enstoolment, was escorted by his two leading ministers to a special hut in the royal compound and there admonished as he knelt: "Young man, all your life you have heard Dahomey, Dahomey, but you have never until today seen the true Dahomey, for Dahomey is its people and here they are."[23]

With this declaration, the two elders pointed to sacks of pebbles, each pebble representing a person, each sack representing a sex or age group. The young king was then told that he must never allow the contents of the sacks to diminish and that every year the pebbles would be counted to see whether their number had increased or declined. He was then given

21 S. F. Nadel, "Nupe State and Community," *Africa,* Vol. VIII, p. 303.

22 Engels, p. 133 (see N. 58).

23 M. J. Herskowitz, *Dahomey, an Ancient West African Kingdom,* New York, 1938, p. 73.

an old gun (in earlier times a hoe handle) and advised, "Fight with this. But take care that you are not vanquished."[24]

The census figures represented the potential power of the state and were carefully guarded; perhaps they were the first state secret. The act and intent of the census turned persons into ciphers, abstractions in civil perspective; people did all they could to avoid being counted. Suspicion persists; even in the United States the authorities during the period of census taking find it necessary to assert that census information will not be used to tax or otherwise penalize the individual, and, in fact, to do so is said to be against the law.

The double meanings of certain critical terms in common English use—"custom," "duty," and "court," reveal this conflict between local usage and the census-tax-conscription system of the early state. We have been speaking of custom as traditional or conventional non-legal behavior, but custom also refers to a tax routinely payable to the state for the transportation of goods across territorial borders. All such taxes are clearly defined legal impositions, frequently honored in the breach, and they do not have the traditional command of custom. In Dahomey, the "Grand Customs" held at the unveiling of a new king, presumably in honor of his ancestors, were the occasion for the payment of taxes, the large-scale sentencing and sacrifice of criminals, and the prosecution of other state business. Camus has Caligula describe such an event in a passage that could have been extrapolated from a Dahomean chronicle: "It's only the Treasury that counts. And living is the opposite of loving ... and I invite you to the most gorgeous of shows, a sight for gods to gloat on, a whole world called to judgment. But for that I must have a crowd—spectators, victims, criminals, hundreds and thousands of them. Let the accused come forward. I want my criminals, and they are all criminals. Bring in the condemned men. I must have my public. Judges, witnesses, accused—all sentenced to death without a hearing. Yes, Ceasonia, I'll show them something they've never seen before, the one free man in the Roman Empire."[25] Along with the annual "customs," the "Grand Customs" paralleled the form of local ceremonies, but the substance had entirely changed. Fiscal or legal coercion, political imposition were not the purpose of these ancestral ceremonies which ritually re-enacted reciprocal bonds. The "customs" of the sovereign were laws, the ceremonies of the kin groups were customs.

Similarly, the term "duty" implies a moral obligation on the one hand and a tax on the other. Naturally, we assume that it is the duty of citizens to pay taxes: the paradox inherent in the term becomes more obvious, as one might imagine, as we examine archaic civilizations.

The term "court" is analogously ambivalent. On the one hand, it refers to the residence or entourage of the sovereign; on the other, to a place where civil justice is dispensed, but at

---

24 *Ibid.*

25 Albert Camus, *Caligula and Three Other Plays*, Stuart Gilbert (trans.), New York, 1958, p. 17.

their root the functions fuse. The prototypical juridical institution was, in fact, the court of the sovereign where legislation was instituted, for which no precedent or formal analogue existed on the local level. Peristiany, speaking of the Kipsigis, sharpens the latter point: "One of the most significant differences between the ... council of elders and a European judicature is to be found in the relation between officer and office. The Council elders do not hold their office from a higher authority. They are not appointed ..."[26] As Seagle, among others, indicates, the court is the first, most important, and perhaps the last legal artifact. In Montaigne's words, "France takes as its rule the rule of the court."[27] Put another way, the court is a specialized legal structure and it embraces all those particular and determinate legal bodies which are peculiar to civilization.

Clearly, the function of the court was not primarily the establishment of order. In primitive societies, as in the traditional sectors of proto-states, there already existed built-in mechanisms for the resolution of conflict. Generally speaking, as Max Gluckman, among others, has shown, in such societies conflicts generated by the ordinary functioning of social institutions were resolved as part of the customary ritual cycle integral to the institutions themselves.

With regard to more specific breaches, we recall Rattray's observation on the Ashanti: "Corporate responsibility for every act was an established principle which survived even the advent of ... the administration of public justice." That is to say the kin unit was the juridical unit, just as it was the economic and social unit. Furthermore, "Causes which give rise to the greater part of present 'civil' actions were practically nonexistent. Inheritance, ownership of moveable and non-moveable property, status of individuals, rules of behavior and morality were matters inevitably settled by the customary law, with which everyone was familiar from childhood, and litigation regarding such matters was ... almost inconceivable. Individual contract, moreover, from the very nature of the community with which we are concerned, was also unknown, thus removing another possible, fruitful source of litigation."[28]

The primary purpose of the historically emerging court, the sovereign's entourage and habitation, was to govern. The distinguished British jurist Sir John Salmond has observed, "Law is secondary and unessential. ... The administration of justice is perfectly possible

---

26 Peristiany, *op. cit.*, p. 42.

The contrast is well remarked by V. C. Uchendu: "Under a constitution like that of the Igbo, which does not provide for a specialized court, judicial matters are ad hoc affairs. The injured party takes the initiative. He may appeal to the head of the compound of the offender or to a body of arbitrators. ... Since the arbitrators have no means of enforcing their decision, for it to be respected it must be acceptable to both parties." Uchendu, *op. cit.*, p. 43.

27 Montaigne, (see N. 56 for full citation) p. 197.

28 Rattray, *op. cit.*, p. 286.

without law at all."[29] And Sir William Markby writes, "Tribunals can act entirely without law."[30] The perhaps unintended point here is that justice, commonly defined, is neither deducible from the law, nor was the legislation of the court a measure of justice, but of the political thrust of the early state, and that flowed from the implementation of the census-tax-conscription system.

In the census-tax-conscription system, every conceivable occasion was utilized for the creation of law in support of bureaucracy and sovereign. We observe no abstract principle, no impartial justice, no *precedent,* only the spontaneous opportunism of a new class designing the edifice of its power. It should be re-emphasized, however, that in certain instances formal analogues for civil imposition existed on the local level, but no formal or functional precedents. Civil taxation, for example, can be rationalized in the context of reciprocal gift-giving in the localities, but the latter was not confirmed by law, or specifically used by the sovereign; similarly, corvee labor is a political analogue of local cooperative work groups. But such evolutionary, and dialectical, relationships are most important for their distinctions.

Stubbs writes about the Norman kings that "it was mainly for the sake of the profits that early justice was administered at all."[31] Burton relates that at Whydah, in native Dahomey, in the event of a financial dispute the Yevogan, the leading bureaucrat in the district, sat in judgment. For his services, he appropriated half the merchandise involved, in the name of the king, and another quarter for various lesser officials. The remainder presumably went to the winning contestant in the judicial duel.[32] Among the Ashanti, the central authority relied on the proceeds of litigation as a fruitful means for replenishing a depleted treasury. Litigation, Rattray notes, came actually to be encouraged.[33]

Tolls were an important source of revenue. In Ashanti, the king had all the roads guarded; all traders were detained until inquiries were made about them, whereupon they were allowed to pass on payment of gold dust.[34] W. Bosnian writes that in early eighteenth century Whydah, the king's revenue "in proportion to his country is very large, of which I believe, he hath above one thousand collectors who dispose themselves throughout the whole land in all market roads and passages, in order to gather the king's toll which amounts to an incredible sum, for there is nothing so mean sold in the whole kingdom that the king hath no toll for it. ..."[35]

---

29 Sir John Salmond, *Jurisprudence,* 1920, p. 13.

30 Sir William Markby, *Elements of Law,* 1905, p. 21.

31 William Stubbs, *The Constitutional History of England,* London, 1890, Vol. I, p. 48.

32 Burton, Richard F., *A Mission to Gelele, a King of Dahomey,* London, 1864, Vol. II, p. 211.

33 Rattray, *op. cit.,* p. 292.

34 Rattray, *op. cit.,* p. 111.

35 W. Bosman, *A New and Accurate Description of the Coast of Guinea,* London, 1705, p. 362.

The punishment for the theft of property designated as the king's was summary execution by "kangaroo courts" organized on the spot by the king's agents.[36] This is echoed in the code of Hammurabi: "if a man steals the property of a god (temple) or a palace, that man shall be put to death; and he who receives from his hands the stolen (property) shall also be put to death."[37] Where the king's property was concerned, no judicial duel was possible. In these instances, which could be endlessly multiplied, we witness the extension of the king's peace, the primary form of the civil "order," actually the invention and application of sumptuary law through the subsidiary peaces of highway and market. In Maitland's words, "the king has a peace that devours all others." If, in these proto-states, the sovereign power is not yet fully effective, it nonetheless strives to that monopoly of force which characterizes the mature state.

The purpose and abundance of laws inevitably provoked breaches. The civil authority, in fact, continually probed for breaches and frequently manufactured them. In Dahomey, for example, a certain category of the king's women were distributed to the local villages and those men who made the mistake of having intercourse with them were accused of rape, for which the punishment, following a summary trial, was conscription into the army.[38] Thus, rape was invented as a *civil* crime. If rape had, in fact, occurred in the traditional joint-family villages—and such an occurrence would have been rare, as indicated by the necessity of civil definition—the wrong could have been dealt with by composition (the ritualized giving of goods to the injured party), ritual purification, ridicule, and, perhaps, for repeated transgressions, banishment; the customary machinery would have gone into effect automatically, probably on the initiative of the family of the aggressor. Such instances as this only sharpen the point that in early states crimes seem to have been invented to suit the laws; the latent purpose of the law was punishment in the service and profit of the state, not prevention or the protection of persons, not the *healing* of the breach. As Seagle indicates, "The criminal law springs into life in every great period of class conflict," and this is most obviously the case during the initial phases of state formation.

In its civil origins, then, a correlation existed between law and crime which partook of entrapment. One may even state that the substantial rationale for law developed *after* the fact of its emergence. For example, civil protection of the market place or highway was certainly not necessary to the degree implied in the archaic edicts at the time they were issued. Joint-family markets and village trails were not ordinarily dangerous places, if we are to

36 R. Norris, *Reise nach Abomey, der Hofstadt des Königs von Dahomey an von Guinea im Jahr 1772*, Leipzig, 1790, p. 221 ff.

37 *Code of Hammurabi*, Harper translation, 1904, paragraph 6, p. 13.

38 A. Le Herisse, *L'Ancien Royaume du Dahomey*, Paris, 1911, p. 72.

believe the reports of the earliest chroniclers, as well as those of more contemporary observers. Moreover, if trouble had developed, the family, clan or village was capable of dealing with it. But, in an evolving conquest state, the presence of the king's men would itself be a primary cause of disruption. Indeed, as M. Quénum, a descendant of Dahomean commoners, informs us in a remarkable work, the soldiers were referred to as bandits and predators who victimized many people. Sometimes their forays were confined to a single compound, where someone, whether man, woman or child, resided who had spoken badly of the sovereign or whom the king suspected.[39] In common parlance, the very names of the elite army units became insults; one meant "nasty person," another "arrogant person," and one would say of a tragic event that it was worthy of yet another military cadre. It is, therefore, understandable that the peace of the highway became an issue.[40]

As the integrity of the local groups declined, a process which, in the autochthonous state, must have taken generations or even centuries, conditions doubtless developed which served as an *ex post facto* rationalization for edicts already in effect. In this sense, laws became self-fulfilling prophecies. Crime and the laws which served it were, then, co-variants of the evolving state.

Just as entrapment was characteristic of early civil law, the idea of protection, in the sense of a protection racket, also inheres in its origins. In Dahomey, we are told by Norris and others, prostitution was encouraged by the civil power and prostitutes were distributed through the villages, the price of their favors being set by civil decree. They were obliged to offer themselves to any man who could pay the moderate fee and once a year were convened at the "annual customs" where they were heavily taxed.[41] Skertchly notes that the prostitutes were licensed by the king and placed in the charge of the Mew, the second leading bureaucrat, who was entrusted with the task of "keeping up the supply."[42] Bosman observes at Whydah that "for every affair that can be thought of, the king hath appointed a captain overseer."[43] *What the king permits, he commands; what he "protects" he taxes.*

The intention of the civil power is epitomized in the sanctions against homicide and suicide, typical of early polities; indeed they were among the very first civil laws. Just as the sovereign is said to own the land, intimating the mature right of eminent domain, so the individual is ultimately conceived as the chattel of the state. In Dahomey, persons were conceived as *les choses du monarque*. Eminent domain in persons and property, even where

39 M. Quénum, *Au Pays des Fons*, Paris, 1938, p. 7.

40 Quénum, pp. 21–22.

41 Norris, *op. cit.*, p. 257.

42 Skertchly, *Dahomey As It Is*, London, 1874, p. 283.

43 Bosman, *op. cit.*, p. 361.

projected as a fiction, is, of course, the cardinal prerequisite of the census-tax-conscription system. We recall that Maine designated the individual the unit of which the civil law steadily takes account. Seagle stated the matter as follows: "By undermining the kinship bond, they (the early civil authorities) made it easier to deal with individuals, and the isolation of the individual is a basic precondition for the growth of law."[44]

Homicide, then, was regarded as an offense against the state. In Rattray's words, "The blow which struck down the dead man would thus appear to have been regarded as aimed also at the ... central authority."[45] In Ashanti homicide was punishable by death in its most horrible form; in Dahomey, by death or conscription into the army. There is a nuance here which should not be overlooked. By making homicide, along with the theft of the king's property, a capital offence, the sovereign power discouraged violent opposition to the imposition of the civil order.

Traditionally, murder in a joint-family village was a tort—a private, remediable wrong—which could stimulate a blood feud, not to be confused with the lex talionis, until redress, which did not imply equivalent injury, was achieved. But a breach was most often settled by composition. As Paul Radin put it: "The theory of an eye for an eye ... never really held for primitive people ... rather it was replacement for loss with damages."[46] And this is echoed by Peristiany: "... they claim restitution or private damages and not social retribution."[47] In any case, the family was fully involved. "The family was a corporation," said Rattray, "it is not easy to grasp what must have been the effect ... of untold generations of thinking and acting ... in relation to one's group. The Ashanti's idea of what we term moral responsibility for his actions must surely have been more developed than in peoples where individualism is the order of the day."[48] This more or less typical anthropological observation makes it clear that the law against homicide was not a "progressive" step, as if some abstract right were involved which the state, coming of age, finally understands and seeks to establish. "Anti-social conduct (is) exceptional in small kinship groups," writes Margery Perham of

44 Seagle, *op. cit.*, p. 64. Quénum had a poor opinion of the ethnographers who claimed to understand and interpret his country. They failed, he believed, because of inadequate sources of information, and (or) ignorance of social customs. "Most of our ethnographers," he wrote, "have had as collaborators princes and ex-ministers of state and have believed their tales." He adds that ignorance of the native language and deficient sympathy compounded the problem. The point to note here is that Quénum is objecting to the view from the top which is a critical issue in the writing of all political history.

45 Rattray, *op. cit.*, p. 295.

46 Radin, *op. cit.*, p. 252.

47 Peristiany, *op. cit.*, p. 43.

48 Radin, *op. cit.*, p. 62.

the Ibo.[49] Crimes of violence were rare, Richard Burton reported of Dahomey, and "murder virtually unknown."[50] Of course, as with other crimes defined by civil law, they may have increased as the social autonomy, economic communalism, and reciprocity of the kin units weakened. But this is much less important than Dalzel's observation that in Dahomey "many creatures have been put to death ... without having committed any crime at all,"[51] thus exemplifying the power of the sovereign literally to command the lives of his citizens. The threat and example of summary execution, especially but by no means exclusively evident at the mortuary celebrations of "Grand Customs" on the enstooling of a king, encouraged obedience to civil injunctions.

The law against suicide, a capital offense, was the apotheosis of political absurdity. The individual, it was assumed, had no right to take his own life; that was the sole prerogative, presumably, of the state, whose property he was conceived to be.

The fanatical nature of the civil legislature in claiming sole prerogative to the lives of its subjects is conclusively revealed among the Ashanti, where, if the suicide was a murderer, "the central authority refused to be cheated thus and the long arm of the law followed the suicide to the grave from which, if his kinsmen should have dared to bury him, he was dragged to stand trial."[52] (One recalls Antigone's defiance.) This contrasts remarkably, if logically, with the behavior of the more primitively structured Ibo, as reported by Victor Uchendu, an anthropologist who is himself an Ibo: "Homicide is an offense against ala—the earth deity. If a villager is involved, *the murderer is expected to hang himself,* after which ... daughters of the village perform the rite of ... sweeping away the ashes of murder. If the murderer has fled, his extended family must also flee, and the property of all is subject to raids. When the murderer is eventually caught, he is required to hang himself to enable the daughters of

49 Margery Perham, *Native Administration in Nigeria,* London, 1962, pp. 229 ff.

50 Burton, *op. cit.,* p. 56.

Acts of violence must be distinguished from *crimes* of violence. The incidence, occasions for, and character of violence in primitive, as opposed to civilized societies, is a subject of the utmost importance, which I have discussed elsewhere (see footnote 52). But the question here has to do with crimes in which violence is used as a means for, e.g., the theft of property. In contemporary societies unpremeditated acts of personal violence which have no ulterior motive, so-called crimes of passion, may not be penalized or carry minor degrees of guilt, that is, their status as legally defined crimes is ambiguous. This would certainly seem to reflect a historically profound distinction between crime and certain types of violence. In primitive societies violence tends to be personally structured, non-dissociative, and, thereby, self-limiting.

51 A. Dalzel, *The History of Dahomey, an inland kingdom of Africa,* etc., London, 1793, p. 212.

52 Rattray, *op. cit.,* p. 299.

the village to perform their rites. It is important to realize that the village has no power to impose capital punishment. In fact, no social group or institution has this power. Everything affecting the life of the villager is regulated by custom. The life of the individual is highly respected; it is protected by the earth-goddess. The villagers can bring social pressure, but the murderer must hang himself."[53]

It can hardly be argued that the purpose of the civil sanction against suicide was to diminish its incidence or to propagate a superior moral consciousness. Dare we say, as with other crimes, that attempts at suicide increased as society became more thoroughly politicized? The law against suicide reveals, in the extreme, the whole meaning and intent of civil law at its origins. In the proto-state, the quintessential struggle was over the lives and labor of the people, who, still moving in a joint family context, were nonetheless conceived to be *less choses du monarque.*

III

If revolutions are the acute, episodic signs of civilizational discontent, the rule of law, in seven millennia of political society, from Sumer or Akkad to New York or Moscow, has been the chronic symptom of the disorder of institutions. E. B. Tylor stated, "A constitutional government, whether called republic or kingdom, is an arrangement by which the nation governs itself by means of the machinery of a military despotism."[54]

The generalization lacks nuance but we can accept it if we bear in mind Tylor's point of reference: "Among the lessons to be learnt from the life of rude tribes is how society can go on without the policeman to keep order."[55] When he alludes to constitutional government, Tylor was not distinguishing its ultimate sanction from that of any other form of the state: all political society is based on repressive organized force. In this he was accurate. For pharaohs and presidents alike have always made a public claim to represent the common interest, indeed to incarnate the common good. Only a Plato or a Machiavelli in search of political harmony, or a Marx in search of political truth, has been able to penetrate this myth of the identity between ruler and ruled, of equality under law. The tradition of Plato and Machiavelli commends the use of the "royal" or "noble lie," while that of Marx exposes and rejects the power structure (ultimately the state) that propagates so false a political consciousness. On this issue, I follow Marx.

---

53 Uchendu, *op. cit.*, pp. 42–43.

54 E. B. Tylor, *Anthropology*, Vol. II, London, 1946, p. 156.

55 *Ibid.*, p. 134.

Tylor distinguishes the civilized from the primitive order. Such a distinction has been made at every moment of crisis in the West but nowhere so pertinently as in Montaigne's contrast of a primitive society with Plato's ideally civilized republic: "This is a nation, I should say to Plato, in which there is no sort of traffic, no knowledge of letters, no science of numbers, no name for a magistrate or for political superiority, no custom of servitude, no riches or poverty, no contracts, no successions, no partitions ... no care for any but common kinship. How far from this perfection would he find the Republic he imagines!"[56] The issue of law and order implicit in Montaigne's contrast between primitive and civilized societies has been a persistent underlying theme for the most reflective and acute minds of the West. The inquiry into the nature of politics probably demarcates most accurately the boundaries of our intellectual landscape. The evolution of the state toward what Max Weber called maximally politicized society, the unprecedented concentration of bureaucratic and technological power, which economically and culturally dominates the rest of the world, creates a climate in which all problems cast a political shadow. We may flee from the political dimension of our experience or we may embrace it in order to do away with it, but we are obsessed by politics. It was perhaps Plato's primary virtue that, at the very origin of the Western intellectual tradition, he understood that, in civilization, all significant human problems have a political aspect and he insisted upon the solution of the latter as a coefficient of the creative resolution of the former. *The Republic* is the first civilizational utopia, and it maintains its force both as a model of inquiry and as antithesis to all projections of the nature of primitive society. Any contrary view of the possibilities of human association must take *The Republic* into account.

The legal order, which Plato idealized, is as Tylor maintained and Marx understood, synonymous with the power of the state. "The state," writes Paul Vinogradoff, "has assumed the monopoly of political co-ordination. It is the state which rules, makes laws and eventually enforces them by coercion. Such a state did not exist in ancient times. The commonwealth was not centered in one sovereign body towering immeasurably above single individuals and meting out to everyone his portion of right."[57] And Engels, reflecting on the origins of the

56 Michel de Montaigne, *The Complete Essays,* trans. Donald Frame, Stanford, 1965. In ignorance of Montaigne's contrast between primitive society and Plato's ideal republic, I published an article, "Plato and the Definition of the Primitive," *Culture in History,* New York, 1960, which explicates some of the points briefly noted above. For a more comprehensive model of primitive society see my "The Search for the Primitive" in *Man's Image in Medicine and Anthropology,* New York, 1963, edited by I. Galdston, pp. 62–115. In order to understand the functioning of custom in primitive society fully, one should have such a model in mind. Unfortunately, in this [reading] I can only suggest its outlines.

57 Paul Vinogradoff, *Outlines of Historical Jurisprudence,* Vol. I, London, 1920, p. 93.

state, asserts: "The right of the state to existence was founded on the preservation of order in the interior and the protection against the barbarians outside, but this order was worse than the most disgusting disorder, and the barbarians against whom the state pretended to protect its citizens were hailed by them as saviors."[58] Moreover, "The state created a public power of coercion that did no longer coincide with the old self-organized and (self) armed population."[59] Finally, in a passage that epitomizes the West's awareness of itself, Engels writes: "The state, then, is by no means a power forced on society at a certain stage of evolution. It is the confession that this society has become hopelessly divided against itself, has estranged itself in irreconcilable contradictions which it is powerless to banish. In order that these contradictions, these classes with conflicting economic interests may not annihilate themselves and society in a useless struggle, a power becomes necessary that stands apparently above society and has the function of keeping down the conflicts and maintaining 'order.' And this power, the outgrowth of society, but assuming supremacy over it and becoming more and more divorced from it, is the state. ..."[60] In a word, the state is the alienated form of society: and it is this process which has fascinated the Western intellect and which may, in fact, have led to the peculiar intensity of the reflective, analytic, and introspective consciousness in the West, to our search for origins and our inexhaustible concern with secular history. A knowledge of one's present, as Montaigne maintained, implies not only a knowledge of one's past but of one's future.

However we project, imagine, or reconstruct the past, we recognize the division, the objective correlate of the division within ourselves, between primitive and civilized society, between moral and civil order, between custom and law. Interpretation of the nature of the primitive and the civilized has, of course, not been uniform. Hobbes versus Rousseau is paradigmatic. But most theorists tend to see civilization as a kind of fall from a "natural," or at least more natural, to a legal or more repressive order. No matter how the virtues of civilization are weighed, the price exacted is inevitably noted. This is as true of Plato as of Freud or Engels. Plato, for example, notes, however inadequately, a condition of existence prior to the city-state, a type of rusticity which he views nostalgically and whose destruction he maintains was socioeconomically determined. I suspect that even the great majority of anthropologists, despite professional illusions of dissociated objectivity, sense that primitive societies are somehow closer than civilized societies to the realization of "natural" law and "natural" right. I believe this emphasis in the Western tradition to be the sounder, and it serves as the basis of my own thinking. There is, as Montaigne noted, an "amazing

---

58 Friedrich Engels, *Origin of the Family, Private Property and the State,* Chicago, 1902, p. 179.

59 *Ibid.,* p. 207.

60 *Ibid.,* p. 206.

distance" between the primitive character and our own. In the contrast between these two sides of our historical nature, which we existentially re-enact, we come to understand law as the antonym and not the synonym of order.

IV

I agree with Nadel that in the transition from primitive to political society the means of control and integration employed were, in a wider sense, "all ... deliberately conceived and (executed): they are agencies of an assimilation conscious of itself and of the message which it carries."[61] Finally, we are led to ask, as did Nadel about the Nupe: "What did the tax-paying law-abiding citizen receive in return for allegiance to king and nobility? Was extortion, bribery, brutal force, the only aspect under which the state revealed itself to the populace? The people were to receive, theoretically, on the whole, one thing: security—protection against external and internal enemies, and general security for carrying out the daily work, holding markets, using the roads. We have seen what protection and security meant in reality. At their best, they represented something very unequal and very unstable. This situation must have led to much tension and change within the system and to frequent attempts to procure better safeguards for civil rights."[62]

The struggle for civil rights, then, is a response to the imposition of civil law. With the destruction of the primitive base of society, civil rights have been defined and redefined as a reaction to drastic changes in the socioeconomic structure, the rise of caste and class systems, imperialism, modern war, technology as a means of social exploitation, maldistribution and misuse of resources, racial hatred. The right to socially and economically fruitful work, for example, which did not come into question in a primitive society or in a traditional sector of an early state (and therefore was not conceived to be a stipulated right) becomes an issue under capitalism. The demand implies a need for profoundly changing the system and indicates that our sense of the appropriately human has very ancient roots indeed. However, we are reminded by the struggle for civil rights, that legislation alone has no force beyond the potential of the social system that generates it. From the study of proto-states we also learn that the citizen must be constantly alert to laws which seek to curb his rights in the name of protection or security. Restrictive legislation is almost always a signal of repressive institutional change, but is, of course, not the cause of it.

The major focus of the defense of the citizen as a person can only be on procedure or, as we call it in our own society, due process. Quénum reports, of the early state of Dahomey,

---

61 S. F. Nadel, *A Black Byzantium,* London, New York, Toronto, 1942, p. 144.

62 Nadel, "Nupe State and Community," *Africa,* Vol. VIII, p. 287.

"There was no penal code promulgated ... punishment had no fixity ... the Miegan (leading bureaucrat, chief judge, and executioner) would become restive if capital punishment would be too long in coming."[63] In the words of Dalzel, "There was a vast disproportion between crimes and punishments."[64] And in early states, most if not all civil breaches were what we would define as crimes, just as in primitive societies "civil crimes" were considered, where they were not unprecedented, torts or private remediable wrongs. As every intelligent lawyer knows, the substance of the law can hardly be assimilated to morality. It is clear, therefore, why Jhering insisted that "Form is the sworn enemy of unlimited discretion (of the sovereign power) and the twin sister of freedom."[65] The degrees of theft or homicide, the question of double jeopardy, habeas corpus, the right to counsel, the question of legitimate witness, trial by jury and the selection of jurors, protection against summary search and seizure, the very division between civil and criminal law—these intricacies of procedure are the primary, but far from absolute, assurance of whatever justice can be obtained under the rule of law.

For example, the only way dissidents in Russia can defend themselves against summary punishment and make their cases universally understandable is by calling attention to abuses of procedure. The spirit of the laws, mummified in the excellent constitution of 1936, is irrelevant, abstract. The tribunal that discharges the intentions of the state can discard, suspend, reinterpret, and invent laws at will. The court, not the constitution, is the primary legal reality. And the politically inspired charge of insanity, which can remove dissidents from the body politic altogether, is the ultimate étatistic definition of the person—a non-being incapable of autonomy. And that, I should note, is foreshadowed in the consummate anti-Socratic Platonism of the Laws, the heavenly city brought to earth, wherein the ordinary citizen is "to become, by long habit, utterly incapable of doing anything at all independently."

Procedure is the individual's last line of defense in contemporary civilization, wherein all other associations to which he may belong have become subordinate to the state. The elaboration of procedure then, is a unique, if fragile, feature of more fully evolved states, in compensation, so to speak, for the radical isolation of the individual. In the proto-states, the harshness of rudimentary procedure was countered by the role of the kinship units which, as we recall, retained a significant measure of functional socioeconomic autonomy and, therefore, of local political cohesion.

But "law has its origin in the pathology of social relations and functions only when there are frequent disturbances of the social equilibrium."[66] Law arises in the breach of a prior

63 Quénum, *op. cit.*, p. 22.

64 Dalzel, *op. cit.*, p. 212.

65 Jhering, *op. cit.*, Vol. II, p. 471.

66 Seagle, *op. cit.*, p. 36.

customary order and increases in force with the conflicts that divide political societies internally and among themselves. Law *and* order is the historical illusion; law versus order is the historical reality.

In the tradition of Rousseau, Lévi-Strauss, in a moment of candor, declares, "We must go beyond the evidence of the injustices and abuses to which the social order gives rise, and discover the unshakable basis of human society ... Anthropology shows that base cannot be found in our own civilization, ours is indeed perhaps the one furthest from it."[67]

The progressive reduction of society to a series of technical and legal signals, the consequent diminution of culture, i.e., of reciprocal, symbolic meanings, are perhaps the primary reasons why our civilization is the one least likely to serve as a guide to "the unshakable basis of human society."

CHAPTER 6 QUESTIONS

1. What is Paul Bohannan's re*institutionalization* (Diamond uses *double institutionalization* instead) (See What is Law for a definition)? According to Diamond, what does he get right and what does he get wrong?
2. Why does Diamond state that morality is confused with legality?
3. What does Diamond mean when he says that law and custom are historically linked? How does this relate to Bohannan's notion of *reinstitutionalization?*
4. For Diamond, what is the connection between the many laws passed by the Nazi government and German customs?
5. Diamond tells us that custom does very little to influence law. What about the inverse? Can law influence custom?
6. For Marxists, what is the future of law?
7. Briefly describe the transition from custom to law that societies undergo.
8. Does the family or individual take priority as the state develops?
9. Diamond takes the side of custom over law. Do you agree with him? Would you rather be governed by law or custom?
10. How does Diamond's statement at the end of Reading 6.1 that "Law and order is the historical illusion; law versus order is the historical reality" encapsulate his argument?

---

67 Claude Lévi-Strauss, *A World on the Wane,* New York, 1961, p. 390.

Chapter 7

Law and Racial Discrimination

On December 7, 1941, the Japanese Imperial Navy attacked Pearl Harbor, an American naval base harboring much of the American fleet. The surprise attack provoked nationalism and strong anti-Japanese sentiment in the United States. President Franklin D. Roosevelt responded to the attacks in part by issuing an executive order that interred Americans of Japanese descent in camps.

In 1942, Fred Korematsu, a 23-year-old Japanese American, defied orders by the American government to leave his home in San Leandro, California, and relocate to a camp. Following his arrest and subsequent detainment, Korematsu challenged his arrest and conviction on the grounds that the government's actions violated the Constitution's Fifth Amendment, which reads, "No personal shall ... be deprived of life, liberty or property, without due process of law" (US Constitution, amend. 5, sec. 1).

In *Korematsu v. United States* (1944), which advanced to the US Supreme Court, the justices ruled in a 6–3 decision that the government acted appropriately. In his majority opinion, Chief Justice Hugo declared that "Korematsu was not excluded ... because of hostility to him or his race." Justice Frank Murphy was nonetheless not convinced, writing "Racial discrimination in any form and any degree has no justifiable part whatever in our democratic way of life."

This was not the first time that the justices of the Supreme Court had ruled on cases addressing race. The most infamous ruling was in *Dred Scott v. Sandford* (1857). In the case, Dred Scott, a slave, sued for his personal freedom first in the Missouri courts and then the federal courts after his "owners" had taken him to Illinois and the Wisconsin Territory, where slavery was not allowed.

Ultimately, the Court ruled against Scott, and it did so based on race. Chief Justice Roger Taney stated that Black people were seen as "beings of an inferior order" by the "civilized portion of the white race" at the time the Declaration of Independence and Constitution were written;

additionally, African Americans were not citizens of the United States. Consequently, Scott did not have the right to bring his case to federal court.

The courts have continued to decide cases that involve race. Often, these cases involve the conduct of the police. In 1991, police officers beat Rodney King, a 25-year-old Black man, during a traffic stop in Los Angeles. A protest erupted after jurors acquitted three of the four officers. Similarly, the death of George Floyd sparked protests after Floyd, a 46-year-old Black man, died in police custody in Minneapolis.

Black Americans have increasingly found themselves behind bars. Attorney Michelle Alexander describes the historical development of mass incarceration beginning with presidents Richard Nixon and Ronald Reagan in her book *The New Jim Crow: Mass Incarceration in the Age of Colorblindness* (2020).

Alexander argues that mass incarceration was by design. In the 1980s, the United States and its courts moved in a conservative direction. The Rehnquist Court gave more power to police, weakening Fourth Amendment search and seizure protections (2020, 87–89). In addition, the Reagan administration gave money and other incentives to local police departments to aggressively enforce the laws against drug trafficking, selling, and use (100–102).

Once convicted, Black Americans discovered themselves caught in a caste system very similar to ones that had existed in the past. Shunned by society, those convicted of minor offenses found themselves unable to gain equal access to employment, housing, and other necessities (124–127).

Alexander notes that surveys show that today most white people do not affirm racist beliefs (132). If Americans have truly embraced "colorblindness," it is unlikely that Black people and people from other minority groups are disproportionately incarcerated because of their race. The assumption, then, is that they must run afoul of the law because they commit more crime.

Both the courts and social scientists have considered whether policing is racially biased. Today police can search you based on both reasonable suspicion and probable cause. In *Floyd v. City of New York* (2013), judge Shira Scheindlin found that the New York City Police Department's "stop and frisk" policy was racially discriminatory and violated the equal protection clause of the Fourteenth Amendment.

In her opinion, Judge Scheindlin noted that 88 percent of those stopped were innocent, with only 6 percent of apprehensions resulting in either an arrest or summons. Scheindlin also observed that whites who were frisked were the most likely to have a weapon on them yet they were much less likely than Blacks and Hispanics to have physical force used against them.

A subsequent study agreed with Scheindlin, finding that stop-and-frisk programs in New York and other cities violated the constitutional rights of Black people and people from other minority groups (White and Fradella 2016). A study of traffic stops in Los Angeles by Ian

Aryes and Jonathan Borowsky for the American Civil Liberties Union (2008) reached the same conclusion. A Maryland study found that Black drivers were stopped 70 percent of the time on Interstate 95 near Baltimore. Yet they were only 17 percent of the drivers (Alexander 2020, 141). A study of the New Jersey Turnpike found that police pulled over Black drivers in 42 percent of the stops, thought these drivers represented only 15 percent of all drivers on the turnpike (131–132).

In *Suspect Citizens: What 20 Million Traffic Stops Tell Us*, Frank R. Baumgartner, Derek A. Epp, and Kelsey Shoub try to answer this question using data collected by the State of North Carolina beginning in 1999. The data included each traffic stop, regardless of whether an arrest or citation occurred, and included demographic information about the driver.

In their first chapter (Reading 7.1), they summarize their findings, which agree with the research described above: police in North Carolina stopped and detained Black and minority drivers at a disproportionately high rate. They also describe some of the issues and debates surrounding police bias. These include the new versus old policing style, the erosion of Fourth Amendment protections, the effect that aggressive policing has on communities, racial profiling, and causes of disparities in interactions with police.

Reading 7.1

Suspect Citizens: Fighting the War on Crime with Traffic Stops

Frank R. Baumgartner, Derek A. Epp, and Kelsey Shoub

On a cold December morning in 2012, Durham Police Officer Kelly Stewart, working undercover from an unmarked car, observed Carlos Riley drive off from a "known drug area" (actually, not far from the Duke University campus) in his red two-door car after conversing with an individual through the open passenger window. Officer Stewart pulled the car over, identified himself as a detective, asked the driver to get out of the vehicle, frisked him and checked his identification. After submitting to the frisk, Mr. Riley got back into his car, with the engine still running, and attempted to drive away. Officer Stewart, standing right at the open door to the car, lunged inside and was able to put on the emergency brake, bringing the car to an abrupt stop. Then, while engaged in a close physical struggle, he tried to put handcuffs on the driver, but Riley fought off that attempt. The officer pulled his service revolver from his holster, pointed it at the driver, and the struggle continued. With the officer holding his gun with both hands and Mr. Riley attempting to deflect it from being aimed directly at him, a shot was fired. The officer was hit in the leg; accounts differ as to who was holding the gun. With the officer shot and in pain, Mr. Riley pushed him from the car and drove off. The officer's badge and handcuffs had fallen into the car, and Riley had possession of the gun.

In a Durham courtroom three years later, Carlos Riley was acquitted on all charges associated with the shooting of Officer Stewart. Evidence presented showed that Officer Stewart had engaged in a pattern of racially profiling drivers, with Attorney Alex Charns noting that more than 76 percent of the traffic stops he made had been of African-American males. The particular stop that led to the confrontation was not recorded at all in the police database. Community organizers and minority residents in Durham argued that the case reflected broad patterns of "racial profiling, police abuse, and illegal searches" (Bridges 2015a). Riley faced charges of reckless driving, robbery with a dangerous weapon, assault on a law enforcement officer inflicting serious injury, assault on a law enforcement officer with a vehicle, and assault on a law enforcement officer with a gun. In the 2015 Durham trial, the jury likely concluded that Officer Stewart had conducted a legally suspect search following a racial profiling incident, that he had shot himself during a struggle, and that Mr. Riley was guilty only of robbery (driving away in possession of the officer's gun, handcuffs, and badge). In any event, none of the charges of assault on the officer were sustained, nor was the reckless driving charge which was the initial justification for the stop (see Bridges 2015b). We can never know, of course, exactly what the jury was thinking or collectively concluded, but with their verdict they made clear that the official version of events, presented by the officer and his legal team, did not sway them.

This is highly unusual. How was it that a jury acquitted a person accused of shooting an officer, particularly a young African-American male with a felony record? (Carlos Riley had previously pled guilty to federal gun possession charges.) What drove a jury of twelve North Carolinians to such a verdict? In most American communities, citizens trust the police. Police testimony in court is typically treated with considerable deference, especially in comparison with young men accused of serious crimes and with previous felony convictions. Moreover, the facts of the case, in particular the shooting of an officer in an altercation with a civilian, were not seriously disputed. Rather, who shot whom, and under what circumstances, was in doubt. There was no doubt that an officer ended up with a bullet in his leg. Obviously, from the outcome of the Carlos Riley trial, trust in the police was lacking in that particular courtroom on that particular day in Durham in 2015.

This [reading] is about how community trust in the police can be enhanced or eroded. We conduct the most comprehensive analysis to date of traffic stops in a single state, North Carolina, in order to explore the complex relations between police and the communities they serve. By looking in detail at over 20 million traffic stops over more than a decade, we explore the patterns apparent in the data. These make clear that powerful disparities exist in how the police interact with drivers depending on their outward identities: race, gender, and age in particular. These disparities could be justified by differences in the likelihood of criminal behavior, they could be based on stereotypes, or a mixture of both factors might explain what we document here. Regardless, as we explore the patterns of racial, gender, and age-based difference in how police interact with members of the public, several things become clear. First, there are stark differences. Second, young men of color are clearly targeted for more aggressive treatment. Third, these differences are not fully justified by differences in criminality. Fourth, the aggressive use of traffic stops as a tool to investigate possible criminal behavior, though justified as part of the war on crime, is surprisingly inefficient, rarely leading to arrests for contraband. When we contrast the costs of targeted and aggressive policing with the benefits of it, we find that the social and community costs are high (in terms of reduced trust in and cooperation with the police) but that the number of crimes solved by traffic stop-related investigations is minimal. Finally, we show that there are feasible solutions to these issues, and that they can actually enhance community safety while simultaneously restoring trust. In fact, they enhance safety precisely because they restore trust. When large pockets of the population lose their trust and confidence in the local police, no one wins.

Two reasons explain the disjuncture between the low benefits but high costs of aggressive traffic policing of those who fit police profiles. First, the very targeting which characterizes a "criminal patrol" ensures that most middle-class white Americans are unaware of it. That is, police behavior seems normal, respectful, and appropriate to most of us. To individuals who fit into certain demographic profiles, however, it is anything but. Since most Americans, particularly voters, are not subjected to these behaviors, however, it has remained off the radar, far from mainstream political discussion, and supporting the police has remained the accepted norm. The second reason why we have not compared the costs to the benefits of these new police practices has been that we have assumed the costs to be zero. If the costs of the policy are zero, and there are any benefits at all, then by definition the benefits outweigh the costs. As we will see in detail below, traffic stops, and the detentions and searches that sometimes result from them, have traditionally been considered only as momentary, trivial inconveniences, meriting no special concern. We argue that this perspective is misguided. If police searches within a neighborhood or of a certain class of citizens are repeated, intrusive, and upsetting, these can place a significant burden on that group of individuals, a high cost indeed. Only if we assign a value to those detentions and searches can we reasonably assess whether that cost is greater or lesser than the corresponding benefit.

As America continues to struggle to understand how to balance public safety needs with respect and equity for all its citizens, in particular its most socially vulnerable, we hope that this analysis can inform reasoned debate. Such debate must be based on the best available evidence, and our goal is to provide that here. While we have no simple solutions, we can document very clearly the extent and nature of those racial disparities that do exist. These are substantial, growing, and unjustified by the crime-fighting value of the policies that lead to them.

Traffic Stops and Public Perceptions of Them

No one likes being pulled over by the police. But we can all recognize when we have been caught after perhaps inadvertently applying a little too much gas. We know when we deserve a speeding ticket (though we hope to avoid it), and we know when failing to signal a lane change merits and does not merit police attention; typically it does not. A long line of legal research has established that while no one likes to come into contact with the law, even those who receive a judicial sanction can accept it if they feel the process has been fair. John Thibaut and Laurens Walker (1975) found that individuals' assessment of court proceedings is affected not only by the outcome, but by their sense of whether the procedures were fair. Tom Tyler and Robert Folger (1980) expanded on this idea outside of the courtroom setting, looking at citizen interactions with police. They found that here too when citizens call the police, or are stopped by them, their perception of how fairly they were treated by the police affects their satisfaction. This was independent of the outcome, such as whether they were issued a citation or whether the officer solved the problem that led to the contact. Tom Tyler and Jonathan Jackson (2014) make the point that people comply with the law because they perceive it to be legitimate.

While white Americans typically have very high ratings for the legitimacy of the police and courts, these numbers are lower for African-Americans. Crucially, this sense of legitimacy is linked to cooperation with the police (e.g., helping to solve a crime) and appears to affect citizens' interactions with government in general, beyond the judicial system. For example, rates of voting move from 36 percent among those with high legitimacy to just 23 percent among those ascribing low levels of legitimacy to the police and the courts (Tyler and Jackson 2014, 89). So feelings of how one is treated by the police, or the courts, affect both future cooperation as well as more general factors of democratic participation such as voting. Recall that legitimacy, throughout Tyler's various works, is unrelated to the favorability of the outcome the individual received in their interaction with the legal system; rather it has to do with the sense of fairness of the procedures.

Since 1999, the US Department of Justice has conducted a Police–Public Contact Survey every three years, drawing from a large sample of Americans aged sixteen and older. Between 17 and 21 percent of the public reported contact with an officer in the previous twelve months in surveys between 2002 and 2008. Consistently, across all the surveys, traffic stops and traffic accidents were the most common reason for the contact: between 53 and 59 percent of all citizen contact with the police related to this (in 2008, 44 percent were drivers in a traffic stop, 3 percent were passengers, and 12 percent were involved in a traffic accident). Other reasons for interactions with the police were (in declining order of frequency): reporting a crime or a problem to the police (21 percent in 2008), receiving assistance or service from the police (6 percent), police investigating a crime (6 percent), and police suspecting the citizen of wrongdoing (3 percent). Altogether, fewer than 10 percent of citizen interactions with the police involve criminal investigations, and almost 60 percent involve traffic stops or accidents, with routine traffic stops by far the most common source of all police contact (see Eith and Durose 2011, 3, Tables 2 and 3).

It is no exaggeration then to say that traffic stops are the epicenter of police–citizen interactions. Perceptions about their fairness will go a long way toward shaping citizens' opinions of the police and even the government more broadly. So it is good news that, among those having contact, the vast majority felt that the interaction was legitimate and that the police acted respectfully. Whereas 74 percent of African-American drivers pulled over in 2008 for a traffic stop perceived that they were stopped for a legitimate reason, this number was much higher (79 percent) when it was a speeding stop than when it was for a vehicle defect

(61 percent). Among White drivers, 92 percent of those stopped for speeding, and 87 percent of those stopped for a vehicle defect believed the stop was for a legitimate reason (Eith and Durose 2011, 8, Table 11). These are high numbers in both cases, but clearly white drivers perceive some extra legitimacy for the police, and there may be good reasons for this racial divide. A recent study by a team of Stanford psychologists and computer scientists analyzed audio transcripts taken from police body cameras in Oakland California in April 2014. Looking at the language used in the interactions, and comparing how the officers interacted with black and white drivers, this study of 981 traffic stops and over 36,000 utterances found that officers used more respectful language when interacting with white drivers: they were more likely to refer to them by their last names rather than by their first name or by a nickname, more likely to say "please," less likely to use negative words, and so on (see Voigt et al. 2017). If officers are apologetic, hesitant, grateful, and formal in their addresses to white drivers, but informal, disfluent, negative, and commanding in their interactions with blacks, then there should be no surprise that the two population groups express different levels of satisfaction following such interactions. To be clear, the differences in the Voigt et al. study were subtle rather than stark. But they were consistent and statistically meaningful.

This sense of the appropriateness of police interaction is fundamental to how citizens can be expected to respond to it. Virtually all Americans appreciate the value of the police investigating crimes. Everyone understands the need to patrol the highways for unsafe drivers. But given the enormous range of traffic laws, we all know that we routinely violate some of them. We do not expect to be given a problem by the police for such issues, however, and we have an intuitive sense of whether a police stop was legitimate or may have been based on a technical violation of the law that was then used as a pretext. Legally speaking, we may understand that a technical violation is indeed a violation, but seeing that used as a pretext for a police interaction would be recognized as just that: a pretext for something else based on a suspicion. We may be prepared to "face the music" when caught driving 15 mph over the posted limit, but would understandably be annoyed if pulled over for driving just 2 mph over the limit.

We will come back to the question of how the police interact with the public, and pay particular attention to the question of whether the member of the public is likely to feel that their traffic stop or interaction was legitimate, or may have been motivated by something other than safety on the roads.

A Transformation in Police Crime-Fighting Strategies

Our interest in the subject of police traffic stops and their repercussions draws from a gradual shift in police practice that occurred over several decades. As Tom Tyler, Jonathan Jackson, and Avital Mentovich (2015) describe it, the police moved from working on crimes in progress, or on solving crimes that had previously occurred,

> to a proactive strategy of preventive measures aimed at deterring future crimes. This more proactive approach to policing has led to more frequent police-initiated nonvoluntary public contacts with the legal system, both through increased stop, question, and frisk activities and via zero-tolerance policies that bring more people within the criminal justice system through arrests, court appearances, and even time in jail.
>
> (604)

That is, rather than seeking the cooperation of the public to help solve crimes that have already occurred, the "new" model of policing seeks to stop the crime in the first place. Rather than contacting citizens to help them solve a crime that all may want to see resolved, in the new model of policing, police interactions with members of the public are more aggressive and suggest that individuals are under suspicion. While sometimes that suspicion is well warranted, often it is not. This shift in the style of public contacts "so that they have increasingly communicated police suspicion and mistrust of members of the public with whom the police are dealing" (603) is of particular interest in this [reading].

Especially problematic is that the "risk-management" model is applied unevenly across racial lines; to a considerable extent white neighborhoods still enjoy the old, community-based style of policing, while minority neighborhoods receive more intense scrutiny. The result of this is a significant decline in citizen perceptions of police legitimacy within minority neighborhoods, which has negative consequences for public–police cooperation in fighting crime. Tyler, Jackson, and Mentovich explain:

> Our argument is that it is not contact with the police per se that is problematic. In fact, the results of the study suggest that when the police deal with people in ways that they experience as being fair, contact promotes trust and a variety of types of desirable public behavior. Rather, it is contact that communicates suspicion and mistrust that undermines the relationship between the public and the police.
>
> (603)
>
> At the same time as these non-voluntary contacts have increased, their nature has changed. The police now more frequently approach members of the public with an attitude of suspicion and distrust as they search for signs of

> criminal character and likely future criminal behavior (e.g., 'a regulatory gaze'). Consequently, an increasing number of people are having involuntary interactions with the police during which they are more likely to be treated as if they are suspected of having deviant tendencies and suspect character. Rather than communicating reassurance, trust, and respect, the police communicate suspicion, mistrust, and fear.
>
> (604)

As these strategies were applied to traffic stops, several innovations occurred. One related to the way sheriffs and highway patrol officers patrolled mostly rural areas with interstate highways. They developed "drug courier profiles" and stopped hundreds or thousands of drivers, often fitting a particular demographic profile, in a needle-in-a-haystack strategy of finding a small number with significant contraband.

The US Drug Enforcement Agency (DEA) promoted the use of profiles largely on the basis of the work of Florida state trooper Bob Vogel, later elected Sheriff of Volusia County, Florida. In a laudatory profile in the *Orlando Sentinel*, Charles Fishman (1991) explains Vogel's laser-like focus on drug couriers, in spite of the fact that they typically were only in transit through his rural stretch of I-95 near Daytona Beach. Fishman writes: "The pipeline wasn't causing much of a law enforcement problem for Vogel. (An early element of the courier profile, in fact, was that cars obeying the speed limit were suspect–their desire to avoid being stopped made them stand out.)" In fact, according to Webb (2007), Fishman's early work on drug interdiction was thrown out by various judges who considered his "hunch" that drugs may be in the car an unconstitutional violation of the need to have probable cause before conducting a search. Vogel responded by studying the Florida vehicle code, finding that there were hundreds of reasons why he could legally pull a car over.

> He found them by the hundreds in the thick volumes of the Florida vehicle code: rarely enforced laws against driving with burned-out license plate lights, out-of-kilter headlights, obscured tags, and windshield cracks. State codes bulge with such niggling prohibitions, some dating from the days of the horseless carriage.
>
> "'The vehicle code gives me fifteen hundred reasons to pull you over,' one CHP [California Highway Patrol] officer told me."
>
> (Webb 2007)

So, while it was those patrolling rural areas of the country, often focused on "oustiders" in transit through their jurisdictions who developed these profiles, Sheriff Vogel's discovery that he could scrutinize the highway code for various technical violations of the law was later adopted more generally. Anyone driving in a car is at risk for a technical violation, especially when such things as "driving in an unsafe manner" are determined by the observations of the officer, not according to objective criteria. This legal innovation, however, represented a powerful transformation of policing practice.

The shifts associated with "old" and "new" style policing were slow in coming and predate Officer Vogel. In fact, the constitutional seeds of this shift go back to the 1960s, when the Supreme Court ruled in *Terry* v. *Ohio*, 392 U.S. 1 (1968) that police officers may legally "pat down" or frisk an individual based on "reasonable suspicion" rather than "probable cause." These interpretations were solidified and extended a generation later, in *Whren* v. *United States*, 517 U.S. 806 (1996). This landmark decision validated the police strategy of targeting individuals who fit a "profile" said to be associated with drug activity. Here the Court validated the right of police officers to pull over a car for any traffic violation, but ruled that there was no constitutional requirement of equity in treatment of traffic offenders. By breaking the law, any law, offenders opened themselves up to the possibility of police action. That action need not be equitable, the Court said. The police were not expected to stop all speeders, all those veering slightly out of their lane as they drive, all those driving in the passing lane of a freeway, or all of those with a cracked brake light, a dangling mirror, or an obscured license tag. Officers could pick and choose those offenders who seemed to be of greater interest. And, with hundreds of traffic laws and great discretion in their interpretation, officers could pull over virtually any car. Once pulled over, officers could seek consent or use probable cause to conduct a search of the driver, passengers, or the vehicle. Effectively, the Court permitted the use of routine traffic stops for targeted criminal investigations. The war on crime was the justification for these actions.

Two Fundamental Supreme Court Cases Create a New Regime

To those readers who are not lawyers, the 1968 movement from "probable cause" to "reasonable suspicion" may not appear to be an important distinction, but suspicion is a very low standard as compared to probable cause. It meant that the police could stop and frisk great numbers of people even if they had no reason to believe they were actively engaged in any illegal activity. Today police use the phrase "Terry stop" to describe situations where they detain an individual momentarily in order to investigate them, including conducting a physical search of their body. Note that even in a Terry stop, the police must be able to point to "specific and articulable facts" that generate a reasonable suspicion toward the individual about to be searched or patted down. Many traffic stops fall under the legal umbrella of a Terry stop: a momentary detention based on suspicion rather than a longer detention based on arrest, or a search based on probable cause.

Justice William O. Douglas was highly critical of the "new regime" he said we were entering in 1968 with the *Terry* decision. He wrote in his dissent in *Terry* v. *Ohio*:

> Until the Fourth Amendment ... is rewritten, the person and the effects of the individual are beyond the reach of all government agencies until there are reasonable grounds to believe (probable cause) that a criminal venture has been launched or is about to be launched.
>
> There have been powerful hydraulic pressures throughout our history that bear heavily on the Court to water down constitutional guarantees and give the police the upper hand. That hydraulic pressure has probably never been greater than it is today.
>
> Yet if the individual is no longer to be sovereign, if the police can pick him up whenever they do not like the cut of his jib, if they can "seize" and "search" him in their discretion, we enter a new regime.
>
> (Justice Douglas, dissenting, *Terry* v. *Ohio*, p. 39)

We may well have entered a "new regime" with policing in the USA with the development of the war on crime, beginning in the 1960s and accelerating in the 1980s and 1990s. While *Terry* was an important shift, the Justices confronted something even more generic in *Whren*, and the combined result of both *Terry* and *Whren* was clearly as Justice Douglas indicated, to "give the police the upper hand." Whereas in *Terry* the Court allowed for a pat-down based on mere suspicion rather than probable cause, in *Whren* the Court acquiesced to the idea that the police may stop a car for virtually any reason. Although the Court ruled in *Whren* that race by itself would be unconstitutional as grounds to decide which cars to stop and which to let alone, it also sustained the legitimacy of a search resulting from a selective traffic stop. Since there was no doubt that the traffic stop had been legally justified (as almost any traffic stop would be), the resulting search was not unconstitutional. The opinion contains this passage, recognizing the allegation of the petitioners that virtually any car on the road can be found to be in violation of some law, and that the police should not be able selectively to enforce the law when they please:

> Since, they contend, the use of automobiles is so heavily and minutely regulated that total compliance with traffic and safety rules is nearly impossible, a police officer will almost invariably be able to catch any given motorist in a technical violation. This creates the temptation to use traffic stops as a means

of investigating other law violations, as to which no probable cause or even articulable suspicion exists. Petitioners, who are both black, further contend that police officers might decide which motorists to stop based on decidedly impermissible factors, such as the race of the car's occupants.

(*Whren*, p. 810)

But, in a unanimous decision written by Justice Scalia, the Court held:

Petitioners urge as an extraordinary factor in this case that the "multitude of applicable traffic and equipment regulations" is so large and so difficult to obey perfectly that virtually everyone is guilty of violation, permitting the police to single out almost whomever they wish for a stop. But we are aware of no principle that would allow us to decide at what point a code of law becomes so expansive and so commonly violated that infraction itself can no longer be the ordinary measure of the lawfulness of enforcement.

(*Whren*, p. 818)

And, finally: "The temporary detention of a motorist upon probable cause to believe that he has violated the traffic laws does not violate the Fourth Amendment's prohibition against unreasonable seizures, even if a reasonable officer would not have stopped the motorist absent some additional law enforcement objective" (*Whren*, p. 806). That is, if the stop itself was legal since there was reason to believe a traffic infraction (however minor) had occurred, then any fruit of that traffic stop was legal as well. We moved from "probable cause" to "articulable suspicion" in 1968 and in 1996 we moved to a full constitutional protection for selective application of the letter of every traffic law, including as a pretext for "some additional law enforcement objective." The war on crime was in full swing, and the police now had the legal backing to conduct it as broadly as they saw fit.

Throughout the period from the 1960s through the 1990s, Court interpretation of reasonable search and seizure moved in the direction of greater powers for the police to conduct searches. To be clear, *Whren* would indeed authorize an officer to observe a car or driver, develop a suspicion or an inkling that something may be of interest, and then wait for the driver to violate one of hundreds of different traffic laws, including driving too fast (speeding), driving too slow (impeding traffic), touching a lane marker, or any of a number of equipment or regulatory violations. Once pulled over for what the Court then recognizes as a legitimate enforcement purpose, the officer can then follow up on their suspicion by interviewing the driver, peering into the car, and so on. *Whren* was a watershed moment.

While of course we expect legal professionals to be sure to be operating within the scope of what has been determined to be constitutionally acceptable, members of the public have a different conception of what is fair and what is not. For an officer to follow a driver until that driver commits a traffic infraction is legally permissible, but many would question whether it is fair. Of course, many others would encourage and applaud the police for tracking those who look suspicious and thereby keeping the community safer. Because the cost of increased surveillance is borne largely by young men of color, most Americans are immune to it, ignorant of it, and may well be in favor of it. But it certainly can be expected to generate mistrust and that mistrust should be particularly acute within the demographic communities that receive extra police scrutiny. Thus as Tracey Meares, Tom Tyler, and Jacob Gardener (2016) explain, police officials may justify their actions as being constitutionally permissible, but members of the public might think they are simply unfair. Legal professionals and ordinary citizens thus speak a different language. One of our conclusions in this [reading] is that the ordinary citizens' understanding of fairness is important to incorporate. This, not the legal details, determines how people think about and respond to disproportionate police scrutiny. It may be legal, but it is not fair.

Community Mistrust as a Response to Disparate and Aggressive Policing

One of the fundamental questions of interest in this [reading] is how community mistrust is generated. Since the 1970s, aggressive police targeting within the minority community has been justified by the war on crime and then more specifically by the "war on drugs." Even routine traffic stops were seen as a means by which the police could target drug couriers and put an end to the epidemic of drug abuse that has long generated so much concern. Here we seek to document what has not been fully documented before: this strategy is a poor tool for catching "bad guys" and instead generates distrust, anger, and alienation among those the police are sworn to protect. Concerns about government waste are always politically salient and so we offer the "risk-management" model of policing as a prime example.

Consistently in implementing the war on drugs, police agencies have made clear that "you have to kiss a lot of frogs before you find your prince"—very large numbers of traffic stops would have to occur before an officer might interdict a significant drug shipment (see Webb 2007). Unstated in that calculation was that many Americans would be subjected to police investigations so that a small number could be searched or arrested in the hope of finding a large cache of drugs. Those who were momentarily detained were said by the Court to have suffered only a trivial inconvenience. The key element in this targeting, which kept it hidden for so long from those who might have objected, was that middle-class Americans were largely exempt from its consequences. On the other hand, members of minority groups, especially young men, were subjected to a lot more than just an occasional trivial inconvenience. Police routinely targeted poor neighborhoods, individuals with certain forms of dress, males rather than females, younger people rather than older ones, and minorities rather than whites. Police cruisers allow officers to look up the license plate numbers of the cars in front of them at a stop light, identifying those with outstanding court warrants. This may be a fantastic opportunity to track down wanted criminals. But statistically it is routinely used to identify those with unpaid tickets, court fees, and other small charges which appear small only to those with the means to pay them. The poor are particularly targeted because of the number of vehicle violations associated with broken tail-lights, equipment problems, and expired registration tags, issues that are more likely to occur among the poor than among the middle class. Where these sociodemographic groups overlap is where police attention is most focused. Thus, millions of Americans have been targeted for more intensive police attention outside of the gaze or knowledge of most middle-class whites. And it has not been trivial at all. It has been humiliating, frustrating, and unfair. Beyond all that, it has been ineffective.

While civil rights attorneys and members of minority communities have long complained of these police activities, the targeted nature of them kept them from the consciousness of most middle-class white Americans. Americans all understand that excessive speeding may well lead to flashing lights in the mirror, and no one enjoys a police encounter leading to a ticket. But we also know the difference between a legitimate, if unwelcome, traffic ticket and a pretextual or targeted enforcement. Being stopped and ticketed is one thing, being asked to justify or explain your whereabouts, your destination, or the car you are driving is something else entirely. When Philando Castile was shot and killed in St. Paul, Minnesota in 2016 after a routine traffic stop, he had been pulled over at least forty-six times from the time he learned to drive until his death fourteen years later; he had had various suspensions of his license and fines for such violations as driving without a license or not having valid insurance. Altogether these violations totaled over $6,000, meaning that he had spent virtually his entire young life as a driver fighting various fines, court fees, and license suspensions (see Peralta and Corley 2016). Many low-income drivers, especially in minority communities, do the same. Of course, these troubles are virtually unheard of in middle-class America. In contrast, poverty keeps many from paying the initial fine, leading to accumulating court sanctions, fees, and penalties.

We should not be surprised that these more aggressive tactics, which effectively (though perhaps inadvertently) treat as criminal suspects large numbers of individuals depending on where they live or work, how they dress, and how they look, would have generated a great deal of mistrust, anger, and alienation. A key but underappreciated element of the new police tactics has been that the cost has been borne almost exclusively by one demographic group: young men of color. Their alienation, frustration, and anger with government is understandable when we consider the disproportionate targeting that they have suffered through these policies and their ratification through the courts.

Increased Attention to an Old Problem

Since the shooting of Trayvon Martin in 2012 and the organization of the Black Lives Matter movement in 2013, police–community relations have been in the news. Of course, friction between police departments and the communities they serve is a perennial issue in urban America. The 1992 Los Angeles riots were in response to the acquittal of police officers for the beating of Rodney King, an unarmed black man pulled over on the freeway for speeding (and who attempted to evade the police, leading them on a high-speed chase). The 1967 Detroit rebellion was sparked by a police raid of a black nightclub. Many of the riots of the 1960s erupted in communities where black neighborhoods were policed by largely white police forces and where trust had eroded beyond the breaking point. There is nothing new, in other words, about problems of trust between the black community and the men and women in blue. However, the last several years have seen unprecedented and consistently high levels of concern, media discussion, and community engagement that have forced or allowed many difficult conversations about race, policing, and citizenship. What is different between the current and previous situations? One key point is shifting social understandings based on changing media coverage.

A turning point in a previous generation of the civil rights movement was when peaceful demonstrators marched from Selma to Montgomery, Alabama in 1965. These marchers were fully aware that Bull Connor's police dogs would attack them, officers would beat them with clubs, drench them with fire hoses, and that some might die. But the iconic photos and national news coverage of these events changed the views of many white Americans living far from the areas where the civil rights demonstrations were taking place. This larger public was appalled, and suddenly more aware, of what had long been happening in communities throughout the South (see McAdam 1988).

Cell phone videos of police shootings may be playing a similar role today. For example, officer Michael T. Slager pled guilty in a Charleston, SC court to firing eight rounds toward the back of fleeing unarmed motorist Walter Scott (see Blinder 2017). Without the cell phone coverage of the shooting, it is unlikely that such a case would have even gone to trial. Dramatic cell phone coverage of many publicized incidents have changed the conversation, giving much greater credence to long-standing but previously discounted complaints in the minority community about differential standards for police encounters with majority and minority populations. The power of the videos, constantly replayed in social media and in the mainstream press, to show the brutality of shooting to kill when a police life is not in danger has galvanized many inside and outside of the minority community. A key element in this conversation is that the videos have created attention, and generated concern, in communities that are not directly affected by such actions.

Until individuals such as Mr. Castile were cast into the national spotlight when videos of their violent deaths were played on national television and reporters delved into their backgrounds, few were asking about the collateral consequences of these large-scale police dragnets. But dry data analytics have backed up these vivid illustrations. New data analytic tools made possible by the routine collection of traffic stop and other types of data on police encounters with citizens have allowed us to document surprisingly large but previously undocumented disparities in the treatment of different racial groups. We will be focusing on the NC case, the longest running statewide data collection of traffic stops data, throughout the chapters to come. While these data do not explain the causes of any disparities, they certainly make clear that they are large. Studies in various states have found the same. The US Department of Justice investigation of the Ferguson (Missouri) Police Department used similar data to show that citizen complaints were indeed based on real, tangible, measurable disparities in treatment of citizens of different race. A particularly egregious finding of the Ferguson report was the degree to which the city had come to use court fees as a source of municipal revenue. The city relied on its poorest residents for traffic fines, court fees, and arrests because all of these were income-generating activities for the city. In effect, the city was financed through selective and targeted enforcement of various laws that did little to make people safer, but which imposed a severe burden on those least able to bear it (see US DOJ 2015).

As mentioned above with respect to Mr. Philando Castile, many individuals living in poverty accumulate traffic and court fees and when they are unable to pay them may be subject to a warrant for arrest. Items which to a middle-class American might be a mere inconvenience or embarrassment can cause others to lose their jobs or go to jail if they cannot pay bail. Walter Scott, shot in North Charleston, SC after a traffic stop for a brake light failure, was behind on child support payments and may have been concerned about the consequences of the traffic stop, as he had an outstanding warrant. Previously, he had gone to jail for this, leading him to lose a job (see Robles and Dewan 2015). Rodney King, whose beating sparked the 1992 Los Angeles riots, attempted to flee from the police in his car, leading to a high-speed chase; he was concerned that the traffic stop would lead to his parole being revoked (see Frontline n.d.). With millions of Americans under some kind of judicial control or supervision, and with many outstanding warrants for such things as unpaid court debts, a "routine" traffic encounter can have very powerful consequences; people can lose their jobs, their homes, or go to jail (see for example Goffman 2014). In other words, whereas the typical middle-class American might be slightly bothered by a traffic stop, they would likely recognize it as a momentary inconvenience with very little chance of long-lasting consequence. For others, those more commonly targeted with more aggressive policing, the calculus is entirely different.

A consequence of the war on drugs and the *Whren* decision is to allow police great leeway in using the traffic laws as they please to target certain individuals. If drug couriers all shared some obvious indicator making them easily identifiable on the roadways, then these police powers would find an appropriate outlet. But, the data reveals that traffic stops only rarely lead to significant contraband hits. Whereas 3 percent of traffic stops lead to a search, only about one-third of those searches lead to contraband. Further, only about half of those contraband hits lead to arrest, which is not surprising because when we look at the amounts of contraband found, it is typically that associated with a user, not a distributor, of the item in question. In the rare instances when large amounts have been found, bona fide drug dealers or couriers may hire qualified attorneys to search deeply into the arresting officer's background and patterns of traffic stops. If they find that the officer has indeed "kissed a lot of frogs" before "finding his prince"—that is, subjected hundreds or thousands of law-abiding minority citizens to traffic stops or searches while letting white motorists go on their way—the charges may be dropped or reduced. Wearing a certain type of cap or driving a car registered in another state do not constitute probable cause. So, throughout the [reading] we will want to compare the costs associated with racially disparate policing with the benefits of the policy. If the benefits are high, perhaps they could be argued to outweigh the costs. But if the benefits are very low, this becomes more unlikely, and we have to look at other reasons to understand why such disparities exist.

Causes of Racial Differences

Throughout this [reading] we will be looking at patterns of police interactions with motorists and looking at how they differ by race, age, gender, and other factors. We want to be clear that the mere existence of a disparity in any given outcome does not mean that the disparity is unjustified. For example, young people commit more violent crime than older people, and males more than females. If the police arrest people in the exact proportion that they commit crimes, then arrests and police contacts will also show these disparities. In plain English, some disparities are caused by differences in the likelihood of breaking the law, not by any bias or differential treatment by race. There is no doubt that blacks and other minorities are vastly over-represented in the criminal justice system, and in this [reading] we will show that North Carolina traffic stops show similar patterns.

Racial Profiling versus Racial Difference

Racial disparities are ubiquitous in criminal justice, housing, education, health care, and in other areas of American life. The presence of a difference does not by itself mean that it was the result of profiling. Jack Glaser defines racial profiling as "the use of race or ethnicity, or proxies thereof, by law enforcement officials as a basis for judgment of criminal suspicion" (Glaser 2015, 3). He does not say that race must be "the" basis for judgment, just "a" basis. Glaser notes that others disagree, and some even find racial profiling to be a positive. Lorie Fridell, a respected voice in the debate, prefers simply to avoid the term:

> We believe "racial profiling" has frequently been defined so restrictively that it does not fully capture the concerns of both police practitioners and citizens. For instance, racial profiling is frequently defined as law enforcement activities (e.g., detentions, arrests, searches) that are initiated solely on the basis of race. Central to the debate on the most frequently used definitions is the word "solely." In the realm of potential discriminatory actions, this definition likely references only a very small portion.
>
> (Fridell et al. 2001, 3; quoted in Glaser 2015, 15)

Fridell and her team prefer the phrase "racially biased policing" (see Glaser 2015, 15; Fridell et al. 2001, 3–4). One reason she gives for this is apparent in the two definitions just given. Glaser's definition (race as any part of a judgment) is close to what many civil rights advocates use; Fridell's definition (race as the sole basis of a decision) is close to what police officers themselves might recognize as profiling. Indeed Fridell's team avoided the term partly because they found that stakeholders used the term to mean very different things.

Our sense is close to Glaser's in that the US Constitution guarantees equal protection of the law without regard to race, ethnicity, and other demographic features. Racial differences are clear in many areas of life, but race itself should not be the basis (or even a basis) of decisions by the police which generate those differences: behavior should. The police perspective that profiling only occurs if race is the "sole" determinant of a decision is so restrictive that it would virtually never come into play. When we look for evidence of profiling, as opposed to mere disparities, we will be looking for instances where racial differences remain even after we remove other possible reasons for an observed disparity. For example, if blacks and whites are equally likely to break the law but blacks are arrested more often, this would be a sign indicating that profiling may be occurring. But if blacks commit more crimes than whites, and are arrested in proportion to that, then this is a disparity with no sign of having been caused by police profiling; it would be a difference or a disparity, but would not indicate biased policing.

No matter what we call it, racial differences in criminal justice are real, and they may stem from a great number of possible causes. To the degree that differences are caused by differences in actual criminal behavior, we certainly cannot suggest that profiling has occurred or that police practices should be called into question. If poverty, housing, job, educational and health-care opportunities are systematically different across groups, then we certainly cannot expect the police to solve those problems, and it may be those larger problems which are generating differences in the propensity to be involved in crime. The police simply come to reflect these social pathologies. So we certainly want to be careful to attribute criminal behavior an important place in our analyses, controlling for it whenever we can before we assess the residual impact of race, over and above differences in behavior.

On the other hand, there can be additional factors which generate differential policing [...].

Four Causes of Racial Disparities

Racial differences in traffic stop outcomes could logically come from four distinct sources. First, as Michael Tonry (1995) makes clear, there is no reason to expect that white and black motorists break the law at the same rate. If black motorists are more likely to speed egregiously, or carry illegal contraband in their cars, then we would expect that the police would be relatively more likely to stop and search black drivers. Differential criminality is the first possible cause of differential contact with the police. Second, there could be some number of "bad apple" police officers who simply do not live up to the standard of fair and impartial policing. Whether because of "old fashioned" racism, implicit bias, or a lack of proper training, racial disparities might be traceable to a small fraction of the police force who treat black drivers much differently than white drivers. Third, there could be widely shared, but relatively subtle, differences in how white and minority drivers are treated following a traffic stop. These differences might be statistically only moderate but widely spread across the vast majority of officers in a given department. Perhaps, due to implicit bias shared by most Americans, a large share of officers tends to treat black drivers just slightly more aggressively than white drivers. Consider the recent study in Oakland, California finding subtle differences in how officers spoke to white and black citizens they encountered (Voigt et al. 2017). These subtle but system-wide differences could be due to inaccurate statistical assumptions or over-wrought stereotypes. Fourth and finally, there could be institutional practices which lead to racial differences in outcomes. For example, a given department might emphasize regulatory traffic stops, stops for equipment failures, or it might have more aggressive search policies in certain neighborhoods or precincts which themselves might differ by race. If there are more police assigned to a given area, and that area is a predominately black neighborhood, then blacks will have a higher chance of coming into the criminal justice system, even with an equal likelihood of engaging in criminal behavior.

Given our extensive statistical evidence, we will differentiate among these different possible causes of the racial differences we observe. Note that institutional practices such as differential policing in different neighborhoods could have a significant racial impact, but might be an inadvertent, unintentional corollary or consequence of policing decisions that were made for other reasons. From the data, we cannot always judge whether those reasons might justify the racially disparate outcomes, but by pointing out the racial disparities that may stem from them, we can allow a conversation that has not previously been made explicit.

Differential Criminality

Tonry (1995) notes that the first explanation of dramatic racial differences in blacks compared to whites in prison, jail, or under some kind of judicial oversight has to be different rates of criminal behavior. He cites observers from W. E. B. DuBois (writing in 1899) to Thorsten Sellin (in 1928), Guy Johnson (1941), and Gunnar Myrdal (1944) all making essentially the same argument: given 400 years of American history, systematic and institutionalized lack of access to education and jobs, and differences in poverty, health care, housing, wealth, and income, it would be astounding if the racial groups did not differ in levels of criminality. And indeed they do. Tonry writes:

> For as long as the FBI has collected and reported national arrest data in its *Uniform Crime Reports*, blacks have experienced substantially higher arrest rates than whites relative to their respective shares of the population. This should surprise no one. Criminality and other serious antisocial conduct flow from social disorganization and social and economic disadvantage.
>
> (1995, 52)

The key point, according to Tonry, then, is to attempt to estimate what share of the difference in differential outcomes from the criminal justice system can be attributed to different levels of criminal behavior versus differential treatment once the justice system comes into contact with individuals of different racial groups. His evidence clearly points in two directions: racial differences in criminality are real and should not be ignored, but also the war on drugs had a dramatic and unjustified effect magnifying the criminality of the black population disproportionately compared to whites.[1] Something changed in policing during the

1 Of course, even when disparities are indicative of actual rates of criminal behavior in underlying populations that does not mean that such disparities are harmless or legitimate. As Tonry points

1980s in particular, leading to dramatic increases in black arrest, over and above what could be explained by differences in rates of involvement with crime. That something was the rise of a new style of policing, focused on drugs (see Tonry 1995, chapter 4). So while some elements of the story are long-lasting, some are new. The new part relates to an aggressive style of policing focused on drugs and minor crimes (for more detail, see Withrow 2004, 2006; and various works by David A. Harris: 1997, 1999a, 1999b, 2002a, 2002b).

"Old Fashioned" Racism versus Implicit Bias

Whereas Bull Connor and other enforcers of the legal separation of blacks and whites during the Jim Crow period explicitly laid out their beliefs in the superiority of whites, we rarely see such "old fashioned" or explicit statements of racial hierarchy, at least in official documents. At the same time, the American experience, reinforced in everyday life, movies, television, and popular culture, makes race a prominent signal or marker, and most Americans harbor implicit, subconscious biases even if they are careful to be racially neutral in their conscious decision-making and would hate to think of themselves as having any racial prejudices. Kristin Anderson (2010) starts her book, *Benign Bigotry*, by pointing out that racial stereotyping has "gone underground" and is much more difficult to see today than when it was written into law as it was during the Jim Crow period. Whereas once one could look for explicit and unabashed outward signs of racism, today's racism must be found in different forms. She explains:

> Explicit prejudice is a set of feelings about others that are consciously accessible, seemingly controllable, and self-reported. Racism based on explicit prejudice is referred to as *old-fashioned* or *overt* racism. Implicit prejudice may or may not be consciously accessible, and may be difficult or impossible to control. Implicit prejudice is believed to be a consequence of years of exposure to associations in the environment, it tends to be impervious to conscious control, and it is relatively stable. Racism based on implicit prejudice has various names: *subtle*, *covert*, *modern*, *ambivalent*, or *aversive*.
>
> (Anderson 2010, 4)

Particularly important is one group's set of stereotypical assumptions about another group. As Anderson writes, this might be about men or women, about gay, married or single

---

out, the roots of criminal behavior are closely tied to larger social inequalities in health care, education, and employment.

people, people of a given nationality, or by racial group. People from another group are wrongly assumed to be "all the same," that is, out-group homogeneity is a common assumption (see Anderson 2010, 22–81).

The sources of covert racial bias are found all around us and are parts of US history. They are not particular to the criminal justice system, but given the powerful effects of race on criminal justice matters, and the over-representation of minorities in the criminal justice system, there should be no surprise that many associate crime with minorities, particularly young males. Crucially, according to the accumulated social psychological literature, no one growing up in mainstream US culture would be immune to these pressures (see for example Gillian and Iyengar 2000). Furthermore, within the police profession, there is ample reason to expect that such biases may be especially strong. In particular, as relates to the decision to shoot or not to shoot a hypothetical suspect in an ambiguous experimental setting, the black suspects are typically shot in a higher percentage of the cases than an identically situated white suspect (see for example Correll et al. 2002; Correll et al. 2007; Correll 2009).

Clearly, a police officer stopping a moving vehicle, or approaching a driver after a traffic stop is called upon to make quick decisions. Just as clearly, officers go through training and are required to treat all citizens in the same manner. [...] Implicit biases are not the only possible reason for racial disparities in traffic stops outcomes, but they are a strong contender. Social psychologists have found covert or subtle bias throughout various experimental settings and there is no reason not to expect it in the context of a traffic stop. In fact, there are reasons to believe that the circumstances governing traffic stops, particularly, the high-volume nature of modern police patrolling tactics, encourage officers to act upon subtle biases.

Inaccurate Profiling and Stereotyping

Jack Glaser has written extensively about the causes and consequences of racial profiling, which he defines as "the use of race or ethnicity, or proxies thereof, by law enforcement officials as a basis for judgment of criminal suspicion" (2015, 3). He also notes: "Reasonable people can and do disagree over whether racial profiling is legal, fair, ethical, and effective" (3). He cites US government (Bureau of Justice Statistics) data projecting that as of 2003, 5.9 percent of white boys born will serve time in prison as compared to 17.2 for Latinos and 32.2 percent for blacks (6). So, he notes, there can be no question about differential likelihood of imprisonment. Much of this, he notes, is related to differential offending rates, but a large percentage of the difference relates to drug offenses, where there are few racial differences in use by race (with the notable exception of powder versus crack cocaine use). He cites a Centers for Disease Control (CDC) study noting the rates at which young men reported having carried a gun in the past thirty days: 17.2 for blacks, 18.2 for whites, and 18.5 for Hispanics. But blacks were three times as likely to be arrested on weapons charges as compared to whites (Glaser 2015, 7). These and other unexplained disparities led Glaser into an investigation of whether the profiles used by police might be inaccurate.

Police agencies and the FBI have long used criminal profiles; attempts to understand the common patterns of how individuals engage in certain types of crimes. Airplane hijackers, for example, were the subject of extensive psychological efforts to generate a profile, even before 9/11, and similar efforts are made for school shooters, serial killers, and Islamic terrorists. By building a profile, police officials hope to be able to focus on those most likely to commit a crime. Some of the first drug courier profiles were constructed by airport security personnel attempting to understand which of tens of thousands of airplane passengers might be transporting drugs. These profiles often targeted individuals who: travelled alone, stayed in their destination city for a very short time, had little baggage, and who were travelling between two cities with significant traffic in drugs (see for example Glaser 2015, 43ff., Harris 2002a).

More generally, police have extensive information about criminals based on those they apprehend. They know where they commit crimes, their age, race, gender, mode of dress, type of car, where they live and work, and many other characteristics. There should be no surprise, and there is no problem, when this information is put to work in order to fight crime. Glaser refers to this as an "actuarial" police profile; constructing these can be a sign of good policing. The problem comes in when particular elements of the "actuarial" profile are over-emphasized, particularly the demographic elements. As discussed in previous sections in this [reading], stereotyping is a common, if not ubiquitous human tendency; members of an "out-group" are wrongly assumed to share traits more than they really do. Therefore it is only a small step from creating a profile to over-emphasizing it.

Glaser (2006 and 2015) provides an example and a statistical illustration. Imagine two groups with the same level of criminality. If one is policed more heavily than the other, it is obvious that one will have more members in prison. But assume perhaps more realistically that one group has higher criminality than the other. What will profiling do in that case? His various simulations, using a wide variety of different parameters, show that the effect of profiling is to exaggerate whatever criminality differences might be in the population. That is, if one group commits twice as much crime (per capita) than the other, but is policed more closely, the ratio of arrests will be significantly higher than two-to-one. The targeted group is over-arrested with respect to their criminality, and the other group is under-policed, leading to fewer arrests in that group than their underlying criminality would warrant.

Of course these are hypothetical examples, but the logic is powerful and the mathematics are very consistent.

One key element in Glaser's simulation should be particularly disturbing: if the targeting is inaccurate with respect to the underlying criminality, then a lower percentage of the total number of criminals will be arrested. As the targeting gets further away from that which is statistically justified by behaviors, so the overall proportion of criminals who are arrested declines. Increased percentages of criminals within the targeted group are arrested, but decreasing percentages in the (larger) non-targeted group are found. Therefore, his simulations show not only much sharper disparities in who is arrested than could be explained only by differences in criminality, but they reach a point where they produce fewer arrests altogether. Profiling, combined with stereotyping, can be counter-productive.

Glaser's (2006 and 2015) simulations do not explore changes in the behaviors of possible criminals in response to the inaccurate targeting by the police. As he notes, some suggest that racial targeting can be justified because it may deter crime in communities where crime rates are highest (see for example Schuck 2006). But, Glaser notes, if the deterrence argument is to be introduced, it has to work both ways: while one group recognizes it is under increased surveillance, another group sees the police moving away—"reverse deterrence." If the police are looking disproportionately for criminals in one neighborhood, or among one demographic group, then individuals with criminal tendencies who are immune to that targeting may decide to commit more crime. Consider an experiment. Amy Hackney and Jack Glaser (2013) put subjects in a situation where cheating was possible. In one treatment group, black subjects were clearly and loudly singled out for cheating and in the other monitoring for cheating was racially neutral. In the case where blacks where targeted, white subjects cheated more, presumably because they felt they were unlikely to be caught: the monitors were so focused on the black subjects the whites knew they could get away with it. "The effect of the profiling of blacks was consequently a net increase in cheating" (Hackney and Glaser 2013, 348). Glaser's point in assessing the likely impact of over-targeting is that if the police devote their limited resources inefficiently, over-policing one group, then by definition they will be under-policing another. That other group will certainly notice and adjust its behavior accordingly. When the cat is away (or distracted by other prey), the mice will play.

There are many potential problems with inaccurate profiling. As Glaser has persuasively argued, it can be inefficient. But we should also recall that differential policing calls into question the constitutional guarantee of equal protection of the law. By putting particular individuals into the position of "suspect" merely because of where they live or work or their membership in a certain demographic group (rather than on the basis of their observed criminal behavior), we collectively send a powerful message that they are not full members of the community, that they are not to expect equal treatment, and that the most visible government agents they are likely to encounter view them as dangerous threats. No wonder people subjected to this respond with anger and withdrawal [...].

Differential Policing by Place

Policing in the USA is a highly local affair, with almost 18,000 state and local police departments in operation in 2008, including over 12,500 local police agencies, more than 3,000 county sheriff's offices, fifty state agencies, and over 2,000 special jurisdiction and constable/marshal's offices (see Reaves 2011). With such an emphasis on local control, there should be no surprise that different local agencies might have different characteristics. So, for example, if a given agency has, say, a 6 percent search rate, and officers in another agency search only 2 percent of the drivers, then there could be racial disparities in search rates driven entirely by institutional practice combined with different racial make-ups of the populations served by various police agencies. In a review of 649 publicly available annual traffic stops reports from 132 different agencies, Baumgartner, Christiani, and colleagues (2017, Table 3) found that highway patrol departments had search rates of 2.12 percent on average, whereas police departments had much higher rates (6.33 percent on average). Further, black, white, Hispanic, and overall search rates typically varied greatly from agency to agency. Clearly, to understand policing as it is experienced by citizens we must take into account the dramatic differences that stem from the localized nature of policing in the USA.

Just as we must be attuned to agency-effects in policing, within larger agencies there may also be substantial "precinct" effects or neighborhood differences in how the police interact with citizens, including during traffic stops. Because of racial differences in residential patterns, these neighborhood, or place-based differences in policing, may have substantial racial implications and can help explain differential outcomes in policing by race.

Indeed, the very localized and place-based patterns of policing are strong possible explanations of racial difference. With housing substantially segregated by race (see Sharkey 2013), a simple cause of racial difference in contact with the police could simply be that the police patrol more intensively on one side of town than the other. Naturally, the police go where the crime is, whether by design or by responding to calls for service. And this may bring them into contact with minorities with greater frequency than whites. But, crucially, while sending more patrol units to crime-ridden neighborhoods is a perfectly reasonable approach to fighting crime, developing different thresholds for searching (higher in some neighborhoods, lower in others) is more problematic. In a country governed by laws, probable cause should mean the same thing regardless of the zip code. Still, we want to be careful throughout our analyses to look within police departments since many racial differences might be due to institutional or agency-level differences across them. Simply put, we will want to ensure that our analyses do not mistakenly attribute to race something that might only be associated with place.

When Community Trust Evaporates

A number of scholars have addressed the high cost of intensive policing of particular social groups. Todd Clear and Natasha Frost (2014) assess what they call "the punishment imperative" in describing the confluence of trends that led to increasingly punitive crime policies from the 1960s to the 1990s. Most notably, they note that the number of individuals imprisoned per 100,000 population was steady for many decades at about 100, but began a dramatic rise in the 1970s until it reached over 500 in the 2000s. Remarkably, this dramatic rise has not been correlated with a rise in either property or violent crime (p. 35). Because imprisonment is a function of how many individuals commit crimes, the proportion of those sentenced to prison, and the length of those prison sentences, it is clear that one could expand net imprisonment by increasing sentencing rates or sentence lengths even in the absence of rises in crime. And this is exactly what occurred in the late 1990s.

Further, the rise in imprisonment was highly concentrated geographically: specific neighborhoods were particularly affected. Clear and Frost cite the influential work of Tucker and Cadora, who wrote: "There is no logic to spending a million dollars a year to incarcerate people from one block in Brooklyn—over half for nonviolent drug offenses—and return them, on average, in less than three years stigmatized, unskilled, and untrained to the same unchanged block" (2003, 2). Tucker and Cadora suggest that a better use of incarceration funds would be to invest in jobs, economic vitality, health care, and social services in those neighborhoods hardest hit by crime. The highly localized nature of crime, and the police response to it, is an important element of the patterns we will explore [...].

A number of authors have explored the dynamics of life in these places of crime and marginality. Alice Goffman (2014) writes of a strongly disordered neighborhood in Philadelphia, based on intensive fieldwork there over six years during which she observed hundreds of police actions and was able to come to know many of those living "on the run." In a neighborhood where police surveillance is a daily occurrence, where large percentages of the young male population are under judicial supervision—on parole or subject to an outstanding warrant (often for an unpaid court fee)—many social pathologies develop. Injured individuals avoid the hospital, fathers avoid their children's schools, people cannot keep regular hours and so cannot work even if they find a job, as all these things create opportunities to be found by the police. Not only do "dirty" individuals (those on the run) suffer from such a life but their "clean" neighbors, friends, and relatives do as well (that is, those with no legal entanglements). As she describes, there is no doubt that the "6th Street" neighborhood that she studied was crime-ridden. But, she writes, "under these conditions the role of law enforcement changes from keeping communities safe from a few offenders to bringing an entire neighborhood under suspicion and surveillance" (2014, 201). She continues:

> Under these conditions, the highly punitive approach to crime control winds up being counterproductive, creating entirely new domains of criminality. The level of social control that tough-on-crime policy envisions ... is so extreme and difficult to implement that it has led to a flourishing black market to ease the pains of supervision. A new realm of criminal activity is produced as young people supply the goods and services that legally compromised people seek to evade the authorities or live with more freedom and comfort than their legal restrictions permit. This black market runs second to the fugitive status as a kind of corollary illegality. Moreover, mothers and girlfriends find themselves committing a seemingly endless series of crimes as they attempt to hide, protect, and provide for their legally entangled sons and partners. Thus, the great paradox of a highly punitive approach to crime control is that it winds up criminalizing so much of daily life as to foster widespread illegality as people work to circumvent it. Intensive policing and the crime it intends to control become mutually reinforcing. The extent to which crime elicits harsh policing, or policing itself contributes to a climate of violence and illegality, becomes impossible to sort out.
>
> (Goffman, 2014, 201–202)

Naturally, she writes, this generates frustration and anger:

> From the perspective of 6th Street residents, distrust and anger at the police are understandable. The police (along with the courts, the jails, and the prisons) are not solving the significant problems of crime and violence but instead are piling on additional problems to the ones residents already face.
>
> (2014, 202)

The police, of course, are not solely to blame: they are called upon to solve social problems but are equipped only with "handcuffs and jail time" (203). Goffman is not the only one to review these processes; important work has also been done by such authors as Elija Anderson (1978, 1990, 1999), Bruce Western (2006), Sudhir Venkatesh (2006), Devah Pager (2007), and Loic Wacquant (2009). These authors collectively paint a picture of poverty being addressed with punitiveness, and the consequences of that. Of course, crime is more complicated than poverty, but the point here is simply that where punitiveness is a logical response to criminality, it has become a response to poverty, and by subjecting entire communities to harsh policing practices it has eroded trust sometimes to a breaking point.

Traci Burch (2013) addresses a different point: many of the most disordered and heavily policed areas of American life have been socially and politically destroyed as well. Fear and mistrust of the authorities extends to voting, making use of government services, and even engaging in political action. Far from mobilizing the poor to demand change, aggressive policing and incarceration policies alienate and demobilize them.

Our analysis [...] focuses on traffic stops, not policing in general, and not incarceration at all. So what is the connection between our analyses and these studies? There are two important linkages. First, these studies document and explain a puzzle: how can community trust be eroded so greatly that juries fail to convict an individual when a police officer is shot with his own service revolver during a scuffle following a traffic stop? This was one of the central questions for Epp et al. (2014), whose analysis of citizen experiences with traffic stops poignantly included a discussion of drive-by shootings where dozens of witnesses proceeded to avoid the police despite clearly seeing more than fifty shots fired on a crowded street (152). Understanding how community trust can be so severely eroded is an important goal.

Second, the tight geographic focus of the aggressive policing tactics documented in the studies cited above, and the consequences of these, explain a paradox: most middle-class white Americans can be completely unaware of the different experiences of others. This creates what we can refer to as an "empathy gap." By that we mean a lack of understanding at the most basic level. For example, most middle-class white Americans, including the authors of this[reading], have never been treated with disrespect during a traffic stop. Many members of the white middle class responded with disbelief or surprise when they saw video of the shooting of Walter Scott in April 2015 in North Charleston. Mr. Scott had been stopped for an equipment violation and attempted to flee; he was shot in the back while running away. Similarly, Sandra Bland, who was found dead in a jail cell in Waller County, Texas in July 2015, had been stopped by a trooper for a traffic violation, but the traffic stop quickly escalated into a heated argument leading to a charge against Bland for assaulting an officer. The ideas of running to escape, or getting into a verbal or physical altercation with an officer following a routine traffic stop, seem alien to most middle-class Americans. Given our experiences with the police, this behavior just does not make sense; we cannot empathize.

We want to close this empathy gap. By documenting and exploring stark differences in how individuals are treated by the police following a traffic stop, we want to give credence to those members of minority communities who say to middle-class Americans: you just don't get it. We hope that our data and explorations here will move us some way to better mutual understandings.

Using Traffic Stops Data to Explore Racial Disparities in Policing

[...] Traffic stops, of course, are but one way in which the police interact with the community. They are certainly not the reason for the massive increase in incarceration of the 1980s and beyond that we referred to earlier in this [reading]. But, as we also noted, they are by far the most common avenue by which citizens encounter law enforcement. Wesley Skogan (2008) studied citizen interpretations of their encounters with the police, emphasizing the long-lasting negative consequences of interactions judged to be painful, unhelpful, or disrespectful on the part of the police toward the citizen. In Skogan's view, positive, respectful interactions have little impact but negative ones can have a strongly detrimental impact on citizen views of the police. Tom Tyler, Jeffrey Fagan, and Amanda Geller (2014) review young adults' experiences with "stop and frisk" policing behaviors in New York. They note, logically enough, that adolescents and young men often have many encounters with the police, and that each one of these is a "teachable moment" in the lives of that young man. They find that about 20 percent of all these pedestrian encounters "appear to fall short of constitutional grounds of legal sufficiency" and that "almost none turn up guns (0.11 percent of all stops) or other contraband (1.5 percent). The high rate of error in these stops, both constitutionally and in effectiveness, is a potential sore spot that could poison citizen support for and cooperation with the police" (Tyler, Fagan, and Geller 2014, 752).

When the police interact with citizens rarely, respectfully, and lightly, we can expect little effect on citizen feelings of belonging. But when the interactions are common, aggressive, and seemingly unjustified, then the citizen so treated may well develop an angry response. Given that traffic stops are the most common type of encounter that Americans have with the police, we believe it is an important place to start. What lessons are different demographic groups being taught?

Why Bother?

One might think that it is unnecessary to document in a book-length study that there are strong racial disparities in traffic stops. Others have already shown strong differences in how blacks and whites are treated throughout the criminal justice system, so why should there be any surprise if we find differences here as well? We believe it is important for a number of reasons. First, we fill a gap that was intended in the original NC law when it was discussed, debated, and passed; indeed the 1999 law mandated periodic reports to ascertain whether there might be important and statistically significant disparities in traffic stops, but no official state analysis was ever done, and the most extensive study done so far focused only on the State Highway Patrol for calendar year 2000 (see Smith et al. 2004). Second, more generally, even if we may not be surprised that disparities exist, we need to put numbers to it: a

10 percent difference is not the same as a 300 percent difference, and we do not know until we do the study how strong any disparity may be. Third, we want to know if the disparities are widening or lessening, and again the only way to know is to look. Fourth, we want to know the various avenues that these disparities may take: are they similar between black and Hispanic drivers compared to whites; how do they differ by age and gender, for urban and rural areas, across police departments, sheriffs, and the highway patrol; whether they are caused by just a few officers or are more widespread; and so on. By understanding the shapes and contours of the disparities, we can understand better what may be causing them. Finally, we want to know what explains them, what correlates with high and low scores on our measures of disparity, and what policies therefore might be effective in curtailing them. The North Carolina dataset ... is uniquely suited to answering these questions as it is by far the most comprehensive record of police traffic stops currently available. Not to spoil the punchline, we will indeed document racial disparities. But our point in writing [...] goes much deeper than that simple question. We aim to understand the scope and nature of them so that we can know what to do about it.

The Plan of the [Reading]

North Carolina was the first state in the nation to mandate the collection of demographic data following any traffic stop, passing the law in 1999. Beginning on January 1, 2000 for the State Highway Patrol, and in 2002 for all but the smallest police agencies, officers have recorded the age, race, and gender of every driver pulled over, why they were stopped, and the outcome of that stop. Based on the analysis of over 20 million of these records, we focus on racial differences in the likelihood of various outcomes, with a particular focus on whether the officer searches the driver of the car. Very few traffic stops lead to a search; just about 3 percent. But searches are highly targeted at young men of color; over 20 percent of those stopped are searched in some jurisdictions. The majority of these searches yield no contraband, and when there is a contraband "hit" the amounts involved are rarely those associated with a dealer or a courier. In fact, courier-level contraband hits are vanishingly rare.

If searches associated with traffic stops were justified as a means to catch drug "kingpins" or couriers, they have been extremely ineffective. In North Carolina alone, millions have been pulled over for minor violations—equipment problems, expired registration tags, and for other reasons that could well be pretexts (fully allowed by the Court in *Whren*) rather than because of excessive speeding, drunk driving, or other serious safety concerns. Disproportionately, these traffic stops, and hundreds of thousands of fruitless searches that followed from them, have been targeted at those fitting a "drug courier profile": young men of color. The disproportionate weight of the war on drugs in these communities is an important component of a larger discussion about mass incarceration, citizenship, and belonging.

We focus on traffic stops and document sustained and troubling disparities in how racial groups are treated in routine traffic stops. These disparities are robust to controls for the purpose of the stop and whether the stop occurred on a weekend evening, late at night, or during the morning rush hour. They are both institutional and officer-based. That is, we can identify individual "bad apple" officers who have particularly wide disparities in their treatment of drivers by race. But the causes of the disparities are much broader than only a few bad apple officers.

Across the state, various police and sheriff's departments have higher and lower levels of disparity in their treatment of drivers of different racial, ethnic, age, and gender groups. Further, the disparities vary over time. Looking both over time and across different agencies, we explore the causes and consequences of racially targeted search and arrest patterns. Individual police officers, sheriff's deputies, and state troopers are identified by a unique ID number. While the identity of the officer is unknown, and therefore we cannot analyze whether officer demographics influence their traffic stops, we can identify individual officers who have high and low rates of search, high and low rates of racial disparity in their stops and searches, and from that identify "bad apple" officers: those with the most marked disparities in the rates at which they search drivers by race. With that information, we can then test whether these officer-level differences explain the patterns of racial disparities seen across the database. While they contribute to them (by definition they must), they by no means explain the bulk of the variance in racial disparity that we observe.

When we compare every community in the state both across space and time, we find that those with the highest levels of racial disparity are systematically related to: higher poverty, smaller size, and lower political power for blacks. That is, controlling for the poverty rate and the size of the city, greater political empowerment of the black community generates lower rates of racial disparity in the police department. We measure black political empowerment as a combination of three factors: the black shares of the population, the voting population, and the elected officials. These three factors are of course highly interconnected, so we treat them as one. The bottom line in our research predicting where disparities are high and low, however, comes down to this: where blacks are politically weak, disparities are strong; where blacks are fully mobilized politically and share in the governance of their local community for example by having seats on the city council, the local police have lower rates of disparity. Lerman and Weaver (2014) documented that disparate treatment by police can stimulate reduced voting turnout and involvement in politics by those affected by their interactions with police. We provide further evidence of the importance of this finding: where disparities are high, the voting share of the black population is lower.

Racial disparities in the outcomes of traffic stops naturally generate alienation among those who sense they have been targeted for unequal treatment. Largely unremarked in this debate is that those not targeted may not even be aware that the targeting is occurring, unless a family member or close friend is routinely targeted. This lack of awareness, we believe, has contributed to a large-scale lack of empathy and understanding. Since the rise of the Black Lives Matter movement beginning in 2012, however, cell-phone videos documenting harsh, sometimes fatal, police interactions with young men of color have awakened all Americans to these realities. The massive scale of what we observe convinces us that the diversion of routine traffic patrols into a targeted practice of aggressive search for those who fit a "profile" in the name of the war on drugs has been extremely costly, much more so than has previously been identified. Further, while members of our nation's minority communities have long been aware of these disparities, middle-class whites are only slowly being made aware of them. Of course, understanding can only start with knowledge and acknowledgment. And repair and reform can only come from understanding.

In this [reading], based on a comprehensive analysis of one state's experience with traffic stops, we add to our collective understanding of the high cost and the low benefit of diverting routine traffic patrols into the wars on crime and drugs. This decision, dating back a generation, has paid little benefit in terms of fighting crime, but has secretly tarnished our democracy. The tarnish has been real, as very few young men of color have escaped the knowledge that they could be pulled over for a pretext, potentially subjected to search, and possibly arrested while their white equivalent on the other side of town would not have to fear these events. The tarnish has been secret as well, since those not targeted by the practice may be completely unaware of it. Of course, police are not allowed to pull over drivers unless they break the law. But many of our traffic and vehicle laws allow for considerable officer discretion, and others put all of us routinely on the wrong side of the law. While the Court has not so ruled, the disproportionate application of the law in some groups but not in other groups has generated resentment, alienation, and a sense of degraded citizenship. Many Americans are only now becoming aware that this is even happening, though it has been going on for decades.

References

Anderson, Elijah. 1978. *A Place on the Corner*. Chicago, IL: University of Chicago Press.

Anderson, Elijah. 1990. *Streetwise: Race, Class, and Change in an Urban Community*. Chicago, IL: University of Chicago Press.

Anderson, Elijah. 1999. *Code of the Street*. New York: W. W. Norton.

Anderson, Kristin J. 2010. *Benign Bigotry: The Psychology of Subtle Prejudice*. New York: Cambridge University Press.

Baumgartner, Frank R., Leah Christiani, Derek A. Epp, Kevin Roach, and Kelsey Shoub. 2017. Racial Disparities in Traffic Stop Outcomes. *Duke Forum for Law and Social Change* **9**: 21–53.

Blinder, Alan. 2017. Ex-officer who shot Walter Scott pleads guilty in Charleston. *New York Times*. May 2.

Bridges, Virginia. 2015a. Durham police officer describes 2012 shooting, struggle. *Raleigh News and Observer*. August 4.

Bridges, Virginia. 2015b. Riley found guilty of robbery, not guilty of shooting Durham officer. *Raleigh News and Observer*. August 14.

Burch, Traci. 2013. *Trading Democracy for Justice*. Chicago, IL: University of Chicago Press.

Clear, Todd R., and Natasha A. Frost. 2014. *The Punishment Imperative: The Rise and Failure of Mass Incarceration in America*. New York: New York University Press.

Correll, J. 2009. Racial Bias in the Decision to Shoot? *The Police Chief* **76**, 5: 54–58.

Correll, J., B. Park, C. M. Judd, and B. Wittenbrink. 2002. The Police Officer's Dilemma: Using Ethnicity to Disambiguate Potentially Threatening Individuals. *Journal of Personality and Social Psychology* **83**, 6: 1314–1329.

Correll, J., B. Park, C. M. Judd, B. Wittenbrink, and M. S. Sadler. 2007. Across the Thin Blue Line: Police Officers and Racial Bias in the Decision to Shoot. *Journal of Personality and Social Psychology* **92**, 6: 1006–1023.

Durham, North Carolina, City of, Executive Command Staff of the Durham Police Department. 2014. Durham Response to the FADE Coalition Policy Recommendations: Final Report to the Durham City Manager. Retrieved September 1 2014 from: http://durhamnc.gov/ich/op/DPD/Documents/FADE%20Coalition%20Response.pdf

Eith, Christine, and Matthew R. Durose. 2011. *Contacts between Police and the Public, 2008*. Washington, DC: US Department of Justice, Bureau of Justice Statistics, NCJ 234599 (October).

Epp, Charles R., Steven Maynard-Moody, and Donald Haider-Markel. 2014. *Pulled Over: How Police Stops Define Race and Citizenship*. Chicago, IL: University of Chicago Press.

Fishman, Charles. 1991. Sheriff Bob Vogel: He's the mayor of I-95, and a terror to drug smugglers. *Orlando Sentinel*, August 11.

Fridell, Lorie, Robert Lunney, Drew Diamond, and Bruce Kubu. 2001. *Racially Biased Policing: A Principled Response*. Washington, DC: Police Executive Research Forum.

Frontline. n.d. The Legacy of Rodney King. Available at: www.pbs.org/wgbh/pages/frontline/shows/lapd/race/king.html

Gilliam, Franklin D., Jr., and Shanto Iyengar. 2000. Prime Suspects: The Influence of Local Television News on the Viewing Public. *American Journal of Political Science* **44**, 3: 560–573.

Glaser, Jack. 2006. The Efficacy and Effect of Racial Profiling: A Mathematical Simulation Approach. *Journal of Policy Analysis and Management* **25**, 2: 395–416.

Glaser, Jack. 2015. *Suspect Race: Causes and Consequences of Racial Profiling*. New York: Oxford University Press.

Goffman, Alice. 2014. *On the Run: Fugitive Life in an American City*. Chicago, IL: University of Chicago Press.

Hackney, Amy A., and Jack Glaser. 2013. Reverse Deterrence in Racial Profiling: Increased Transgressions by Nonprofiled Whites. *Law and Human Behavior* **37**, 5: 348–353.

Harris, David A. 1997. Driving While Black and all other Traffic Offenses: The Supreme Court and Pretextual Traffic Stops. *Journal of Criminal Law and Criminology* **87**, 2: 544–582.

Harris, David A. 1999a. *Driving While Black: Racial Profiling on our Nation's Highways. ACLU Special Report*. New York: American Civil Liberties Union. Available at: www.aclu.org/racial-justice/driving-while-black-racial-profiling-our-nations-highways

Harris, David A. 1999b. The Stories, the Statistics, and the Law: Why "Driving While Black" Matters. *Minnesota Law Review* **84**: 265–326.

Harris, David A. 2002a. *Profiles in Injustice: Why Racial Profiling Cannot Work*. New York: New Press.

Harris, David A. 2002b. Racial Profiling Revisited: "Just Common Sense" in the Fight against Terror? *Criminal Justice* **17**: 36–41, 59.

Lerman, Amy E., and Vesla M. Weaver. 2014. *Arresting Citizenship*. Chicago, IL: University of Chicago Press.

McAdam, Doug. 1988. *Freedom Summer*. New York: Oxford University Press.

Meares, Tracey L., Tom R. Tyler, and Jacob Gardener. 2016. Lawful or Fair? How Cops and Laypeople perceive Good Policing. *Journal of Criminal Law and Criminology* **105**, 2: 297–344.

Pager, Devah. 2007. *Marked: Race, Crime, and Finding Work in an Era of Mass Incarceration*. Chicago, IL: University of Chicago Press.

Peralta, Eyder and Cheryl Corley. 2016. The driving life and death of Philando Castile. *NPR Morning Edition*. July 15. Available at: www.npr.org/sections/thetwo-way/2016/07/15/485835272/the-driving-life-and-death-of-philando-castile

Reaves, Brian A. 2011. *Census of State and Local Law Enforcement Agencies*, 2008. Washington, DC: US Department of Justice, Bureau of Justice Statistics, NCJ 233982 (July).

Robles, Frances, and Shaila Dewan. 2015. Skip child support. Go to jail. Lose job. Repeat. *New York Times*. 19 April.

Schuck, Peter H. 2006. *Meditations of a Militant Moderate: Cool Views on Hot Topics*. Lanham, MD: Rowman and Littlefield.

Sharkey, Patrick. 2013. *Stuck in Place: Urban Neighborhoods and the End of Progress Toward Racial Equality*. Chicago, IL: University of Chicago Press.

Skogan, Wesley G. 2008. Assymetry in the Impact of Encounters with Police. *Policing and Society* **16**, 2: 99–126.

Smith, William R., Donald Tomaskovic-Devey, Matthew T. Zingraff, H. Marcinda Mason, Patricia Y. Warren, and Cynthia Pfaff Wright. 2004. *The North Carolina Highway Traffic Study*. US Department of Justice, Office of Justice Programs, Final Report Document No.: 204021. Available at: www.ncjrs.gov/pdffiles1/nij/grants/204021.pdf

Thibaut, John, and Laurens Walker. 1975. *Procedural Justice: A Psychological Analysis*. Hillsdale, NJ: Lawrence Erlbaum Associates.

Tonry, Michael. 1995. *Malign Neglect: Race, Crime, and Punishment in America*. New York: Oxford University Press.

Tucker, Susan B., and Eric Cadora. 2003. Justice Reinvestment. *Ideas for an Open Society* **3**, 3 (November). New York: Open Society Institute.

Tyler, Tom R., and Robert Folger. 1980. Distributional and Procedural Aspects of Satisfaction with Citizen–Police Encounters. *Basic and Applied Social Psychology* **1**, 4: 281–292.

Tyler, Tom R., and Jonathan Jackson. 2014. Popular Legitimacy and the Exercise of Legal Authority: Motivating Compliance, Cooperation and Engagement. *Psychology, Public Policy and Law* **20**, 1: 78–95.

Tyler, Tom R., Jeffrey Fagan, and Amanda Geller. 2014. Street Stops and Police Legitimacy: Teachable Moments in Young Urban Men's Legal Socialization. *Journal of Empirical Legal Studies* **11**, 4: 751–785.

Tyler, Tom R., Jonathan Jackson, and Avital Mentovich. 2015. The Consequences of Being an Object of Suspicion: Potential Pitfalls of Proactive Police Contact. *Journal of Empirical Legal Studies* **12**, 4: 602–636.

United States Department of Justice (US DOJ), Civil Rights Division. 2015. *Investigation of the Ferguson Police Department*. Washington: US DOJ. March 4.

Venkatesh, Sudhir. 2006. *Off the Books: The Underground Economy of the Urban Poor*. Cambridge, MA: Harvard University Press.

Voigt, Rob, Nicholas P. Camp, Vinodkumar Prabhakaran, William L. Hamilton, Rebecca C. Hetey, Camilla M. Griffiths, David Jurgens, Dan Jurafsky, and Jennifer L. Eberhardt. 2017. Language from police body camera footage shows racial disparities in officer respect.

Wacquant, Loic. 2009. *Punishing the Poor: The Neoliberal Government of Social Insecurity*. Durham, NC: Duke University Press.

Webb, Gary. 2007. Driving While Black: Tracking Unspoken Law-Enforcement Racism. *Esquire*, January 29. Downloaded from www.esquire.com/news-politics/a1223/driving-while-black-0499 on May 21, 2015. [Originally published as: DWB, *Esquire* 131, 4 (April 1999): 118–127.]

Western, Bruce. 2006. *Punishment and Inequality in America*. New York: Russell Sage Foundation.

Withrow, Brian L. 2004. Driving while Different: A Potential Theoretical Explanation for Race-Based Policing. *Criminal Justice Policy Review* **15**: 344–364.

Withrow, Brian L. 2006. *Racial Profiling: From Rhetoric to Reason*. Upper Saddle River, NJ: Pearson Prentice Hall.

CHAPTER 7 QUESTIONS

1. Why did the jury did not convict Carlos Riley on charges related to the shooting of Officer Stewart?
2. Frank Baumgartner and his coauthors announce their study's results on traffic stops and race in North Carolina in the first chapter of their book. What did they find?
3. Do the authors believe that there is a high or low cost to society from aggressive policing?
4. Why do Black Americans regard the courts as less legitimate than whites in surveys?
5. What was the old style of policing? What is the new one?
6. What is the significance of *Terry v. Ohio*? Why did Justice William O. Douglas dissent?
7. Nowadays, why do police "kiss a lot of frogs"?
8. Why can a routine traffic stop have lasting and powerful consequences for many Americans?
9. In Jack Glaser's simulation, what happens when police targeting is inaccurate?
10. What happens when a community's trust in the police erodes?

Bibliography

Alexander, Michelle. *The New Jim Crow: Mass Incarceration in the Age of Colorblindness*. New York: The New Press, 2020.

Ayres, Ian, and Jonathan Borowsky. "A Study of Racially Disparate Outcomes in the Los Angeles Police Department." ACLU of Southern California report, Los Angeles, October 2008. https://www.aclusocal.org/en/racial-profiling-lapd-study-racially-disparate-outcomes-los-angeles-police-department.

Babcock, Barbara. "'Defending the Guilty' after 30 Years." In *How Can You Represent Those People?*, edited by Abbe Smith and Monroe H. Freeman, 1–13. New York: Palgrave Macmillan, 2013.

Black, Donald J. "The Boundaries of Legal Sociology." *Yale Law Journal* 81 (1972): 1086–1100.

Chambliss, William J. "A Sociological Analysis of the Law of Vagrancy." *Social Problems* 12, no. 1 (1964): 67–77.

Carlin, Jerome E. *Lawyers' Ethics: A Survey of the New York City Bar*. New York: Russell Sage Foundation, 1966. https://www.russellsage.org/lawyers-ethics.

———. *Lawyers on Their Own: The Solo Practitioner in an Urban Setting*. New Orleans, LA: Quid Pro Books, 2011.

Chemerinsky, Erwin. *Closing the Courthouse Door: How Your Constitutional Rights Became Unenforceable*. New Haven, CT: Yale University Press, 2017.

Dred Scott v. Sandford, 60 U.S. 393, 15 L. Ed. 691, 15 L. Ed. 2d 691 (1857).

Dror, Yehezkel. "Law and Social Change." *Tulane Law Review* 33 (1959): 787–802.

Friedman, Lawrence M. *A History of American Law*. 3rd ed. New York: Simon and Schuster, 2005.

———. *Total Justice*. New York: Russell Sage Foundation, 1994.

Floyd v. City of New York, 959 F. Supp. 2d 540 (S.D.N.Y. 2013).

Gideon v. Wainwright, 372 U.S. 335, 83 S. Ct. 792, 9 L. Ed. 2d 799 (1963).

Griswold v. Connecticut, 381 U.S. 479, 85 S. Ct. 1678, 14 L. Ed. 2d 510 (1965).

Heinz, John P., and Edward O. Laumann. *Chicago Lawyers: The Social Structure of the Bar*. New York: Russell Sage Foundation, 1982. https://www.russellsage.org/publications/chicago-lawyers.

Hoebel, E. Adamson. *The Law of Primitive Man: A Study in Comparative Legal Dynamics*. New York: Atheneum, 1979.

Howard, Philip K. *Life without Lawyers: Liberating Americans from Too Much Law*. New York: W. W. Norton & Co., 2009.

Kidder, Robert L. *Connecting Law and Society: An Introduction to Research and Theory*. Englewood Cliffs, NJ: Prentice-Hall, 1983.

Korematsu v. United States, 323 U.S. 214, 65 S. Ct. 193, 89 L. Ed. 194 (1944).

Ladinsky, Jack. "Careers of Lawyers, Law Practice, and Legal Institutions." *American Sociological Review* 28, no. 1 (1963): 47–54.

Lippman, Matthew. *Law and Society*. Thousand Oaks, CA: SAGE Publications, X.

Llewelyn, Karl N., and E. Adamson Hoebel. *The Cheyenne Way: Conflict and Case Law in Primitive Jurisprudence*. Norman: University of Oklahoma Press, 1941.

Lortie, Dan C. "Laymen to Lawmen: Law School, Careers, and Professional Socialization." *Harvard Educational Review* 29, no. 4 (1959): 352–369.

Malinowski, Bronislaw. *Crime and Custom in Savage Society*. New Brunswick, NJ: Transaction Publishers, 2013. First published 1926 by Harcourt, Brace & Co. (New York).

Marbury v. Madison, 5 U.S. 137, 2 L. Ed. 60, 2 L. Ed. 2d 60 (1803).

Mayhew, Leon H. "Stability and change in legal systems" in *Stability and Social Change*. Boston: Little, Brown and Co, 1971.

National Archives. *The Constitution of the United States: A Transcription*. U.S. National Archives and Records Administration, May 4, 2020, www.archives.gov/founding-docs/constitution-transcript.

O'Neill, Timothy. "'The Stepford Justices': The Need for Experiential Diversity on the Roberts Court." *Oklahoma Law Review* 60, no. 701 (2007): 701–35.

Pascoe, Peggy. *What Comes Naturally: Miscegenation Law and the Making of Race in America*. Oxford: Oxford University Press, 2009.

Pennington, Kenneth. "Innocent until Proven Guilty: The Origins of a Legal Maxim." *The Jurist* 63 (2003): 106–124.

Pollak, Louis H. "Why Trying to Rank Law Schools Numerically Is a Non-Productive Undertaking: An Article on the *U.S. News & World Report 2009 List of 'The Top 100 Schools.'*" *Drexel Law Review* 1, no. 1 (2009): 52–68.

Ramseyer, J. Mark, and Eric B. Rasmusen. "Comparative Litigation Rates." The Harvard John M. Olin Discussion Paper Series No. 681, Cambridge, MA, November 2010. http://www.law.harvard.edu/programs/olin_center/papers/681_Ramseyer.php.

Rhode, Deborah L. *Adultery: Infidelity and the Law*. Cambridge, MA: Harvard University Press, 2016.

Savigny, Friedrich Carl von. *Of the Vocation of Our Age for Legislation and Jurisprudence*. Translated by Abraham Hayward. New York: Arno Press. 1975 [1831].

Seiff, John A. "The Presumption of Innocence." *Journal of Criminal Law & Criminology* 25, no. 1 (1934): 53–64.

Selznick, Philip. *The Moral Commonwealth: Social Theory and the Promise of Community*. Berkeley: University of California Press, 1992.

Seron, Carroll. *The Business of Practicing Law: The Work Lives of Solo and Small-Firm Attorneys*. Philadelphia: Temple University Press, 1996.

Sumner, William Graham. *Folkways: A Study of the Sociological Importance of Usages, Manners, Customs, Mores, and Morals*. Reprint, Good Press, 2019. First published 1906 by Ginn and Co. (Boston, MA).

Tomlinson v. Congleton Borough Council, 2003 U.K.H.L. 47, 2004 A.C.1 46 (2003).

Turley, Jonathan. "It's Their Private Court." *Los Angeles Times, May 12, 2010.*

Van Hoy, Jerry. *Franchise Law Firms and the Transformation of Personal Legal Services*. Westport, CT: Quorum Books, 1997.

White, G. Edward. Introduction to *The Common Law*, by Oliver Wendell Holmes, vii–xxxiv. Cambridge, MA: The Belknap Press of Harvard University Press, 2009.

The White House Archives. "President Bush Calls for Medical Liability Reform" (transcript and video). Speech at Baptist Health Medical Center, Little Rock, Arkansas, January 6, 2004. https://georgewbush-whitehouse.archives.gov/news/releases/2004/01/20040126-3.html.

White, Michael D., and Henry F. Fradella. *Stop and Frisk: The Use and Abuse of a Controversial Policing Tactic*. New York: New York University Press, 2016.

Wice, Paul B. *Criminal Lawyers: An Endangered Species*. Beverly Hills, CA: SAGE Publications, 1978.

www.ingramcontent.com/pod-product-compliance
Ingram Content Group UK Ltd.
Pitfield, Milton Keynes, MK11 3LW, UK
UKHW050950290926
15470UKWH00005B/1746

9 798823 369527